Culture, Capital and Representation

Other publications by Palgrave Macmillan in association with the Institute of English Studies

Brycchan Carey et al. (eds), *Discourses of Slavery and Abolition: Britain and Its Colonies, 1760–1838*
Gail Marshall and Adrian Poole (eds), *Victorian Shakespeare*, Vol. 1: *Theatre, Drama and Performance*, Vol. 2: *Literature and Culture*
Andrew Nash (ed.), *The Culture of Collected Editions*
Jerome McGann, *Radiant Textuality: Literary Study after the World Wide Web*
Elizabeth James (ed.), *Macmillan: A Publishing Tradition*
Elizabeth Maslen, *Political and Social Issues in British Women's Fiction, 1928–1968*
Angelique Richardson and Chris Willis (eds), *The New Woman in Fiction and Fact: Fin-de-Siècle Feminisms*
Warren Chernaik, Martin Swales and Robert Vilain (eds), *The Art of Detective Fiction*
Rebecca D'Monte and Nicole Pohl (eds), *Female Communities 1600–1800*
Isobel Armstrong and Virginia Blain (eds), *Women's Poetry in the Enlightenment: The Making of a Canon, 1730–1820*
Isobel Armstrong and Virginia Blain (eds), *Women's Poetry, Late Romantic to Late Victorian: Gender and Genre, 1830–1900*
Warren Chernaik and Martin Dzelzainis (eds), *Marvell and Liberty*
Andy Leak and George Paizis (eds), *The Holocaust and the Text: Speaking the Unspeakable*
Warwick Gould and Thomas F. Staley (eds), *Writing the Lives of Writers*
Ian Willison, Warwick Gould and Warren Chernaik (eds), *Modernist Writers and the Marketplace*
John Spiers (ed.), *George Gissing and the City: Cultural Crisis and the Making of Books in Late Victorian England*
Mary Hammond and Shafquat Towheed (eds), *Publishing in the First World War*
Mary Hammond and Robert Fraser (eds), *Books without Borders*, Vol.1: *The Cross-National Dimension in Print Culture*, Vol. 2: *Perspectives from South Asia*
Gina Potts and Lisa Shahriari (eds), *Virginia Woolf's Bloomsbury*, Vol. 1: *Aesthetic Theory and Literary Practice*, Vol. 2: *International Influence and Politics*

Culture, Capital and Representation

Edited by
Robert J. Balfour

In association with the Institute of Commonwealth Studies, and the Institute of English Studies (School of Advanced Study) University of London

Selection and editorial matter © Robert J. Balfour 2010
Individual chapters © contributors 2010

All rights reserved. No reproduction, copy or transmission of this publication may be made without written permission.

No portion of this publication may be reproduced, copied or transmitted save with written permission or in accordance with the provisions of the Copyright, Designs and Patents Act 1988, or under the terms of any licence permitting limited copying issued by the Copyright Licensing Agency, Saffron House, 6–10 Kirby Street, London EC1N 8TS.

Any person who does any unauthorized act in relation to this publication may be liable to criminal prosecution and civil claims for damages.

The authors have asserted their rights to be identified as the authors of this work in accordance with the Copyright, Designs and Patents Act 1988.

First published 2010 by
PALGRAVE MACMILLAN

Palgrave Macmillan in the UK is an imprint of Macmillan Publishers Limited, registered in England, company number 785998, of Houndmills, Basingstoke, Hampshire RG21 6XS.

Palgrave Macmillan in the US is a division of St Martin's Press LLC,
175 Fifth Avenue, New York, NY 10010.

Palgrave Macmillan is the global academic imprint of the above companies and has companies and representatives throughout the world.

Palgrave® and Macmillan® are registered trademarks in the United States, the United Kingdom, Europe and other countries.

ISBN 978–0–230–24645–4   hardback

This book is printed on paper suitable for recycling and made from fully managed and sustained forest sources. Logging, pulping and manufacturing processes are expected to conform to the environmental regulations of the country of origin.

A catalogue record for this book is available from the British Library.

Library of Congress Cataloging-in-Publication Data

Culture, capital, and representation / edited by Robert J. Balfour.
   p. cm.
  "In association with the Institute of English Studies, School of
  Advanced Study, University of London."
  Includes bibliographical references and index.
  ISBN 978–0–230–24645–4
  1. European literature—History and criticism 2. Capitalism in literature.
  3. Economics in literature. I. Balfour, Robert J., 1971–
PN710.C85 2010
809'.894—dc22
                                                              2010023748

10 9 8 7 6 5 4 3 2 1
19 18 17 16 15 14 13 12 11 10

Printed and bound in Great Britain by
CPI Antony Rowe, Chippenham and Eastbourne

To my parents Leola and Russell Balfour

Contents

List of Illustrations	ix
Acknowledgements	xi
List of Contributors	xii
Introduction: Culture, Capital and Representation Robert J. Balfour	1
1 Colonialism, Displacement and Cannibalism in Early Modern Economic Thought Hugh Goodacre	16
2 Accounting Capital, Race and Benjamin Franklin's 'Pecuniary Habits' of Mind in *The Autobiography* Rekha Rosha	35
3 A System Illusory and Immoral: Jonathan Swift and the Emergence of the Modern Economic Polity Christopher J. Fauske	49
4 Payments of Attention: Epitaphic Cash Flow in Gray and Wordsworth György Fogarasi	67
5 Money, Manhood and Suffrage in *Our Mutual Friend* Ruth Livesey	83
6 Feverish Speculation: the Railway Across the Isthmus of Panama Marian Aguiar	100
7 Reading Finance Capital Leigh Claire La Berge	116
8 The Gold Standard and Literature: Money and Language in the Work of Jean-Joseph Goux Ben Roberts	132
9 Producing and Consuming Agricultural Capital: the Aesthetics and Cultural Politics of Grain Elevators at the 1937 Paris International Exposition Guillaume Evrard	148

10 Finance and Film: Wall Street Myth and Mythopoeia 169
    Elton G. McGoun

11 Conclusion: Re-presenting Capital in Culture:
    the Necessary Persistence of Memory in a New Century 184
    Robert J. Balfour

Bibliography 202

Index 218

List of Illustrations

Figure 1 Centre rural, Le silo à grain (The Grain Elevator), from Jean Favier, *L'architecture, Exposition internationale, Paris, 1937* (Paris: Éditions Alexis Sinjon, [1938], Portfolio 3, Plate 41 (detail)). Call no. T805.B2 1937, Collection Centre Canadien d'Architecture/Canadian Centre for Architecture, Montréal.   150

Figure 2 Canadian Pavilion, overall view and plan, from *Exposition 1937: sections étrangères*, introduction de Jacques Gréber; présentation de Henri Martin (Paris: Éditions art et architecture, [1937], Plate 38). Call no. T805 1937 (W4034), Collection Centre Canadien d'Architecture/Canadian Centre for Architecture, Montréal.   151

Figure 3 Canadian Pavilion, Transports stand, from Edmond Labbé, *Exposition Internationale des Arts et Techniques dans la Vie Moderne* (1937): rapport général, T. 2 Album annexe, Plate LXIX (Paris: Imprimerie Nationale, 1938–1940). Call no. T805 1937 (8479), Collection Centre Canadien d'Architecture/Canadian Centre for Architecture, Montréal.   152

Figure 4 Battage du blé dans l'ouest canadien (Threshing the wheat in Western Canada), *Pavillon du Canada: Exposition Internationale Paris 1937/Canadian Pavilion: International Exhibition Paris 1937* [1937], p. 20, French side. Collection of the author.   155

Figure 5 Under the Eiffel Tower: on the left, the Belgian Pavilion. On the other side of the Jena Bridge, the pavilions of Great-Britain, Canada, the Press, and Advertising (Sous la Tour Eiffel: A gauche, le pavillon de la Belgique. De l'autre côté du pont d'Iéna, dans l'ordre et en perspective: les pavillons de la Grande-Bretagne, du Canada, de la Presse, de la Publicité...). Pierre-Louis Flouquet (1937) 'Paris 1937: L'Exposition internationale des arts et techniques dans la vie moderne'. *Bâtir* (June): 1227–8 (1227) (Studio Lumière, Bruxelles). Collection of the author. 161

Figure 6 Partie du Port de Montréal, le 5e port du monde (Partial view of Montreal Harbour, fifth harbour of the world), *Pavillon du Canada: Exposition Internationale Paris 1937/Canadian Pavilion: International Exhibition Paris 1937* [1937], p. 5, French side. Collection of the author. 163

Figure 7 A Field of Golden Grain in Western Canada, *Pavillon du Canada: Exposition Internationale Paris 1937/Canadian Pavilion: International Exhibition Paris 1937* [1937], p. 24, English side. Collection of the author. 165

Acknowledgements

I wish to thank the Institute of Commonwealth Studies and the Institute of English Studies (University of London) for providing the support and opportunity to host in 2005 the international colloquium: Representation of Capital 1700–2000: Speculation and Displacement.

I wish to acknowledge Clare Hall (Cambridge University) for the Fellowship extended to me in 2003, and the Institute of Commonwealth Studies (University of London) for the Fellowship extended to me between 2003 and 2005 to enable this project to reach completion.

A special word of thanks is extended to Professor Emeritus Margaret Lenta (University of KwaZulu-Natal) for her support and assistance with editing the book.

Finally, I wish to thank the members of the Editorial Board who assisted with the review process:

Professor Robert Hampson, English, Royal Holloway, London, UK
Professor Margaret Lenta, English, KwaZulu-Natal, SA
Professor Jacques Berthoud, English, York, UK
Professor Robert Williams, Art History, Edinburgh, UK
Professor Hans-Walter Schmidt-Hannisa, European Languages, Galway, Ireland
Professor David Cooper, Economics, Alberta, Canada
Dr Justine Crump, Nuffield, Oxford, UK
Dr Jacqueline Reid-Walsh, Cultural and Media Studies, Bishops University, Canada

List of Contributors

Marian Aguiar's research focuses on the different forms of modernity that appear in the global context. Her forthcoming book *Tracking Modernity: India, Trains, and the Culture of Mobility* explores cultural representations of the modern by considering the imagination of railway space in colonial, nationalist and postcolonial South Asian contexts.

Robert J. Balfour is Honorary Professor in Languages at the University of KwaZulu-Natal in South Africa, and Registrar of St Augustine College, the Catholic University of South Africa. He has held fellowships at the Institute of Commonwealth Studies (London) and Clare Hall (Cambridge). In addition to academic publications in literature, applied linguistics and education, Robert Balfour is also a published poet, writer of short fiction, and an exhibited painter.

Guillaume Evrard is a doctoral candidate in History of Art, and an art history tutor at the University of Edinburgh. His interdisciplinary and cross-national research on the visual arts, architecture and national identity in France, the United States and Canada has appeared in *Regards croisés sur le Canada et la France*, Dir. Paul Guillaume and Laurier Turgeon (2007), and in *La France dans le regard des Etats-Unis/France as seen by the United States*. Ed. Frédéric Monneyron and Martine Xibeyras (2006).

Christopher J. Fauske is Associate Professor of Communications at Salem State College, and co-convenor of the Money, Power, and Print colloquium.

György Fogarasi is Associate Professor of Comparative Literature at the University of Szeged, Hungary. He has published essays in the fields of rhetoric, aesthetics and romantic literature. He is the Hungarian translator of Paul de Man's *Allegories of Reading*, Edmund Burke's *Philosophical Enquiry*, as well as of numerous essays on romanticism and theory. His book on *'English' Necromanticism* (involving analyses of texts by Gray, Wordsworth, Marx and Benjamin) is forthcoming.

Hugh Goodacre is a writer and researcher on the history of economic thought, specialising in the economic thought of the colonial era and the continuing influence of colonialist ideas within the economics discipline today. He has published periodical articles and book chapters on this subject, and has a book in press on *William Petty and the Roots of Economics*. From 1972 to 1996 he was Curator of Books and Manuscripts in the Asia, Africa and Pacific Department of the British Library, and is currently Senior Lecturer in Economics at the University of Westminster, as well as Affiliate Lecturer at Birkbeck College, University of London, and Teaching Fellow at University College London. He lectures on the history of economic thought, as well as on the world economy, money and banking, and UK macroeconomics. He is an active promoter of the history of economic thought in the teaching curriculum and research remit of university economics departments, and a frequent correspondent on this and related issues in the national and international press.

Leigh Claire La Berge is Collegiate Assistant Professor of Humanities at the University of Chicago. She has published articles on politics and the university, psychoanalysis, and the representation of money. She is currently at work on a manuscript examining finance and American literature and film in the 1980s.

Ruth Livesey is Reader in Nineteenth-Century Literature and Thought in the Department of English, Royal Holloway, University of London. She is Assistant Editor of the *Journal of Victorian Culture* and her publications include *Socialism, Sex and the Culture of Aestheticism in Britain, 1880–1914* (2007) and the forthcoming co-edited volume, *The American Experiment and the Idea of Democracy in British Culture, 1776–1914* (2011).

Elton G. McGoun is William H. Dunkak Professor of Finance at Bucknell University and a visiting member of the Economics Faculty of the University of Ljubljana. He has lectured and spoken at universities in Europe and Asia and published books and articles on the philosophy, history and culture of finance and accounting. In past lives he was a lieutenant in the US Navy Supply Corps and the chief financial officer of a credit union in Anchorage, Alaska. In addition to his academic work, he drives a pick-up truck and lives across the road from a corn field.

Ben Roberts is Lecturer in Media Studies at the University of Bradford. He has research interests in philosophy of technology and network media.

Rekha Rosha is a Visiting Assistant Professor in the Department of English at Wake Forest University, where she teaches courses in American literature, from the colonial era through the nineteenth century. Her current book-length project Literary Accounting and the Emotional Life of Capital, from the Revolutionary War to the Great Crash of 1929 explores the question: What do we talk about when we talk about money? Her project traces the interrelated notions of fiscal and moral accountability in six canonical works through the trope of regulative affect – emotions of guilt, blame and shame – to argue that the accountability plot binds a community to circumscribe its affective limits.

Introduction: Culture, Capital and Representation

Robert J. Balfour

J. Z. Muller in his survey of capitalism's development (*The Mind and the Market*, 2003) notes that there has long been a perception, owed in its origins to classical Greek conceptions of the well-governed polis, and in medieval Christianity's notion of the moral ambiguity of wealth, that 'profits from trade were regarded as morally illegitimate', and that 'making money from money' (2003: 5) was considered in an even harsher moral light than trade itself. One need only look to Shakespeare's *Merchant of Venice* (c.1596) for an accurate representation of the relationship between those who practised 'usury', those who benefited from it, and those who made a virtue of despising it. Of course Shakespeare was particularly attuned to the race and gender prerogatives associated with usury, and no doubt drew upon a long-established idea of value in relation to notions of property and person, in which one could become the other in the exchange of worth. Money, therefore, has long been regarded as a base, but nevertheless real definition of worth, antithetical to the ways in which the practice of virtues (located as these are within an altogether more abstracted system of values, in the form of faith or religion) could result in the storing-up of heavenly wealth and favour. In turn that idea would find its corruption in the relationship between worldly goods, good works and their relative value in the form of the indulgences money could buy in the late fifteenth century (most infamously by Johannes Tetzel in 1517). Thus the relationship between money and value is both changeable and always ambiguous.

Of central importance to *Culture, Capital and Representation* is the way in which literature, cultural studies and the visual arts represent, interact with and produce ideas about capital, whether in its early phases (the growth of stock markets) or in its late phase (global speculative capital). Authors in the volume are concerned with the representation of issues such as speculation, displacement, exploitation, capital growth, the decline of the welfare state and the growth of surplus migrant populations. The contributions range over three centuries and attempt to trace issues arising from the dominance of capitalism, the primary means by which we understand our work, organise economies, and ascribe value to people and money, depending on their location within the capitalist system.

The disjunction between sign and reality in a wide range of literature is explored across eleven chapters, with particular reference to fictional representations of commerce, capitalism and credit. Further, the broader cultural, economic and political implications of this disjunction are considered in the light of an exploration and interrogation of literature and the visual arts.

The chapters not only span three centuries but also span various areas of cultural production (film, poetry, novels, journalism) and serve to explore the links between capitalism and power on the one hand, and alienation and disenfranchisement on the other. Discourses that critique capitalism are not always considered legitimate or relevant within the hegemonic frameworks. This may be seen in the economic, moral and ethical debates which present fresh perspectives on free market economies, the exploitation of labour and the marginalisation of women, children and other race groups.

Writing (whether popular or elitist, and irrespective of genre) has long challenged the excesses of unregulated capital. This is evident from the beginning of the eighteenth century in the public debates concerning gambling, and the establishment of the first stock exchange in England and the Netherlands. These issues find interpretation in the writing of the period. These debates may be linked to other topics, for example, the emergence of credit-based commercial practices, gambling, insurance, colonial ventures, stock market 'bubbles', and the legal and cultural restrictions placed upon women and various race groups in financial matters.

More broadly, the book considers how the comprehension of value comes to be enculturated; how it can be manifest, designated, exchanged and possessed. Though not common in literary studies, there is merit here in some discussion of the methodological choices and turns for *Culture, Capital and Representation*. Methodologically the book focuses on a diversity of perspectives on capital over a range of genres over a period of approximately 350 years. While chapters have been grouped in terms of historical period, the book itself does not claim to provide a historical treatment of the range of writing about capital in any given century; in other words the book coheres in terms of the treatment of the issues in relation to the genre highlighted for attention by the reader. In seeking to be widely representative of historical epochs, I have also attempted to ensure that a variety of cultural forms and genres are selected through which the reader may approach representations of, and reactions to, capital as charted in the book. I believe that the broad focus on capital over time, in addition to an equally diverse range of cultural forms and genres, offers the reader a unique intercultural, as well as interdisciplinary perspective. Obviously the cost of that perspective occurs in relation to the loss of focus on a more restricted historical epoch, on just one cultural form or one genre. But, given that research within disciplines provides amply for scholarly coverage in these areas (one need only look to the history of economics for example, or the treatment of capitalism in literature), the contribution that this book makes is to encourage a historicised (though that is not to suggest a historical) treatment of capital and its representation over time. Furthermore, a focus on fairly recent developments of a cultural form, for example film, and the scholarship developed around this would have meant losing the continuity of focus over time on culture, capital and representation precisely to show the continuities between concerns and issues pertaining the effects and uses of capital over time.

The purpose thus has not been to provide a literary account of capital, or an economic account, or a historical account, but rather to bring together scholarly accounts of as many disciplines as possible within the limits of what a book of this kind can reasonably achieve by focusing in the chapters on particular forms of cultural production. Thus the book charts an ideological history of value in the West (GoGwilt, 1995), as it is conveyed/challenged/enacted in a variety of texts – asking the questions, What is happening to value? How can it be constituted? What changes are occurring? Again, the methodological treatment of these questions presupposes a number of issues to be explored by the authors who attempt to develop more closely, and more cogently, the analysis of cultural phenomena in relation to economic phenomena, and the interrelationship between theoretical frameworks in both areas. This book offers a number of hypotheses, explored in the contributions of eleven scholars drawn from fields as seemingly diverse as economics and art history, accounting and film studies. First, that literature makes the first substantive engagement with capital and capitalist ideas, and, by doing so, participates in the fictional debate about these issues, offering cultural/ideological responses to the ideas of capital, credit, speculation, economic expansion and the exploitation of colonised or displaced peoples. Second, literature, both fictional and non-fictional, produced by those who perceive themselves to be critical of, or excluded from, dominant trends by virtue of race and/or gender, interacts with ideas about the different forms of capital irrespective of the period. Whilst not all writing (for example, advertising) is critical of capital, most writing problematises the concept, or at least points to its ambiguities. Third, that the modern world is still subject to a persistent and growing fear of the disjunction between the 'real world' as it is experienced by the populace, and the 'imaginary' realm of economic and political power which exists between texts and between states. Fourth, popular dissatisfaction with the fundamental disjunction between the real world and the economic forces that shape it is everywhere evident in cultural products. The novel, for example, is a genre that because of its popularity as a form over the last three centuries offers an opportunity to understand the variety of means used to negotiate the disjunction between reality and systems of signs like language, currency, class, gender and race. Fifth, the language used to sustain this fantasy is ever-changing – the discourses of credit, industrialisation, colonialism, and now of globalisation (Schuster, 2003). Nevertheless, the effect is the same; that of a 'reality' created and sustained by systems of signs mobilised by the powerful few, in a profitable fantasy that excludes, exploits and damages people peripheral to it. Finally, this fantasy threatens to eclipse the real altogether by making it discursively invisible by means of language, media and ideology which collude in a colonial-global fantasy until the particular sufferings – displacement, deprivation and disenfranchisement – of individuals become invisible (Hardt and Negri, 2001).

Culture, Capital and Representation does not privilege discourses or perspectives on economics but rather recognises that the relationship between material life and literature is always uncertain; that money, and especially speculative capital, is not 'real' either. Literature is like money. The relationship between material life and literature is complex and mutual, but to discount the latter as a mere fictive reflection of the former is to ignore the power of ideology. Literature has strong resemblances to money. It has real power and yet is also preoccupied with representation and value.

For postmodernists there is no distinction between 'fact' and 'fiction'. 'Fact', as a category, is exploded. It is just as likely to be culturally produced and mediated as an airport novel. Both factual and fictional texts are referential to a reality that no longer exists and both are subject only to the constraints of language. Both make themselves intelligible to readers in language, and by reference to ideological and cultural assumptions shared by readers.

The flipside to the idea that no texts can represent reality absolutely is the notion that reality itself is textually produced. Our responses and comprehension of our experience are mediated, thwarted, diverted and quashed by our ideological programming. This, as is argued throughout the chapters, is what makes the 'unreality' merchants, the spin-doctors of capital, so dangerous: they do not just steal pension funds, they imprison consciousness in fictions of their own creating. More importantly, these fictions have consequences for people not regarded as part of the fiction, who are not characters in the plot, surplus populations who are seen as cheap and disposable labour, whose unemployment and migrant status is a consequence of free market capitalist practices.

The understanding it offers of the power of such fictions, irrespective of the genres in which they occur, will make this book a key contribution to the debates about the nature, operation, origins and development of late twentieth-century capitalism and globalisation (Hobsbawm, 2000; Rosenberg, 2000).

The book opens with a discussion by Hugh Goodacre of colonialism, displacement and cannibalism in the writing of William Petty (Hull, 1899). Goodacre argues that Petty's writings in the seventeenth century were precursors of what are regarded as economic orthodoxies in the late twentieth century in which the subject of colonialism and its legacy is confined to the margins of the economics discipline, where it is expected to share the ground with women's issues, racism, the environment and other issues which are similarly subjected to characterisation as positioned on a theoretical fringe. This chapter challenges that standpoint through an exploration of William Petty's writing over a period of some thirty years (1657–87) drawing from the biographical and historical context in relation to other related bodies of literature, including colonialist propaganda, and the literature of Utopianism. Goodacre demonstrates that, while these literatures predate any direct literary representation of capital or its associated phenomena, they display plentiful engagement with its preconditions in their discussion of such issues as the nature of material wealth and the extension of the wage system. The literature of this period is valuable, above all, for its preservation of a viewpoint that was subsequently to be lost in the literature of political economy, let alone in the economics of today – a viewpoint from which the colonised peoples had not yet been rendered invisible, and where their suppression and even extirpation was neither elided from, nor merely implicit in, political and economic discourse, but was an openly proclaimed policy objective. A prime example is Petty's 'proposal to transfer the bulk of the Irish population not westwards to Ireland's province of Connaught, as in the Cromwellian "transplantation" scheme, but eastwards into England, with the aim of increasing the density of England's population'. It is here argued that 'the colonial experience must be brought back from the theoretical periphery to which it is customarily consigned by the hegemonic discourse' within economics (as discipline and profession), and 'restored to the centre of attention which it actually occupied in the writings of those who first forged the analytical apparatus which is still in use by economists today'.

Rekha Rosha draws similarly on the writing of another economist, Benjamin Franklin (1706–90), and explores the extent to which the use of autobiographical genre – Franklin's *Autobiography* (1793) – provides the reader not only with an account of Franklin's pecuniary habits of mind, but serves as a decisive moment of cultural instruction in a capitalist consciousness and the displacement of individual agency. The *Autobiography* is a model for self-making, which Franklin implies is the outcome of two events: first, the subordination of individual thought to social knowledge; and second, the increased political agency which this subject formation grants capitalism. Rosha argues that the ideological shift Franklin narrates is underwritten by accounting, as its form and function control Franklin's narrative, and offers interpretive strategies for comprehending this shift. The chapter suggests that the *Autobiography* provides a starting place for examining the role of economic narration in constructing and governing subjects under capitalism.

For Rosha, Franklin's epigrammatic description of his accounts frames consciousness in particular ways, and this shapes and grooves the 'habits of mind' (Adorno, 1941) necessary to capitalism. The account reduces complexity to its most manageable level and Franklin amplifies this effect in his treatment of proverbs. In offering a definition of knowledge as externally located and in promoting standardised methods of financial and personal behaviour, he addresses the central question of the bourgeoisie in the eighteenth century: how am I to act? He responds to it by synchronising bourgeois behaviour with capital. By treating himself as an object whose every action is traceable to capital, he relieves the reader of the burden of engaging with interiority. In this sense, he represents the personification of capitalist consciousness; mediated by the mechanographical processes of the account book and by collective knowledge.

The *Autobiography* (1793) idealises a mediated subject characterised by intervention and control to such a degree that the individual agency of the subject remains unaccountable. Franklin treats indebtedness as a variant of racial slavery, making capitalism and capitalist behaviour central to preserving freedom. The republican value for freedom militates against the self-interestedness of the marketplace, granting the slavery-based democratic government a moral status grounded in its ability to maintain 'disinterestedness'. The social is managed at a distance by the agency transferred from self to ledger. Accounting represents the means by which self-management becomes the foundation for self-governance.

Prominent in writing about capitalism, the growing significance of the industrial revolution, and its effects on subjects regarded as peripheral to its interests, are Jonathan Swift and Daniel Defoe. As Trotter observes, 'the metaphor of circulation, upon which Defoe's analysis of wealth was founded, attributes a greater significance to trade than to manufacture. The people selling, rather than the people making, are the ones who ensure that wealth is distributed as widely and efficiently as possible' (Trotter, 1910: 3). Christopher Fauske, through an analysis of selected poetry and prose by Swift (1667–1745) points out that his poetry actually mirrors the more sophisticated aspects of his arguments in political tracts. It turns out that Swift's poetry does indeed reflect an understanding demonstrated in his prose. Wealth is not a problem *per se*; the problem lies in the source of that wealth and the use to which it is put.

Fauske makes the point that Swift was firmly of the school that held that land, income generated from the land, and even the people who worked the land as well as, importantly, ancillary industries associated with the land, drapers, weavers, etc., all not only contributed to the wealth of a nation but were, in a fundamental sense, the wealth of the nation itself. In this sense the virtuous accumulation of wealth is not equivalent to the hoarding of money (a practice noted among the Spanish and Portuguese in pursuit of their colonial expansion), but a recognition of the human wealth found when people are adequately at labour. The accumulation of money, because it could be used to buy labour as well as goods, allowed for the development of luxury, and as Muller (2003: 5) suggests, it was luxury that was regarded as morally corrosive.

Although Fauske does not deal to a great extent with the relationship between capitalism and the representation of gender, Defoe in *Moll Flanders* (1722) describes the gender attitudes of his day in ways not dissimilar to Shakespeare, arguing that if wealth was corrosive, it was none more so than when held by women. Appropriate and inappropriate displays of wealth are, as suggested by Fauske, central to the views held by Swift but the very careful delineations of what might be regarded as appropriate or not, are themselves located in a moral system which is shown to delimit and prescribe the value of the value of money. What vexed Defoe and Swift, and many other social commentators of their time, was that moral systems were themselves in doubt; the colonial expansion of the Catholic powers had destabilised the uneasy peace that came with the end of the Wars of Religion (1562–98). In attempting to understand the complexities of value in relation to goods and labour Fauske notes that Swift was keen to endorse the view that trade could not be of mutual benefit since it was based on need, and need, in turn, encouraged an unequal relationship between traders in which the dialectic could only take the form of a win/lose binary. The binaries of trade were not unlike those associated with race, or gender, in which that which was coloured or female was always the weaker or loser. There is, in turn, with the resurgence of state-supported slavery (1450–1850) an endorsement of the relationship between money, property and the person, requiring the formal definition of slavery as the legitimate use of non-believers (as defined by the Catholic Church in *Romanus Pontifex*, 1455) for labour. The alignment of systems of moral value with systems of temporal values has thus always been close and thus it is not surprising that the commodification of discourse is also in some ways about the commodification of values.

The commodification of discourse, the very means by which meaning and value are transacted, is explored further by György Fogarasi in what he terms the 'payments of attention' by which is meant the extent to which value is inscribed in epitaphs in the poetry of Gray (1716–71) and Wordsworth (1770–1850). This chapter traces the economic workings of 'attention' in the eighteenth- and nineteenth-century epitaphic tradition and focuses on the way attention figures as a special currency supporting a whole credit system (a 'pension scheme' of sorts) in which the living pay the dead attention in the hope of being repaid by the future living when they themselves have died. Fogarasi argues that the system traced in this chapter is one of speculation and displacement. The specular (or chiasmic) relation between the living and the dead, or visitor and visited, appears in the close association of the *genius loci* haunting the living, in the figure of the wanderer or passer-by returning to his 'haunt'. Such a circumstance is, in turn, displaced as soon as the latter figure steps into the realm of the dead and awaits similar payments (in the form of attendance and attention) as a recompense for his earlier expenditure (his own perusal of memorials, his own mindful spending of time).

As a prototype for capitalist advertisements (which circulate names of products rather than names of humans) as well as for hypermedial home pages (which are located at specific 'sites' to be 'visited'), the genre of the epitaph offers, according to Fogarasi, a fruitful way of thinking about the logic of cash flow from the perspective of 'necromantic' spectrality. The chapter elaborates this problem by outlining Wordsworth's notion of the capitalist flow of attention as it appears in his description of London in Book VII of *The Prelude*. This reading is preceded by an introductory analysis of Gray's *Elegy* (with references to Adam Smith's writings on morals and economy), and also by some remarks concerning Wordsworth's own *Essays upon Epitaphs* and his poem 'Tintern Abbey'. Having established in this chapter the relationship between speculation and displacement Fogarasi's chapter provides the reader with the critical and theoretical framework to further explore the developmental trajectory of capitalism and its representation as mentioned in the opening paragraphs of this Introduction.

Speculative markets and imperial impulses towards colonial expansion are shown in Livesey's chapter on the representation of the people in *Our Mutual Friend* (1864–5) to be critical in an understanding of manhood or, what Livesey terms 'money suffrage'. Although Dickens's (1812–70) penultimate novel, *Our Mutual Friend*, appeared a couple of years before the passing of the Second Reform Act in 1867, the work took shape amid British parliamentary debates on various other franchise bills, most notably Benjamin Disraeli's proposals of 1859. Livesey reconsiders the text's well-known preoccupation with commodities and speculation in the context of this wider discussion of the relationship between representation and money in the 1860s: a political debate on the criteria to be used in judging a man worthy of the suffrage. Disraeli had proposed that the franchise should be granted to those with a certain amount of money in government funds, or in possession of East India Stock in addition to the automatic political representation of professionals such as doctors, lawyers and certain schoolmasters. The social reformer Frederick Denision Maurice (1866) classified such selection criteria as a form of 'money suffrage' that would eventually implicate the people in a melodramatic plot of popular revolution against the bloated plutocracy. The one thing needful, Maurice argued, was rather true 'manhood suffrage' in which political representation was contingent upon the male population recognising their part in what Livesey terms a romance plot of conservative populism: that all were 'freeborn Englishmen' prior to the imposition of that infamous Norman yoke. Dickens's text critically revisits Disraeli's sites of representation: being 'in the Funns' is a mere matter of speculation and the representatives of the professions are characterised by entropy. The chapter builds on recent work by Juliet John to argue that the displacement of the conventional triangulations of melodrama by a romance plot towards the close of *Our Mutual Friend* enacts the displacement of capital, speculation and class by the populist notion of true, universal manhood.

Returning to the journalistic genre, Aguiar problematises representation in the writings about, and literature of, what she terms feverish speculation, focusing on the railway development across the Isthmus of Panama in the nineteenth century. This chapter echoes the concerns described by Fauske's work on Swift and others where moral degeneration is associated with the mindless pursuit of wealth for purposes only of accumulation. In 1850, the Panama Railroad Company began a short railroad across the Isthmus of Panama. The American project drew speculators from every level of society, gold diggers gambling on riches on the west coast, bankers and businessmen investing in infrastructural development to bring in miners and hotel owners and salespeople capitalising on travellers' expectations. The American government underwrote these financial interests through international manoeuvres. Aguiar analyses mid-nineteenth-century travel narratives from Panama. She considers national and economic interests represented in the cultural space of letters, memoirs, stories and journalistic accounts. Looking at the recurring trope of fever, the chapter suggests the image demonstrates anxiety about a transforming United States. The vision of an unhealthy Panama provided justification for such developments as the railroad. The depictions of fever revealed fears of racial assimilation and moral decay. Aguiar argues in this chapter that the association of this place (recalling Fogarasi's treatment of place in the epitaphic tradition) and this historical time, with fever, shows cultural ambivalence towards an increased emphasis on speculative markets and growing imperial ambitions.

It was Grotius (1583–1645) who offered a rights-based (rather than civic-devotion or morality-based) view of justice in which was stressed the 'right of individuals to use the world for their private purposes' (Muller, 2003: 17). And, how we have understood 'private purposes' has in some measure laid at the base of arguments relating to the role of the state in curtailing or regulating the degree to which private interests could be pursued at the expense of, or for, the common good. Colonialism witnessed the peculiarly close relationship between the pursuit of trade and the creation of captive markets as part of imperial expansion. As a historical phenomenon colonialism gave rise to massive forms of displacement in the form of diasporas abroad and the concentration of capital in industrialised and highly urbanised metropolitan centres. Taking as its focus, not the representation of history, but rather the 'production of time' La Berge also identifies Theodore Dreiser's (1871–1945) *The Financier* (1912) as key to understanding the relationship between representations of time and money. La Berge argues that with the inauguration of a post-industrial moment of capitalism (after 1973), many cultural critics interested in the representation of economic phenomena abandoned studies of production in favour of consumption. La Berge suggests that instead of focusing on consumption, we should look at the regime of accumulation that replaced commodity production, that of finance. La Berge also claims that once isolated and understood, the 'financial form' of value is not unique to a post-1973 context and explores the representation of capital accumulation and temporality in classical and recent Marxist political economy through a reading of several theories of finance capital. The chapter establishes first a link between finance capital and temporality. Second, it suggests that from these readings we may develop what she terms a 'financial form', alongside the commodity form, which may be used as a hermeneutic for cultural and literary criticism. Finally, La Berge considers Dreiser's *The Financier* through a specifically financial optic. Her reading of Dreiser's text reveals the representation of the temporal nature of finance to be co-constitutive with the narrative structure of the novel.

A key feature of late twentieth-century capitalism is the de-linking of objects of production and their value. Nowhere in history is this more clearly signalled than when industrialised nations de-link gold from the value of money in order to survive catastrophic depressions and wars, owed in part to the implosion of inadequate systems of capitalist production as seen in the colonies and the captive markers they represented for empires. Roberts explores the representation of the gold standard in relation to money and language in the work of Jean-Joseph Goux. This chapter begins by exploring the relationship between literature and money in Gide's 1925 novel *The Counterfeiters* (*Les Faux Monnayeurs*). As Jean-Joseph Goux has argued in *The Coiners of Language* (1973), although counterfeit money is marginal to the plot, it is symbolically at the heart of the novel. In particular the theme of the fake and the counterfeit is in constant tension with the key Gidean themes of sincerity and authenticity. Roberts shows how Goux's discussion here develops out of his earlier concerns in Symbolic Economies. This leads to a critical examination of his central claim, namely that the decline of the gold standard in the field of economic currency is paralleled by a decline in the 'gold standard' of literary language, that is, literary realism. Roberts draws on Derrida's criticisms of Goux's historicising claims in his own given time: counterfeit money.

Capital is not only represented in text, or on paper. Its rise has inspired another kind or representation, the skyscraper, the unique architectural form associated with large buildings dedicated to the service of capital, whether these be corporations, banks or international organisations. Evrard suggests that the connections between early capitalism and late capitalism are revealed in the architecture of the early twentieth century, and that nowhere more clearly are such links demonstrated than at international trade fairs. In his discussion of the links between the objects or production and their value, Evrard makes this unique comparison between the architecture of France's and Canada's industrialised mega-agricultural production in the form of the Canadian grain elevators at the Paris 1937 International Exposition. This chapter uses two ephemeral buildings displaying the external shape of a grain elevator, in the specific context of the Paris International Exposition in 1937 – the Canadian pavilion at the foot of the Eiffel Tower and the French replica in the Rural Centre – to examine the representation of capital through architecture.

In the late 1930s, the grain elevator was the perfect building type for intellectual speculation and displacement, in the middle of conflicting values between modernity and tradition, internationalism and national identities, economic matters and social issues. De Certeau's conception of *The Practice of Everyday Life* (1988) is used to interpret both buildings' design and to explain why they appear as the representation of different national circumstances. Evrard argues that these French and Canadian grain elevator structures represented specific procedures in the commodification of agricultural capital. They respectively illustrated both stages of capitalist flows: production and consumption. With its international standard celebrated by the Modern movement, the French grain elevator was part of a space for a national strategy. Evrard argues that it conveyed a centralised message mainly to the French citizens about the improvement of life which was to arise from technological and social progress in France. The grain elevator was a symbol for the production of new agricultural habits, in order to strengthen the national economy in the global market.

While Thomas Aquinas (1225–74) might, as Muller (2003: 8) argues, have 'decried as covetousness the accumulation of wealth to improve one's place in the social order', it is that accumulation of wealth that appears to free Gordon Gekko in the film *Wall Street* (1987) from moral or social obligations to his family, minders or thousands of investors with whose capital he dispenses. Gekko practises an elevated form of usury, trading not on the interest extracted from loans, but on the rise and fall of currencies. His speculation on currencies contributes to market instability and ultimately represents a loss of value, not simply in terms of currency, but also in terms of locality and the value of place. What is evident in Elton McGoun's chapter is that traversing the global market need not mean international travel as the centres of capital (from which it moves and from which surplus populations become valuable or valueless) can, paradoxically, be confined to a single street, traversed as it is by an international financier in *Wall Street*. McGoun explores one of the puzzles of financial markets: the extent to which they are susceptible to manipulation by speculators as has been observed over the past century and a half or so in the United States. Why have regulation and enforcement, however rigorous, never been able to eliminate it? McGoun asserts, with reference to the film *Wall Street*, that financial market manipulation is not an exceptional excess of a few individuals, but an underlying condition inherent in American culture.

Contemporary films show that the characters who manipulate markets have achieved a mythic status. *Wall Street*'s Gordon Gekko displays cunning intelligence and plays the role of the cowboy in the Wild West myth. The West's myth of the cowboy as the myth of *Wall Street* justifies market manipulation. American culture values cunning when it is employed to challenge authority and break the bureaucratic rules and laws that keep the individual from realising his (not yet her) full potential. McGoun argues that audiences admire Gekko and people like him for their attacks on the status quo, and are entertained by their antics. Cowboy iconoclasts are not merely entertaining but are socially and economically necessary. In order to avoid stagnation, we need rules not only to be challenged but to be broken. Wall Street itself, assisted by the media, is engaged in an ongoing process of mythopoeia in which we seek to accommodate conflicting feelings concerning the opposition between law-makers and law-breakers, both of whom our culture has created. The contending forces of manipulation and its detection and punishment are engaged in an ongoing process of myth-making which has as its basis the disconnection between the movement of capital, the signification of value, and the populations affected, displaced and disempowered by such unregulated and erratic speculation. This chapter suggests that one of the effects of late twentieth-century capitalism is that it requires large populations that can be similarly manipulated when value becomes divorced from labour.

In *Globalization and the Dilemmas of the State in the South* (1999) Adams, Gupta and Mengisteab describe with reference to politics, economics and sociology, the movement of peoples in response to advances in technology and the development of speculative capital as a primary force in the global economy. Another important text charts the development of the ideology of Western identity politics. GoGwilt in *The Invention of the West: Joseph Conrad and the Double Mapping of Europe and Empire* (1995) takes as its basis the literature of Joseph Conrad as a lens through which the creation of empires, the development of the notion of 'other' (in terms of race, class and gender) in Western thought is represented. This book is closely aligned with what we attempt in *Culture, Capital and Representation,* but we address these ideas within a historical trajectory that takes into account social, artistic and textual representation of economic phenomena as seen in the development of stock exchanges, bubbles, art, literature, architecture and media. From a theoretical perspective texts such as *The Empire Writes Back* (by Ashcroft, Griffiths and Tiffin, 1989) provide a post-colonial account of the development race and identity areas formerly colonised and problematises metropolitan and colonial assumptions regarding these categories, their invention, and perpetuation in the post-colonial order. Our text does not take the colonial period and its aftermath as a starting point because capital, though intrinsic to colonisation, predates it and its associations with exploitation and marginalisation cannot be limited to geographical entities such as the post-colonial world, but extend beyond this to the very origins of the colonising impulse, Europe itself and the displacement and dispossession associated with the collapse of medievalism, the growth of the nation state and the onset of industrialisation.

A recent text which explores the development of capitalism from a socio-economic as well as philosophical perspective has been referred to at the beginning of this Introduction, *The Mind and the Market* (Muller, 2003). In this important survey concerning the Western intellectual tradition in relation to the development and spread of capitalism, Muller has provided an invaluable reference point for our own book. Unlike Muller's work, however, we have sought to provide a more detailed observation of cultural phenomena over a period of time. And, whilst such a treatment cannot be exhaustive, the advantage of this book over others is that it not only brings together a broad disciplinary range but also a wealth of perspectives which are shown to be developmental (over time in our historical arrangement of the chapters) but also different in terms of emphases and utility. Given the spectacular collapse of the free market system in 2008, the timing of *Culture, Capital and Representation* is apposite because it attempts to illustrate, but not from an economic theory perspective, the cumulative effects of speculation in relation to the displacement of the person and the value of a person's labour.

Finally, Marangoly-George's *The Politics of Home: Postcolonial Relocations and Twentieth-Century Fiction* (1996) is an example of a text that addresses migration, relocation and dispossession within a post-colonial framework. While we see that as valuable, our book attempts to pull back into the eighteenth and nineteenth centuries, to draw out the implications of such research, and to consider the development and representation of capital through a variety of genres (not only literature) and discourses. A volume such as this cannot be exhaustive in its treatment of cultural phenomena over a period of three centuries, and the selection of texts or phenomena has been determined not necessarily by the existing body of research already available. I believe that the book occupies a special niche in the published scholarship on capitalism, achieving as it does an interdisciplinarity between fields of scholarship. The range and span of material covered here is likely also to have a popular as well as scholarly appeal, this especially in view of the recent market instability and media and public interest shown in the collapse of value in currencies and commodities.

1
Colonialism, Displacement and Cannibalism in Early Modern Economic Thought

Hugh Goodacre

Introduction: 'political arithmetic', cannibalism and Enlightenment

The representation of political-economic issues in eighteenth-century literature cannot be adequately understood without an appreciation of what it was that writers of that period were concerned to put behind them – the unvarnished and crude discourse of the bureaucratic-military officialdom of the preceding century, exemplified, in the economic literature, by the 'political arithmetic' of William Petty.[1] The most comprehensive – and for many the definitive – response to writers like Petty was provided by Adam Smith, who skilfully combined the lofty tones of moral philosophy with homely discussions of everyday economic affairs in a determined attempt to rescue the apparatus of economic analysis from its association with those who had forged it and refurbish it in such a way as to make it an acceptable element of a discourse which claimed the mantle of Enlightenment. Accordingly, far from acknowledging any debt to his unenlightened forebears, he breezily dismisses them with the declaration: 'I have no great faith in political arithmetic' (*Wealth of Nations* IV, v).

As is almost inevitable in the case of any comprehensive response to a felt intellectual need, Smith's repudiation of political arithmetic had long been anticipated from within the field of literature. For it was Jonathan Swift, author of *Gulliver's Travels*, who, nearly half a century before the publication of Smith's work, had delivered an opening broadside, in his oft-cited satirical pamphlet of 1729 entitled *A modest proposal for preventing the children of poor people from becoming a burthen to their parents or country, and for making them beneficial to the publick*. This pamphlet takes the form of a gruesome proposal for the breeding of Irish children as livestock. The supposed benefits of this scheme are elaborated in ridiculous quantitative terms which capture Petty's mode of expression with icy accuracy, as do the associated comments on this 'excellent nutritious meat' – 'whether stewed, roasted, baked or boiled'. A panoply of statistical justification is adduced, of a type very familiar to readers of Petty's writings, covering the demographic aspects, the average weight of each carcass, the costs ('about two shillings per annum, rags included'), potential uses for the hides ('gloves for ladies, and summer boots for fine gentlemen'), the export potential, the numbers to be 'reserved for breed', the implications for the revenue of the church, and so on.

William Petty (1623–87) had been a senior official in the Cromwellian military-colonial administration in Ireland. The invasion of 1649 which established that administration had been launched with the declared intention of implementing a punitive programme of mass executions, enslavements and deportations of Irish 'rebels', and the confinement of the remaining Irish population within a kind of reservation in the western province of the country – the notorious policy of 'To Hell or Connaught!' Though it did not prove feasible to carry out this programme in the form originally envisaged, the expropriation of Irish land in favour of English beneficiaries went ahead as planned, and Petty played a pivotal role in the administration of this land redistribution process. Subsequently, after the restoration of the English monarchy in 1660, Petty managed to retain most of the extensive lands he had amassed for himself through sharp practice in the performance of his duties, but he never succeeded in relaunching his official career on the high-flying course it had taken under the Cromwellian regime. In his vain attempts to claw his way back into high office, he continued to the end of his days to advance proposals for all kinds of fiscal, administrative, naval and military reforms – some practical, some prophetic, some fantastic – and it is to the text of these proposals that historians of economic thought have traced much of the analytical apparatus still in use by economists today.

Long after his death, then, Petty's writings remained a byword for the generation of all manner of policy proposals, and even his successors in the field of political arithmetic acknowledged that he epitomised the kind of thought process Swift parodies – a seamless drift from an apparent extreme of rationality and claims of benevolence to the most extravagantly impractical and morally indefensible policy conclusions. Furthermore, not least of his policy concerns was the promotion of Ireland's livestock production. There could consequently have been little doubt in the minds of Swift's readers who had provided the principal inspiration for his pamphlet's central character, the 'modest proposer'. This is not to say that the actual arguments Swift satirises can all be traced back to Petty; on the contrary, in the decades since Petty's death, debates on population issues had generated an extensive pamphlet literature, much of which had specific reference to Ireland and its economic condition, and the actual points at issue had to a great extent moved beyond those centralised by Petty. Swift's pamphlet abounds in satirical allusions to this later literature, contributors to which had, since Petty's death, embraced many of the best-known pamphleteers of the period, including Child, Defoe and Davenant (see Landa, 1942 and Wittkowsky, 1943 for early but still valuable surveys). Not least of those to whom the pamphlet alludes is Swift himself, who did not escape his own merciless self-parody (Rawson, 1978: 121–44). But while the specific arguments alluded to in the pamphlet thus range far beyond those identifiable in Petty's writings, it is hard to avoid the conclusion that it is Petty's characteristic mode of argumentation which provides a connecting thread running through the entire range of Swift's satire.[2]

Petty's own economic preoccupations regarding Ireland had centred around his endeavours to assess and reassess the mixed experience of the Cromwellian colonial administration in Ireland in its attempts to implement its ambitious policy objectives, an experience which had coincided with the height of his own official career. The end result of this prolonged process of assessment was his proposal to transfer the bulk of the Irish population not westwards to the province of Connaught, as in the Cromwellian 'transplantation' scheme, but eastwards into England. The aim was to increase the population density, or 'compactness', of England's population, this being, in his view, the key to the advantages enjoyed by Holland, at that time not only Europe's most densely populated country, but also its most economically advanced. Ireland, conversely, would be transformed into a 'kind of factory' for rearing livestock for England, in other words one vast cattle ranch, which would have the concomitant beneficial effect of putting an end to Ireland's independent national life and its associated anti-colonial traditions, and would accordingly bring about a 'perpetual settlement' (or, the term used prophetically by his editor in 1899, a 'final solution') that could, at last, 'cut up the roots of those evils' which 'have made Ireland, for the most part, a diminution and a burthen, not an advantage, to England' (*TI* 551, 546 (editorial comment), 558 §5).

In short, Petty's writings on Ireland exemplify a viewpoint that was subsequently to be lost in the literature of political economy, let alone in the economics of today – a viewpoint from which the colonised peoples had not yet been rendered invisible, and where their suppression and even extirpation was neither elided from, nor merely implicit in, political and economic discourse, but was an openly proclaimed policy objective. In what follows, it will accordingly be argued that the colonial experience must be brought back from the theoretical periphery to which it is customarily consigned by the hegemonic discourse within the economics profession, and restored to the centre of attention which it actually occupied in the writings of those who first forged the analytical apparatus which is still in use by economists today.³

Representation of material wealth

The concept of capital as an exploitative social relationship operating within the sphere of production was advanced by Marx in the form of a critique of political economy, a body of literature which, he argued, had served to obscure this relationship. If capital is indistinctly conceptualised even by writers such as Smith and Ricardo who were the primary focus of Marx's critique, it is not surprising that it lacks direct representation in the work of Petty. Nevertheless, even in his writings, there is already a clear recognition of the need for some such analytical category. This is particularly evident in his pioneering formulation of a system of national income accounts, where he distinguishes three sources of income, namely land, labour, and a further category which he terms 'money and other personal estates' – a three-fold categorisation which is commonly taken to anticipate the concept of 'factors of production' which still underlies the orthodox economic analysis of today.

Petty's motive in carrying out his national income calculation is to advocate raising the share of the tax burden imposed upon labouring people. He suggests that England's total national expenditure is £40 million per annum, and – on the same principle as that used in national income accounts today – assumes that national income must therefore equal the same amount. He estimates the total value of land and of 'money and other personal estates', and, on the assumption that these each yield roughly the same rate of return (around 6 per cent), reckons that, taken together, they account for £15 million of the £40 million expenditure; consequently, he reasons, the source of the residual amount, i.e. the remaining £25 million, must be labour.

This calculation gives Petty the conclusion he is looking for: if the income of labouring people accounts for five-eighths of total national income (i.e. £25 million out of £40 million), they should pay five-eighths of the tax. This would be a very substantial proportional increase, and was to be accomplished by the regressive virtues of direct taxation on the consumption goods of the poor – the 'excise' – which, in the language of the radical pamphlet literature of the time, ensured that 'the poor labourer, who hath threshed all day for a livelihood, should himself be threshed at night' ('Philo-dicæus' 1647: 116). Petty's standpoint towards labouring people is further revealed in an extension of the same calculation. Since labourers, i.e. 'people', generate an income of £25 million, then, assuming they yield the same rate of return as land and 'money and other personal estates', i.e. 6 per cent, they must be worth £417 million, or (assuming the population to be 6 million) £69 a head. That this calculation of 'the value of the people' brings to mind the slave trade is by no means fortuitous. On the contrary, for Petty there is no conceptual difference between wage labour and slavery; rather, they are placed on a continuum, with slavery at the lower limit, where people are 'forced to as much labour, and as cheap fare, as nature will endure' (*TTC* 68 §12). Correspondingly, his various discussions of this calculation are interspersed with estimates of the price of slaves, both Irish and African.

But to return to the representation of the category of 'money and other personal estates', Petty clearly perceives material wealth to be associated with a particular form of income which is distinct from the rent of land. However, the nature of the income-producing property of this category remains unexplained, and it is more characteristic of his writings as a whole that anything analogous to 'capital' is elided, leaving the two-fold approach epitomised in his celebrated statement that 'labour is the father and active principle of wealth, as lands are the mother' (*TTC*: 68). Accordingly, it is generally agreed that Petty displays no clear awareness of the role of capital – that his economic thought is, quite simply, 'pre-capitalist' (Aspromourgos, 1996: 49–51, 89–95).

It is nevertheless worth noting some of the features of his representation of material wealth, if only to distinguish it from that of writers of the subsequent period. First of all, it is immediately evident that his category of 'money and other personal estates' is closely associated with the luxury consumption of the rich, as exemplified by the estimates he provides of 'utensils of plate and furnitures', 'silks, linen and calicos', 'wines, oils and other liquids', 'grocery and spicery and drugs', 'jewels and hangings, beds and other ornaments too troublesome to particularise', and so on (*VS*: 107). His lists also include items which would now be categorised as physical capital, or as 'produced means of production' (Aspromourgos, 1996: 40), such as 'shops, warehouses, cellars, barns and granaries' (*VS*: 106–7) and 'tradesmen's tools and utensils' (*PP1*: 181), but these are mixed in somewhat indiscriminately, without any suggestion that they merit a separate category distinct from that of the general one of 'money and other personal estates'; if any sub-categorisation is hinted at, it is in the distinction between durable and nondurable items, rather than between consumption and production goods (Aspromourgos, 1996: 40).

As for financial wealth, Petty has only the most limited idea of anything beyond 'coined gold and silver of the kingdom' (*VS*: 106 §10). He was among those who advocated the issue of credit on the security of land, an idea that was subsequently to mature into the 'land bank' proposals of subsequent decades, but in general his views on financial institutions are undeveloped. In particular, he uses the term 'bank' in such a way as to show that it is, for him, effectively synonymous with the monarch's war chest, or a 'stock for war' (*TI*: 572, 557 §3, 567); indeed, the idea of a financial system separate (at least in theory) from the monarch's fiscal-military arrangements only became widely current in England with the formation of the Bank of England in 1694, seven years after Petty's death.

Recent research has, to some extent, modified the formerly negative assessment of Petty's engagement with capitalist ideas. For example, it has been argued that there are elements of capitalistic calculation in his primitive concept of opportunity costs, or 'stock lying dead' (Aspromourgos, 2000: 62). He has even been credited with a concept of the circulation of capital, in his plan to pay workers at his iron foundry in Ireland in iron ore – what might be termed (by analogy with Ricardo's single-commodity 'corn-corn' model) an 'ore-ore' model (Aspromourgos, 2000: 59).

However, whatever anticipations or premonitions of the capitalist system may be discernible in Petty's economic analysis, it remains clear that it would be anachronistic to search there for any substantial or direct representation of capital, or of the associated phenomena which began to exercise the popular imagination in the following century, such as stock market bubbles, and so on. It is, rather, in the representation of the preconditions for the emergence of that new stage in the identification of capital that Petty's writings are most relevant, and to these we now turn.

Representation of labouring people and the wage system

The existence of the capitalist system presupposes, as Marx points out, a 'primitive accumulation' of capital, which precedes capitalist accumulation, which is 'not the result of the capitalist mode of production, but its starting-point', a historical prerequisite which 'plays in political economy about the same part as original sin in theology' (1976: 26). Though Petty's writings undoubtedly bring us face to face with the circumstances of this era in the most vivid manner, it is nevertheless a complex task to establish to what degree he was aware of its defining characteristic – the process through which labour is brought into subjection to the power of capital, so that capitalist accumulation can accordingly be set in train. To explore this question, his writings need to be carefully situated in their biographical and historical context; this makes it possible to distinguish four successive, though overlapping, phases in his perspective on labouring people, each of which illustrates an aspect of the preliminary engagements of early modern economic literature with the newly emerging socio-economic relations of capitalism.

The first phase in Petty's perspective on labouring people can be discerned in his writings of the Cromwellian period and its aftermath. At this time, he was concerned to defend the interests of the dominant faction of large landowners in Ireland who opposed the original plan to 'transplant' the Irish *en masse*. These landowners, of which Petty himself was a prominent representative, were naturally more than happy to see dispossessed 'rebel' landowners out of the way, but they wanted the actual cultivators of the soil to be left where they were so that they could effectively enserf them in 'feudal' style, in the sense that they were to be retained *in situ* as effectively an adjunct to the land.

A second phase in Petty's perspective on labour may be discerned following the restoration of the English monarchy in 1660. He now resided primarily in England for a number of years, during which time a contradiction opened out between his own continuing status as a kind of 'neo-feudal' colonial grandee in Ireland, on the one hand, and his growing interest in the advance of the wage system in England, on the other.[4] In the latter connection, he addressed the issue of the motivation of labour in a way that was characteristic of his time, seeing an excessive wage level, or, in real terms, 'over-feeding of the people', as inevitably resulting in 'indisposing them to their usual labour' (*PA*: 275) – a concept which remains an essential element of the economist's toolkit, in the form of the so-called 'backward-bending labour supply curve' represented diagrammatically in today's microeconomics textbooks.

At the aggregate, or 'macroeconomic', level, Petty actually ran ahead of the times in his system of national accounts, where he categorised the income of the entire labouring population purely and simply – and as yet utterly unrealistically – as 'wages'. Such use of simplifying assumptions and their application to schematic concepts and calculations explains the fascination which his writings hold for historians of economic thought, who find there, in primitive form, such a striking anticipation of the deductive method of economic analysis still in use today. However, in terms of the representation of the conditions of the labouring people of his own time, an assumption of the universality, or even the predominance, of the wage system was anachronistic. Certainly it is true that the dispossession of the peasantry was already far advanced, but it by no means follows that the resulting dispossessed population had as yet become a wage-earning labour force, least of all a homogeneous one such as that suggested by his national income calculations. If such was the case in England, then it was incomparably more so in Ireland, and, when Petty returned to live in that country once again, his writings began to express increasing frustration over the problems involved in establishing a wage-earning labour force at all in the conditions prevailing there. For the Irish socio-economic system, based as it still was on communal as well as individual patterns of land use, remained, even at this time, fully capable of reabsorbing into itself those who might otherwise have constituted the demographic base for a wage-earning class.

Petty roots his comments on this situation in observation. The Irish, he states,

> are able to perform their husbandry with such harness and tackling as each man can make with his own hands, and living in such houses as almost every man can build; and every housewife being a spinner and dyer of wool and yarn, they can live and subsist after their present fashion, without the use of gold or silver money. (*PA*: 273)

Such being the case, the cash economy constitutes, by his estimate, only a fifth of all their 'expense', the rest of their consumption being 'what their own family produceth' (*PAI*: 192); the principal exception is tobacco, which was evidently spearheading the introduction of cash transactions for consumption goods into the agrarian economy – the Coca-Cola of its day. He furthermore asserts that the Irish are able to supply themselves with 'the necessities above-named without labouring two hours per diem' (*PA*: 273). He consequently asks:

> What need they to work, who can content themselves with potatoes, whereof the labour of one man can feed forty, and with milk, whereof one cow will in summertime give meat and drink enough for three men, when they can everywhere gather cockles, oysters, muscles, crabs, etc., with boats, nets, angles or the art of fishing, [and] can build an house in three days? (*PAI*: 201)

Petty's discussions of how the Irish are to be 'kept to their labour' (*PAI*: 189) thus illustrate the obstacles to the subjection of labour to capital in conditions where they have the alternative of an independent livelihood on the land. As Marx was later to point out in the final chapter of the first volume of *Capital*, such conditions were to remain characteristic of the colonial world throughout the centuries that followed.

From frustration and over-simplification it is only a short step to fantasy, and it was accordingly to this that Petty turned in what signalled a third phase in his changing perception of labour – his scheme for the wholesale transfer of the Irish population to England. He is nothing if not explicit in his acknowledgement of the fantastic nature of this scheme:

> And here I beg leave, among the several matters which I intend for serious, to interpose a jocular and perhaps ridiculous digression, and which I indeed desire men to look upon rather as a dream or reverie than a rational proposition ... If ingenious and learned men, among whom I reckon Sir Tho. More and Descartes, have disputed that we who think ourselves awake are, or may be, really in a dream, and since the greatest absurdities of dreams are but a preposterous and tumultuary contexture of realities, I will crave the umbrage of these great men last named to say something for this wild conception, with submission to the better judgment of all those that can prove themselves awake. (*PA*: 285)

But though Petty initially presented his scheme in such terms, in his subsequent writings it begins to take on a more practical and systematic character, until it finally assumes a form which marks the fourth and final stage of his developing perspective on labouring people. Labour and land now appear in a form increasingly analogous to that of the 'factors of production' of subsequent economics, and in particular play the role of, respectively, mobile and immobile factors as they appear in today's spatial-economic analysis, with whose logic his 'transplantation' scheme has much in common (see further in Goodacre 2005 and 2009). Furthermore, far from acknowledging any association of his scheme with the world of 'dream or reverie', he now provides an elaborate apparatus of statistical justification which pioneers the entire genre of the economic policy proposal as it has existed ever since.

In the course of this long and complex biographical and intellectual trajectory, Petty's life and thought at one time or another exemplified all those phenomena which Marx associates with the primitive accumulation of capital – violence, social upheaval, expropriation of the cultivators from their land, the centrality of the state as the prime economic agent, and 'passions the most infamous, the most sordid, the pettiest, the most meanly odious' (1976: 32). Marx characterised Adam Smith as 'the political economist *par excellence* of the period of manufacture' (1976: 14, iii). Petty might equally appropriately be described as 'the political economist *par excellence* of the period of primitive accumulation'.

Colonialist propaganda and the cultural representation of colonised peoples

As part of the preparation for its invasion of Ireland in 1649, the Cromwellian regime sponsored the publication of a body of propaganda setting out, perhaps for the first time in such a systematic way, England's long-term colonial objectives, which it aimed to justify by reference to 'Irish barbarism and the idea of an English civilizing mission' (Carlin, 1993: 210).

In his writings on Ireland, Petty incorporates the doctrines enunciated in this body of literature, but surpasses it all in his relentless efforts at theoretical systematisation. In particular, he sought to explain the supposed backwardness of the Irish in materialistic, rather than religious, terms. He was, for example, prepared to consider the possibility that the problem might lie in their physical make-up, though he concluded that this was not an adequate explanation: 'For their shape, stature, colour, and complexion, I see nothing in them inferior to any other people, nor any enormous predominance of any humour' (*PAI*: 201). It was not that he lacked crude notions in the field of physical anthropology, which he did not hesitate to apply to the 'several species of man' inhabiting other continents. Rather, his observation of Irish society was sufficiently close for him to prefer less fanciful, though nonetheless materialist, explanations: 'Their lazing seems to me to proceed rather from want of employment and encouragement to work than from the natural abundance of phlegm in their bowels and blood' (*PAI*: 201).

But while the intractability of Irish labour to subjection to the wage system could thus not be attributed to their physical characteristics, it was, he suggests, nonetheless deeply rooted, in consequence of 'their ancient customs, which affect as well their consciences as their nature'; for, he asks,

> why should they desire to fare better, though with more labour, when they are taught that this way of living is more like the patriarchs of old and the saints of later times, by whose prayers and merits they are to be relieved, and whose examples they are therefore to follow? (*PAI*: 201–2)

Petty shared with the Cromwellian propaganda a range of arguments commonly used in the period to justify rule by conquest, and in particular urged that the Irish could be made to realise that "tis their interest to join with them and follow their example who have brought arts, civility and freedom into their country' (*PAI*: 203). In connection with the 'arts', a category which then included technology, Petty claims that there were 'not ten iron furnaces' in the whole of Ireland (*PAI*: 209). That which he established on his own estate was manned primarily, if not exclusively, by colonists from England, and his experience in this and his other enterprises doubtless strengthened his prejudice that only colonialism could introduce technological progress into Ireland.

An associated argument, which was once again taken up by Petty from the Cromwellian propaganda, was that, left to themselves, the Irish would fail to develop the natural resources of their country – an argument that was to remain a familiar feature of colonialist writings throughout the subsequent era, and was indeed one of the prime contexts in which the term 'economic development' first came into currency two centuries later. Nor is this by any means the only element in Petty's writings on Ireland which anticipates the perspective of today's orthodoxy on issues of economic development, concerned, as they both are, to represent their objectives as being everywhere frustrated by the supposed shortcomings in the character, morals or motivation of the colonised and formerly colonised peoples.

For example, reflecting on the 'indisposition' of the Irish to take to maritime trade, Petty complains that 'the Irish had rather eat potatoes and milk on dry land than contest with the wind and waves with better food' (*PAI*: 208). With such a failure of a culture of enterprise to take root, it is no surprise that commercial institutions are in a dire state, and he poses the question:

> Why should they [i.e. the Irish] raise more commodities, since there are not merchants sufficiently stocked to take them of them, nor provided with other more pleasing foreign commodities to give in exchange for them? (*PAI*: 201)

Moreover, commercial transactions are impeded by corresponding deficiencies in the financial institutions, in the form of 'difference, confusion and badness of coins, [and] exorbitant exchange and interest of money' (*PAI*: 196), as well as weakness of what development economists now term 'property rights', which leads Petty to ask: 'Why should men endeavour to get estates, where the legislative power is not agreed upon, and where tricks and words destroy natural right and property?' (*PAI*: 202).

Finally, Petty enthusiastically embraces that most characteristic feature of the ideology of conquest – the assertion that the colonised people lacked any history, culture or learning at all prior to the arrival of the invader:

> There is at this day no monument or real argument that, when the Irish were first invaded, they had any stone housing at all, any money, any foreign trade, nor any learning but the legends of the Saints, Psalters, Missals, Rituals, etc., viz. nor geometry, astronomy, anatomy, architecture, engineery, painting, carving, nor any kind of manufacture, nor the least use of navigation or the art military. (*PAI*: 154–5)

The ultimate insult in this connection was the assertion that the Irish were intruders in their own country, a common suggestion being that they were of 'Scythian' origin, an idea which supposedly explained the apparently 'nomadic' aspect of Irish pastoral society, an aspect which in fact reflected the practice of transhumance, or seasonal migration. This idea had been given wide currency by the English poet Spenser (Coughlan, 1990: 207; Morgan, 1985: 268), and has been described as a 'last twist of the knife' comparable with 'white South African claims that the black majority are late arrivals in the area' (Carlin, 1993: 221–2). Petty characteristically advanced his own 'conjecture', which was that Ireland's first inhabitants were likely to have come from Scotland, rather than being 'Phoenicians, Scythians, Biscayers, etc.' (*PAI*: 204), a less outlandish conjecture, perhaps, though doubtless intended to be no less wounding.

Colonialism and Utopia

What the tone of Petty's discussions lacks in fanatical invective is amply compensated by a clinical note which is, arguably, even more chilling. As has been remarked in the course of the call for a 'reappraisal of Irish history', such 'austerely clinical terms' were until very recently seen as an essential prerequisite for an 'academic' approach to the history of that country, resulting in an elision of its 'catastrophic dimension', 'thereby de-sensitising the trauma' of the country's colonial experience (Bradshaw, [1989] 1994: 201–4). While Ireland, as has now been seen, provides a particular vantage point from which to survey some early representations of the emerging capitalist system in their colonial context, the need for such a historical reappraisal is, of course, far from being confined to Ireland alone, being, on the contrary, a common requirement of the vast majority of humankind today.

Petty, who was, like a number of early modern writers on economic thought, a trained physician, takes his use of anatomical imagery to extremes in his attempts to justify his methodological approach to socio-economic analysis. In particular, he regards Ireland as presenting an ideal opportunity for such 'political anatomy', just as 'students in medicine practice their inquiry upon cheap and common animals' (*PAI*: 129; for discussion, see Coughlan, 1990: 213–20). The English state's experiments in this 'laboratory' of Ireland aimed at 'governmental modernization, colonial expansion, religious reformation and identity formation all in process simultaneously' (Morgan, 1999: 9). In the case of each of these processes, everything that constituted an advance from the English point of view necessarily entailed measures to suppress Ireland's cultural, political and religious life and annihilate its national identity: 'the development of "Englishness" depended on the negation of "Irishness"' (Hadfield and Maley, 1993: 7).

This was a time when the state's role as the prime economic agency for any such socio-economic initiative remained ideologically unchallenged, and, in this case as in many others, literary engagement with such policy issues necessarily took indirect forms, one of which was the literature of Utopianism. Petty's writings epitomise the process through which this literature was increasingly divesting itself of any pretence to be 'merely fictional', and was, on the contrary, openly merging with the literature of practical statesmanship. Petty was far from being the first to discuss the colonial dimension of the issues in question; on the contrary, Thomas More's *Utopia* itself has been described as marking 'a watershed in the development of colonial theory' (Morgan, 1985: 269).

A topical pamphlet in the Utopian genre at the time of Petty's arrival in Ireland described a mythical kingdom named 'Macaria', whose 'excellent government' included a number of 'councils' handling the different aspects of state policy, one of these being a 'council for new plantations [i.e. colonies]' (Webster, 1979: 67–8). Petty greatly elaborated such ideas in his later writings, and in his final scheme for the transformation of Ireland into a 'kind of factory', he outlined precisely such a council (a 'council of fitting persons') in terms which vividly illustrate the transition from utopian speculation to the practicalities of administering a planned economy:

> pitching the number of each species of cattle, for every sort of land within the whole territory of Ireland; the same may pitch the number of cow-herds, shepherds, dairy-women, slaughter men and others, which are fit and sufficient to manage the trade of exported cattle, dead or alive, of hides, tallow, butter and cheese, wool and sea-fish, etc.; to appoint the foreign markets and ports where each commodity is to be shipped and sold, to provide shipping, and to keep account of the exportation above mentioned, and of the imported salt, tobacco, with a few other necessaries. (*TI*: 575)

The demographic profile of the population remaining in Ireland is to be subject to 'adjustment', in such a way as to

> pitch how many of them shall be English, or such as can speak English, and how many Irish, how many Catholics and how many others, without any other respect, than the management of this trade, for the common good of all the owners of these lands, and its stock indifferently. (*TI*: 575)

This power of the council extends to 'managing the multiplication' of the population (*TI*: 605), and since the entire population is to be 'all aged between 16 and 60 years' (*TI*: 563), the council will also be obliged to 'carry away children and superannuated persons'.

Despite the normally positive connotations which the term 'Utopia' enjoys today, there has, from Plato's *Republic* onwards, traditionally been, explicitly or implicitly, an associated 'dystopia' for those excluded from its highest privileges, and it is in this sense that the French geographer Yann-Morvran Goblet describes Petty's vision of the relation between England and Ireland as a system of 'twin utopias' (Goblet, 1930: 2, 280–306). The polarity between the two comes across vividly in

Petty's writings as a whole: on the one hand, the variety and luxury of the glittering colonial metropolis of London, with its 'plays, entertainments of the shows of nature and art', its 'fair collections of all natural and artificial rarities', 'all meats, drinks and clothings that the whole world affords', the liberty it provides 'to see beautiful women with and without impunity', its 'great variety of drinks, viz., of all sorts of waters, beers and ales, cider and juices of fruit, of wines from all countries and of distilled spirits and essences', and so on (*PP1*: 41–2); on the other hand stands the dour homogeneity of Petty's scheme for a 'new model Ireland' (*TI*: 567) – housing that reaches a standard of basic habitability (*TI*: 577), clothes that are 'uniform' (*TI*: 569), and a humble country diet of potatoes and dairy products, enlivened only by foraging (*PAI*: 201, as quoted above).

The grimly practical manner in which Petty set out his plan illustrates all the different means he had at various times considered for wiping out Ireland's national traditions – economic, social and cultural – which had proved so resilient to transformation in accordance with the requirements of colonialism and emergent capitalism. His scheme would, he claimed, facilitate the eradication of the Irish language, along with the replacement of 'those uncertain and unintelligible' Irish place names (*PAI*: 208). It would provide ample scope for cross-marriages, in particular between Irish men and English women, so that the offspring would be reared in the language and culture of their mothers (*PAI*: 202–3). In short, 'the manners, habits, language and customs of the Irish ... would all be transmuted into English' (*TI*: 573), and they would thus be rendered, literally, invisible – linguistically, economically, ideologically. (On the concept of transmutation in Petty's schemes for the Irish, see McCormick, 2006 and further works by that author.)

The status of 'neo-feudal' and bureaucratic upstarts such as Petty was predicated on the strength of the state rather than, as in the 'true' feudalism of the medieval period, its weakness. Their fortunes were made through exploiting the opportunities presented by war – civil, international and colonial – and the fiscal arrangements necessary to finance it. Correspondingly, their aspiration was to ensconce themselves ever more securely in the 'fiscal-military state', that bureaucratic-military structure whose growth 'created new social roles, justified by distinctive kinds of legitimisation', requiring 'linguistic resources which justified and explained (and therefore enabled) the growth of fiscal-military power' (Braddick, 2000: 270f.). Petty's engagement with ideas of Utopian derivation was an essential aspect of this process of generating these linguistic and ideological resources.

Displacement, the state and the market

Today's economic orthodoxy, which generally exercises its sway with notorious intolerance, has, as an exception, customarily allowed a degree of heterodoxy to prevail within its sub-discipline of development economics, in a tacit admission that the orthodox analytical apparatus is incapable of addressing issues of 'structural change', obstacles to the extension of the market, and associated topics such as displacement, migration, and so on. However, as part and parcel of this defensive manoeuvre, the subject of colonialism and its legacy is driven out to the margins of the economics discipline, where it is expected to share the ground with women's issues, racism, the environment and other issues which are similarly subjected to characterisation as denizens of a theoretical fringe.

The aim of the present enquiry has been to challenge this perspective, and to argue that an appreciation of the colonial context is necessary not only for the circumscribed range of issues which the orthodoxy wishes to peripheralise in this way, but to the core issues of economic analysis as a whole; the main examples in the present enquiry have concerned early representations of material wealth and the wage system, but the same could equally be argued in respect of similarly central economic concepts such as price, supply, demand and the market, and it is to the last of these that we shall now turn by way of conclusion.

For Petty, it is a well-informed state, rather than the market, which is best fitted to allocate resources and regulate the economy, and it is accordingly to high office in the state that he directs his ambitions. He consequently complains in his correspondence about the frustration of his ambitions at Court: 'I have no luck with my politics. Slight Court tricks have advanced many men, but the solid study of other men's peace and plenty ruins me' (*PSC*: 61). The imagery of gambling is clearly implicit in these references to 'luck' and 'tricks' at Court, and their attendant danger of 'ruin'. Such allusions to gambling become explicit when he writes of the market, where, he remarks, 'particular men get from their neighbours ... rather by hit than wit, and by the false opinions of others, rather than their own judgements' (*TTC*: 52f. §17). All this suggests that Petty did not see the market as an alternative to state agency, but rather as an extreme case of the shortcomings to which the state was also liable if the forces of 'luck' and 'hit' were allowed to prevail over the sound judgement and 'wit' with which he regarded himself as so plentifully endowed.

Ironically, by dismissing the market in favour of the blunter instrument of state action, Petty was turning his back on precisely those forces that were ultimately to achieve what, for him, had been only a 'dream or reverie'. For, as Yann-Morvran Goblet, writing in 1930, tellingly observed, Petty's scheme was grimly prophetic of what was actually to transpire in the two centuries that followed, when Ireland was indeed emptied of the majority of its inhabitants, many of them transported abroad as he had advocated, its language and traditional way of life fighting for survival, and much of the country's territory converted into one vast cattle ranch. This prompted Goblet to ask: 'What politician has ever put forward a plan, be it never so formal and official, which has been realized so comprehensively, point by point, as the "reverie" of Sir William Petty?' (Goblet, 1930: 2, 305).

Conclusion: colonialism and the history of economic thought

Swift's parody of Petty in his pamphlet of 1729 was written at a time when the horrors of the previous era of conflict and despotism had already been exposed in such an all-round way that it would seem impossible to imagine any further depth to the nightmare represented by unrestrained state power. Yet Swift proved capable of mustering the imagination to portray an even worse nightmare scenario still, an ultimate *reductio ad absurdum*, posing as he did the question that if state power is unrestrained, what would stand in the way of Petty's political arithmetic actually being taken seriously? The scheme suggested in the pamphlet is, after all, perfectly logical in terms of that methodology: if it is agreed that a people is to be displaced, rendered invisible or 'transmuted', then it clearly makes sense to proceed to the quantitative stage and calculate what makes the best economic sense. In Petty's new-fangled quantitative version of deductive reasoning, conclusions were represented as 'intellectually binding on anyone who accepted the premises and could find no flaw in the logic' (Letwin, 1963: 136–7), or, to use his own words:

> The observations or positions expressed by number, weight, and measure, upon which I bottom the ensuing discourses, are either true or not apparently false ... and if they are false, not so false as to destroy the argument they are brought for; but at worst are sufficient as suppositions to show the way to that knowledge I aim at. (*PA*: 244–5)

Within half a century of Swift's pamphlet, political economy had received its enlightened facelift, and Adam Smith had presented an alternative vision, that of the market as the basis for a system of 'natural liberty', in which the individual would replace the state as the prime economic agent. In this 'classical' stage of political economy, the potentially subversive project of exposing the nature of economy and society was fatally intertwined with the project of providing ideological justification for the emergence of the market, which was now to become a new Moloch incomparably more voracious than the previous one of Swift's nightmare. It was to be yet another three-quarters of a century before the next exposure of man-eat-man social relations, and, for that, capital had to be represented from a new perspective – that of the people subject to capitalist exploitation and in rebellion against it.

The present enquiry has aimed to establish that no phase of this history of the representation of capital can be adequately comprehended within a single-country perspective that abstracts from the colonial relationship, and that to attempt to apply such a perspective – let alone to impose it by 'disciplinary' means – is to endorse the peripheralisation of the colonised and formerly colonised peoples, and thus to contribute to the perpetuation of the legacy which the era of colonialism has bequeathed to the world of today.

Notes

1. All page numbers for works of Petty refer to those in the following editions:

    EW: Charles Hull (ed.), *The Economic Writings of Sir William Petty*, 2 vols. Cambridge: Cambridge University Press (1899).
    PA: *Political Arithmetic*. Written c.1671–2 and amended in subsequent years. First authorised edition published 1690. In *EW*: 233–313.
    PAI: *The Political Anatomy of Ireland*. Written c.1671. First published 1691. In *EW*: 121–231.
    PP1, *PP2*: *The Petty Papers: Some Unpublished Writings of Sir William Petty*. Edited from the Bowood Papers by the Marquis of Lansdowne, 2 vols. London: Constable (1927).
    PSC: *The Petty–Southwell Correspondence, 1676–1687*. Edited from the Bowood Papers by the Marquis of Lansdowne. London: Constable (1928).
    TI: *A Treatise of Ireland*. Written 1687. First published 1899. In *EW*: 545–621.
    TTC: *A Treatise of Taxes and Contributions*. Published 1662. In *EW*: 1–97.
    VS: *Verbum Sapienti*. Written 1665. First published 1691. In *EW*: 99–120.

2. This view relies on drawing a distinction between the variety of Swift's sources for the specific arguments he parodies, on the one hand, and, on the other hand, the unity and consistency of the modest proposer's mode of argumentation, which surely brings Petty irresistibly to mind. Such a distinction is, admittedly, not drawn so sharply by most other contributors to the very

extensive secondary literature on Swift's pamphlet, though in the majority of cases they agree that Petty is prominent among those whom Swift had in mind (see, for example, Landa, 1942; Wittkowsky, 1943; and, more recently, Fox, 2003: 6–7). Briggs (2005) argues that the modest proposer's mode of argumentation is, like his range of arguments, a 'composite' construct deriving from Petty and other individuals, particularly John Graunt.
3. Much of the extensive secondary literature on Swift's pamphlet places a similarly central focus on attitudes towards the poor in general, rather than on issues arising specifically in the colonial context in Ireland, despite the fact that the latter aspect was clearly uppermost in Swift's mind at the time, as demonstrated by Landa (1942) and Kelly (1998). The cultural and literary aspects of Swift's writings on the Irish and other 'savage' peoples is compendiously reviewed by Rawson (2001), though with only marginal reference to more directly political-economic issues. For a useful survey of comment on the pamphlet emanating from within literary studies, see Briggs (2005), and for further relevant bibliography, DeGategno and Stubblefield (2006).
4. On the concept of 'neo-feudalism' as applied to this phase of Petty's writings, see Goodacre (2005), discussing works of Robert Brenner and others.

2
Accounting Capital, Race and Benjamin Franklin's 'Pecuniary Habits' of Mind in *The Autobiography*

Rekha Rosha

Introduction

Recent biographies of Benjamin Franklin continue to regard him as the representative self-made American man (Brands, 2000; Isaacson, 2003; Wood, 2004). Yet, the psychic interiority Benjamin Franklin's *The Autobiography* (1793) depicts is so densely furnished with rules of economic exchange, the routes of capital, and the slogans of capitalism that the text evinces not a distinctive, self-authored individual but a capitalist wholly patterned by the narrative logic of capital. Franklin's claims of self-making through planning are overwritten by those plans – i.e. the accounts that fill the pages of his life's story. In this chapter I argue that his 'Account', as Franklin calls his memoir, is in many ways just that, a nearly extant copy of his own account ledger.

Keeping a ledger requires the account holder to maintain a written record of every economic transaction – posted either as 'gain' or 'loss' – to calculate expenses and revenue daily, and to balance the books every quarter. Defined this way, the careful monitoring of capital makes further demands of critical evaluation and self-reflection, and read this way I argue that the account book situates consciousness within a narrative of past economic decisions and actions. This link between capital and consciousness that Franklin's 'Account' demonstrates also points to the unusual political status of the account holder; that is, as an account book reports all financial decisions in order to control future outcomes, it presupposes a subject simultaneously powerless to control market forces and at the same time successful in adapting to the changing conditions of capital. As accounting brings intellection under its scheme of management it inscribes Franklin into a subject position defined in strict relationship to capital, and in direct opposition to the kind of radical individualism Franklin is conventionally read as symbolising.

For example, Franklin's description of his promotion to postmaster-general, which he says owes in large part to his careful accounting habits, ends with this advice to his readers: 'they should always render Accounts & make remittances, with great Clearness and Punctuality. – The Character of observing Such a Conduct is the most powerful of all Recommendations to new Employments & Increase of Business' (1793: 112). 'Character' here means the formal testimony of an employer as to the qualities of the employee (*OED*), and therefore Franklin figures his relation to accounts as a relationship between employer and employee, where the account book performs the same function of an employer, as the balanced books testify on the employee's behalf to shape and reinforce the employee's reputation, specifically in regard to accuracy and fairness. His comment reveals the social effects of accounting: the account holder, like an employee, relies on the account book for a favourable letter of recommendation in order to sell his labour or increase revenue. While his accounts are partly responsible for Franklin's ability to climb the ladder of success, curiously, in his description he clearly remains subordinate to them, since, like an employee, his future success depends entirely on his employer's written endorsement. The accounts require Franklin to scrutinise the profitability of his every action and thought – and as his metaphor of the accounts as an employer indicates – this also poses a limit on his freedom of action and thought. In fact, everything in the text points to this same paradox: in a social field defined by capital, the value of commodities, and physical labour as well as intellectual effort, is determined not by the uniquely free individual but by the calculations of the account book.

What reading *The Autobiography* in this way makes possible is not only a new understanding of the symbolic origin of this work – contra literary critics such as Michael Warner (1986), Grantland S. Rice (1997) and Jennifer Jordan Baker (2000) – but also a more complex view of the work overall. In this text and other writings, Franklin's understanding of how consciousness and capitalism are formulated within the narrative of capital, i.e. the account book, is located in direct relation to racial identity, and as he treats indebtedness as a form of racial slavery, he makes calculative thinking a defence against enslavement. Franklin's abolitionist views, like many others', were rife with inconsistencies and hypocrisies, and in *The Autobiography* this is no less the case as Franklin regards slavery not as an economic system to be abolished but as an economic situation to be avoided.

The slippery slope of market capitalism – the further in debt one goes, the closer to slavery one comes – is for Franklin founded on the same ideological grounds the Opposition writers staked out, which depended on the continued existence of slavery to establish the compelling logic of their resistance. For them and for Franklin slavery was not only rhetorically expedient, but its existence helped create the political category of freeholder they sought. And as *The Autobiography* accounts for the financial value of Franklin's every thought and action I argue that the text endorses increased self-regulation constitutive of a white freeholder identity in response to the coercion of labour under slavery. As a model of a national, white subject, Franklin's *The Autobiography* idealises a highly mediated subject characterised by intervention and control to such a degree that, paradoxically, the individual agency of the white, national subject remains unaccountable, and for blacks and slaves, painfully unlocatable.

Epigrams and other 'self-evident' truths of capital

In Franklin's 'Rules Proper to be Observed in Trade', originally published on 20 February 1749/50 in *The Pennsylvania Gazette*, several years before *The Autobiography*, he catalogues the habits of success. In what amounts to a colonial version of Stephen R. Covey's bestseller *The 7 Habits of Highly Successful People* (1990), Franklin provides a list of nine rules, the third of which, following Franklin's exhortations to obey the golden rule and act morally in all things, is this advice: 'Be strict in discharging all legal debts' (1987: 345). This is followed by advice on profitable behaviour for merchants and rule seven, 'Take great care in keeping your accounts well: Enter every thing necessary in your books with neatness and exactness; often state your accounts, and examine whether you gain, or lose; and carefully survey your stock, and inspect into every particular of your affairs' (1987: 345–6). Rule eight expands these meticulous habits to include, 'annually settle your accounts' (1987: 346). To be 'a fair character in the world' (1987: 346) requires acting according to precedents of rational prediction; the golden rule as well as the rules of trade. In this and numerous other passages in *The Autobiography*, various essays, and *Way to Wealth*, the sphere of morals is circumscribed by the sphere of economic action.

All of which seems to confirm the ethos of penny-pinching self-denial Max Weber takes Franklin to embody: 'the *summum bonum* of this ethic, the earning of more and more money, combined with the strict avoidance of all spontaneous enjoyment of life, is above all completely devoid of any eudæmonistic, not to say hedonistic, admixture' ([1930] 2004: 18). Yet Franklin's *Gazette* article makes it clear that capital accumulation depends on more than the steadfast refusal of instant gratification. You have to keep 'meticulous' accounts, which means making sure to enter everything in neat, clear handwriting, and examine and re-examine all entries, as well as annually drawing the balance. Every nickel spent and dime earned (as it were) must be systematically written down in order to be monitored; success is impossible without the accounting methods Franklin so carefully enumerates. Weber is certainly right that Franklin is one of the first American writers to offer a ready way to profits and virtue, but in the *Gazette* passage and throughout *The Autobiography* Franklin does more than moralise: he standardises behaviours and habits of thought according to the narrative structure of capital. In *The Autobiography* Franklin offers accounting as the means by which the reader achieves the appropriate subject disposition that the historical shift from agrarianism to market capitalism demanded; that is, as workers were increasingly subjected to assessment and discipline, Franklin sees a positive political project in self-regulation compatible with capitalism and Republican ideals of self-governance.

For Weber, modern capitalism is defined by 'accounting capital', the narrative that rationalises capital, and by extension, capitalism. Accounting is a necessary narrative condition of capitalist expansionism, and as Franklin's memoir makes clear, it is also a necessary narrative condition of capitalist expression. Turning to the various accounts – financial, moral and personal – that appear throughout Benjamin Franklin's *The Autobiography*, I argue that he uses the form and function of accounting to direct his own narrative attempts to offer interpretive strategies for comprehending and accepting the historical, ideological and material shift from agrarianism to market capitalism.

Franklin seems to treat his memoir like an account book in his explanation that he has applied his meticulous accounting methods to his writing in order to '[bring] all these scatter'd Counsels thus into a Focus' (1793: 107). Franklin's use of accounting tables and methods makes the reader aware of both their historical importance, and their personal significance. Since 1400, accounting has provided merchants, banks and proprietors with a classificatory system that makes the abstract routes of capital and exchange visible and instantly verifiable (see Miller, 1994). Franklin's efforts to tabulate the various transactions of his own life suggest that, in a similar sense, accounting methods render his life visible and verifiable for the reader.

This function of the account book, to consolidate information and value, is rhetorically intensified by Franklin's use of proverbs. Throughout the text, Franklin looks over his accounts in order to draw a moral, as if to balance his mistakes against any unintended benefits. For example: like his account books, Franklin's proverbs neatly summarise universal experience; it is as if the rational prediction of capital lends authority to other narrative modes of predicting human behaviour.

Both Franklin's accounts and proverbs systematise knowledge to offer the reader a set of standards by which everyone can operate; they are for him the universalising democratic principle at work in his text. His reasons for this owe to accounting's importance in agrarian and mercantile economies, and because of its centrality in his own life. Accounts mattered a great deal to him; not only did he owe his promotion to postmaster-general to his ability to keep accounts, but his accounting savvy also helped him maintain a record of all his business transactions with men throughout the colonies and in the Caribbean allowing him to stay on top of an enormous amount of trade. He kept several kinds of accounts as part of running his extensive printing business.

One of Franklin's sets of books, Ledger D, includes 'nearly 900 accounts' (Eddy, 1929: 7) meaning that he maintained business dealings with almost a thousand people. His accounts ranged from Philadelphia, to Boston, Rhode Island (57), Maryland (125), Carolina (52) and Georgia (124), and also included transactions with businessmen in Antigua (116) and Jamaica (51).

Some of Franklin's printing work actually included printing account books. He printed a small volume containing the Library Company's catalogue of books, the company's charter, rules and laws of the company, and its promissory notes, a kind of receipt book. More significantly, Franklin is also credited with publishing the first manual on accounting in America, 'Merchant's-Accompts'; although originally printed in *Bradford's Young Man's Companion* in 1737, Franklin's republication in 1748 was the first to give George Fisher proper credit as author (see McMickle, 1984).

Following his return to Philadelphia in 1785, Franklin resumed writing his memoirs and 'set about putting his affairs into order' (Eddy, 1929: 8). In the spring of the following year, his son, William Temple Franklin, helped his father to settle his affairs, closing Ledger D and transferring all accounts to Ledger E. The timing of these writings – the closing of his financial *and* autobiographical accounts – might explain why Part Two of all the sections of *The Autobiography* is most interested in plans and schedules. I read *The Autobiography* as a moment at which Franklin transfers his economic life to his narrative life.

We see the entanglement of memoir and money in Franklin's use of the 'Tables of Examination' (1793: 99), which are his method of self-improvement and a variant on the kinds of accounting tables that seem to have occupied a considerable amount of his energies. He records the number of times he transgresses against his moral principles by marking a black dot in the row of the corresponding vice. He explains, 'I determined to give a Week's strict Attention to each of the Virtues successively [...] like him who having a Garden to weed, does not attempt to eradicate all the bad Herbs at once, which would exceed his Reach and his Strength, but works on one of the Beds at a time' (1793: 98). The weekly schedules, in which Franklin keeps a daily record of the number of times he gives 'offense' (1793: 98) against any of the thirteen virtues, are kept in a book along with selected proverbs and quotations. These tables allow Franklin to hold himself accountable for his actions in order that he may clear away, 'successively my Lines of their Spots, till in the End by a Number of Courses, I should be happy in viewing a clean Book after a thirteen Weeks daily Examination' (1793: 98).

As Weber argues, Franklin's moralising of capitalist practices and behaviours secured eighteenth-century American culture for capitalism. His tables, schedules and accounting data permanently document his habits and represent his efforts to instruct the reader on how to follow his example economically and morally, and yet they also offer something more. Franklin's 'little Book', cleared of all its black spots, represents what is arguably most powerful about accounting in this period: to rationalise capital and all actions conducted under its sign. While moral accounting like Franklin's had been a spiritual means of self-actualisation going back to the Puritans, it is also first and foremost a narrative of capitalist development primarily because accounting capital provides an influential pattern for all sorts of other human practices making profit-seeking and self-realisation indexes of each other. If capitalist development secures individual progress, that progress, as Franklin demonstrates, is concomitant with the displacement of individual agency.

One explanation for the paradox of individual agency *The Autobiography* reveals is that the semiotic field accounting constructs proposes action and deferral, simultaneously. Jean-Joseph Goux distinguishes accounting, or 'settlement by writing', from other kinds of writing, such as money, cheques and bank transfers (1999: 114) by both presence and absence. In an account book, the fundamental binary terms, 'credit' and 'debit', are not signs of value. Franklin's ledgers are not guaranteed by gold – he cannot cash the ledger nor can he exchange it for anything of value – unlike fiat money which was guaranteed by gold. Credit and debit are categories naming all transactions but equally important they are mathematical operations of addition and subtraction, since every entry of gain is an addition of value to previous entries, and debit is a subtraction of value to previous entries. In this sense, the terms 'credit' and 'debit' are not just signs but operations: they are events that occur on the page.

Yet as an inverse operation, 'credit' always exerts pressure against its opposite, 'debit', so that as credit is posted a debit amount is also posted. (In a single-entry account like Franklin's, for every debit posted on the right-hand side of the account, a '0' is entered under the credit column on the left side of ledger, and vice versa.) So arranged, Goux explains, debt is always simultaneously posted against credit and the one forces the deferral of the other. Accounting statements are always expressed in double-negatives: income is simultaneously credit and not-loss; loss is both debt and not-gain. And because the ledger does not initiate the incomes and outgoes (paying a debt, receiving income) it records, it is a *de facto* trace of a 'real world' event that has already occurred. The ledger as Goux describes it is a social order in which traces of real action simultaneously come to be represented and stand in for economic actions. We might consider the accounting book – the collection of fiduciary statements – a second order of deferral since the book transfigures the 'reality' of exchange, which does not exist outside the calculative documentation of exchange. The tensions of the process of substitution are expressed in the repeated deferrals of presence and absence that occur in each entry and in the sum total of entries.

In Franklin's 'Account', the stasis of the ever-deferring terms credit and debit are analogous to the moral truisms, which render every action an affect of capital. As he records his personal history, Franklin glosses the past in folksy, homespun proverbs to create abstractions from experience. Proverbs are conventionally understood as providing a cultural explanation of knowledge; they state conclusively what a large number of people intuitively believe to be true. Throughout the text, Franklin repeatedly extracts a moral message from the various moments of his life which he describes. To give one of numerous examples, after recounting his efforts to promote civic virtue by forming a local chamber of commerce, he concludes, 'wise Men may probably be more unanimous in their Obedience to [virtues], than common People are to common Laws' (1793: 103). In a sense he is developing 'self-evident' truths. Louis

Masur explains that Franklin suggested that Jefferson substitute '"self-evident" for "sacred and undeniable" in describing immutable "truths"' (2003: 11). Franklin's proverbs thus signify a larger epistemological paradigm shift as the status of universal truths was placed under siege by locally produced truths. Franklin the aphorist shares common cause with Franklin the scientist, diplomat and merchant. It seems certainly true if not self-evident that by translating local experience into universal verities Franklin formed the basis of an epigrammatic philosophy that appeals to the ledger's attentions to the immediate 'reality' of the individual.

Elsewhere in *The Autobiography* Franklin goes a step further in relating proverbs to accounting: 'Habits must be broken and good Ones acquired and established, before we can have any Dependance on a steady uniform Rectitude of Conduct. For this purpose, I therefore contriv'd the following Method' (1793: 89). Methodology helps to create 'uniform' conduct; the maxim's simplicity and directness underlines its rationality and helps the reader imagine enormous complexity in simple ways. Its means-to-goal phrasing is meant to encourage means-to-goal thinking, and because proverbs reduce complexity in this way they construct knowledge particularly well-suited to promoting the kinds of labour which should become routine. Behaviour that poses conflicts with capital must be methodically eliminated, and just as accounting aims to eliminate risk and uncertainty, Franklin also applies it to eliminating the uncertain features of his personality that might stand in the way of profit. In this sense, his proverbs also emphasise the externality of information and they underwrite an interiority constructed according to standards of operation (accounting) and standardised social knowledge (proverbs, witticisms, etc.). In his memoir, the semiotics of book money has a distinct bearing on identity.

In a striking example of the intersection of technocratic and linguistic control, *Poor Richard Improved* (1758) begins with Richard quoting a man quoting him: 'Father *Abraham* stood up, and reply'd, If you'd have my Advice, I'll give it you in short, for a *Word to the Wise is enough,* and *many Words won't fill a Bushel,* as *Poor Richard says*' (*Writings,* 1987: 175). The entire piece goes in this way, as the old man repeats verbatim one proverb after another taken from *Poor Richard's Almanac*. Reprinted as *The Way to Wealth,* Franklin's best-known work during his lifetime, it defines knowledge in the same way Franklin defines it in his memoir: knowledge is not internal but the effect of collective relations. 'Abraham' is a moment of ventriloquism for Richard, in the same way that Franklin ventriloquises Richard. In addition, by using accounting as his narrative model Franklin reveals that it too ventriloquises; that is, the ledger's narrative effectively speaks for capital and in turn extends to the individual account holder an ahistorical, economic subjectivity similar to capital's (presumed) ahistorical status.

Franklin's self-evaluations and assessments are geared towards self-definition by means of self-control, and share features with an increasingly commercialised culture. Yet his 'tables', which require both daily entries and nightly evaluations, go beyond the practical objective of quantifying data as they draw attention to certain intellectual dimensions of the self – critical reflection, self-study and rational coherence – thereby granting greater significance to specific functions of consciousness, and this shapes and grooves the 'habits of mind' (Adorno, 1941) necessary to capitalism. Theodor Adorno offers another perspective on Weber's claim that accounting rationalises capital; under Adorno's definition, accounts also routinise how the capitalist interprets personal motivations (no longer greed *per se*, but improvement, progress, the logical outcome of the rational predictions of his ledger), and the world around him or her. As Adorno points out, the growth of capitalism created a greater demand and need for the kind of intellection central to it, which is why in Franklin's *The Autobiography* we find a troping of knowledge that defines it as nearly inactive. Where the account in his text reduces complexity to its simplest most manageable level, he amplifies this effect in his treatment of proverbs.

In using accounting as the model for a national subject, Franklin's *The Autobiography* idealises the subordination of individual agency to capital, so much so that the national subject remains unaccountable, as individuals like old 'Abraham' 'merely' re-enact values traceable to accounting capital. The trace-event structure of the ledger that governs Franklin's weak intellection and action is analogous to his active resistance to and simultaneous passive endorsement of racial slavery. As Franklin treats racial slavery as a sign of total lack of control over one's labour and of political self-determination, internalising technocratic control becomes the mark of racial freedom because it signals the individual's control over his actions and future. Yet, Franklin's moral slogans, drawn from his successes and failures in the market, offer a form of collective knowledge that the ledger authorises to insist on the uniformity of knowledge. Self-knowledge is oddly lacking in Franklin's memoir; instead, we have an epigrammatic philosophy of capital, by which I mean Franklin's epithets express a wider consensus about the morality of capitalism. All his personal decisions, economic or not, are calculated to determine their broader value, either in dollars or sense.

To this extent, both proverbs and accounts endorse any failure to act in conflict with capital, and therefore offer Franklin an ideological alibi for slavery.

The 'colour' of credit and debt

In 1727, Franklin hit on the idea of forming a group dedicated to increasing business contacts, and more grandly, to influencing public affairs in Philadelphia. It was later called the Junto, and Franklin initially imagined that this proto-rotary club would be called 'the Society of the Free and Easy; Free, as being by the general Practice and Habit of the Virtues, free from the Dominion of Vice, and particularly by the Practice of Industry & Frugality, free from Debt, which exposes a Man to Confinement and a Species of Slavery to his Creditors' (1793: 106). He treats 'debt' as a fairly capacious term, signalling all things antithetical to good business – wasteful expense, moral laxity, dishonesty – and in addition debt signals a particular political status. At the time when he was writing *The Autobiography*, the term 'credit' had come to represent honest, commercial integrity, and for Franklin it also represents political autonomy. Franklin's worry about the moral failure of debt also reflects the ways some eighteenth-century textbooks applied mercantile techniques to spiritual matters. *The Universal Library of Trade and Commerce* observes: '"A Tradesman's Books, like a Christian's Conscience, should always be kept clean and neat; and he that is not careful of both, will give but a sad Account of himself either to God or Man"' (quoted in Yamey, 1974). To prevent such failings, Franklin uses the same successful strategy popularised by writers to keep his moral slate clean: 'I have always thought that one Man of tolerable Abilities may work great Changes, & accomplish great Affairs among Mankind, if he first forms a good Plan, and [...] makes the Execution of that same Plan his sole Study and Business – ' (1793: 106).

Early in his 1748 essay 'Advice to a Young Tradesman, Written by an Old One', Franklin draws a distinct connection between personal behaviour and business practices. He warns merchants that, 'The most trifling Actions that affect a Man's credit are to be regarded. The Sound of your Hammer at Five in the morning or Nine at Night, heard by a Creditor, makes him easy Six Months longer' (1987: 321). He admonishes the tradesman and the reader alike to keep an eye on the little things. Similarly, by keeping an account 'you will discover how wonderfully small trifling Expences mount up to large Sums, and will discern what might have been, and may for the future be saved, without occasioning any great Inconvenience' (1987: 321). Individual agency appears under different levels of magnification; small individual actions, like small expenses, can have larger, more significant effects. While quantification enables us to survey our efforts and decisions, abstraction of this sort also creates a thorny paradox, as self-awareness is at once a self-liberating and self-regulating posture. Without careful monitoring, small trifles, be they debts or a failure to appear industrious or successful, can overtake us.

Not surprisingly, Franklin is anxious about the larger implications of this paradox. If freedom comes from strictly monitored self-regulation then 'free and easy' freemen are not really all that different from heavily regulated slaves. But for Franklin the distinction between freemen and slaves centres on calculative rationality, and not enslavement.

In a discussion between Franklin and Governor Morris over drinks after a formal dinner party, Morris jokingly tells Franklin 'that he much admir'd the Idea of Sancho Panza, who when it was propos'd to give him a Government, requested it might be a Government of *Blacks*, as then, if he could not agree with his People he might sell them' (1793: 137). Morris goes on to compare the Quaker members of the Philadelphia Assembly, who were then stonewalling his efforts to exempt himself and non-colonial landholders from paying taxes, to Panza's blacks. Turning to Franklin, another dinner guest adds, '"Franklin, why do you continue to side with these damn'd quakers? Had not you better sell them? The Proprietor would give you a good Price"' (1793: 137). Appalled, Franklin retorts:

> The Governor, says I, has not yet *black'd* them enough. He had indeed labour'd hard to blacken the Assembly in all his Messages, but they wip'd off his Colouring as fast as he laid it on, and plac'd it in return thick upon his own Face; so that finding he was likely to be negrify'd himself, he as well as Mr Hamilton [the former governor whom Morris had replaced], got tir'd of the Contest, and quitted the Government. (1793: 137)

The rhetorical reversal – he does not deny that the Quakers are 'blackened' but asserts that Governor Morris has not 'black'd' them *enough* – energises Franklin's argument, and in an uncharacteristic moment he comes across as a fiery, upstart patriot. Franklin is clearly enthusiastic over this bit of poetic justice, as the Governor's attempts to 'negrify' the Quakers through slander, or blackening their names, backfires on him. In treating 'blackness' not as an essential physiological property, but as a migratory, linguistic construct, which can be traded back and forth between the antagonists like insults, Franklin seems to treat race as a politically expeditious category, whereby the Governor attempts to debase the Quakers' arguments by devaluing the Quakers by 'blackening' them, and thereby disqualifying them for the political considerations they were demanding.

In light of Morris's comment and Franklin's emphasis on colour and discoloration it is easy to read the metaphorical layers of thick, black 'colouring' that the Quakers used to efface the Governor's whiteness as having a material effect. In Franklin's story, he predicts that Governor Morris is close to becoming so blackened, that is, so devalued, that he will inevitably become black in the sense Morris means it, a slave. Morris's prolonged exposure to blackness leaves him so nearly 'negrify'd' that his status as a political subject is jeopardised. It is as if being associated with blackness eventually generates an association with racial slavery, and it is this chain of associations that threatens Morris's political status as a free subject. Read this way the metaphor of blackening stands in two places at once: it operates as an insult, not defining but prejudicially redescriptive, and at the same time it is a totalising term as it completely renames the subject, or 'negrify[s]' him.

In Franklin's anecdote, blackness cannot be contained; it migrates and its meaning is both partial and totalising. At first glance, Franklin's warning to Morris is that blackness, or racial slavery, is not static but historically and *politically* determined, suggesting that the winners of political contests determine all fortunes and identities. Franklin's suggestion, however, seems at odds with the Opposition writers who sought to pin down blackness by making racial slavery the complete opposite of 'natural' freedom. As historian Joyce Appleby claims, 'By contrasting freedom to slavery, the revolutionaries were giving an absolute value to freedom which it had not previously possessed, even in the intellectual tradition from which they drew' (1992: 158). The revolutionaries ranted against slavery in order to give freedom a deeper meaning even though they too stopped short of seeing it as a fundamental human right. For the patriots, abolishing slavery would have meant denying the very grounds of their arguments for establishing an independent country.

Yet, Franklin's story about the Governor's loss of face appeals, curiously enough, to the Opposition's rhetorical and political tactic. Maintaining control over our credit, losses and gains, as well as our vices, virtues, actions, speech, dress and work is less like the heavy regulation slaves experience than it had first appeared because for Franklin it is precisely the *lack* of control that puts the account holder in danger of indebtedness, which he takes to mean the devaluation of one's credit, reputation, social standing, etc. Read this way, identity is subordinate to the narrative structures of economics rather than prior to them, which is why, as Morris demonstrates, losing credibility is like losing face; it is as if for every political loss a 'black spot' (to borrow Franklin's description of his moral accounting procedures) was entered against Morris's whiteness. This also explains Franklin's metaphor of the account as an employer; the account provides evidence of Franklin's identity as a capitalist thereby making his character visible on its pages. Franklin's equation of indebtedness with racial slavery signals the links between race and material and political valuation established in his anecdote, and indicates the way to avoid getting caught up in that equation. To put it simply, for Franklin indebtedness puts us at risk of becoming 'negrify'd' because it represents the lack of control over determining our financial value: therefore, 'black' means 'devaluation' (the failure to account for and locate one's own value) represented by Morris's defaced whiteness, and 'negrify'd' refers to Morris's zero political credibility. Control over the account book, then, is crucial to defining solvency, freedom and, ultimately, whiteness.

From this ideological position, Franklin distinguishes between slavery – the total lack of control over labour – and freedom – rationally guided actions completely under the individual's control. The slave, of course, cannot be represented within a narrative space under his own control because it is the slave owner and not the slave who keeps the account book. But to define freedom in this way is also to define it in relation to rational and systematic controls governing thought and action. That is, as the freeman emerges from his account book, he also becomes an object of careful monitoring within his account book; for example, Franklin daily scrutinises and modifies his emotions, moral behaviours and social behaviours as they are represented within his account books. In addition, as the 'ideal' subject the reader is meant to emulate, Franklin becomes an object of the reader's scrutiny, and by treating himself as an object whose every action is traceable to capital, he relieves the reader of the burden of imagining or engaging with an interiority that an autobiography generally makes available. This low-intensity engagement which the text seems to promote could be read as the first phase of reproducing capitalist intellection, as Adorno defines it. That is, since capital is the foremost object of the text's contemplation, Franklin invites the reader to develop the habits of capitalist thought.

Conclusion

In spite of its reputation as a celebration of an American success, *The Autobiography* defines the individual in strict relation to accumulating capital, and as it equates indebtedness with racial slavery and profits with a white freeholder status, Franklin posts the successful capitalist under the category of whiteness. To define race according to profit and loss statements is to define whiteness as neither a property of physiognomy nor of capital but an effect of the processes of generating profit. As Franklin uses his account to explain events in his life, he turns it into what Bruno Latour refers to as a 'strong explanation' (1988). Indeed, Franklin seems to go a step further as he insinuates himself into his account as his 'Account' – the narrative of his life – becomes the *only* explanation.

If accounting provides the means of self-management, which in turn becomes the foundation for white male self-governance, in Franklin's account such self-governance means a life detached from the social and divorced from one's own consciousness; a life in which the value of intellectual and social action is handed over from the individual to the account book. If accounting is responsible for giving whiteness a material reality, its consequences for other raced subjects is equally important.

Franklin himself becomes such a highly mediated figure that he seems to be absent from his own account. The lack of personality Michael Warner (1986) sees in Franklin might be owing to the fact that the text is not about him, or the major events of his life (Christopher Looby (1986) points out that he never discusses the American Revolution) because, in the end, the story of his life is a story about the processes of self-management within a social organisation. Part of the conditions of capitalism to which his accounting practices and proverbs contribute is the production and reproduction of 'organizational life' (Miller, 1994: 15). His 'spirit of capitalism' (to return to Weber) is 'that attitude which seeks profit rationally and systematically' (1930: 27). It is an attitude intimately connected with the conditions of capitalism and which capitalism must reproduce in order to maintain its own existence. What Franklin draws our attention to are the ways in which accounting as the narrative form of capitalism shapes a mode of consciousness, and therefore behaviours, necessary to reproducing the conditions of capitalism *and* racial identity.

3
A System Illusory and Immoral: Jonathan Swift and the Emergence of the Modern Economic Polity

Christopher J. Fauske

Jonathan Swift, Dean of St Patrick's Dublin, sometime Drapier, has entered history at least in part for his writings about money. He was a man of his time – at least in so far as an understanding of economics was concerned – and even a cursory reading of Swift's work should make it clear that his reflections on how money influenced the functioning of society owe nothing to modern economic theory or practice, drawing, instead, upon traditional understandings of the interconnection of wealth and societal welfare. It is a distinction often overlooked, at least in part because of modern readers' own confusions about the connection between money and economics, and, additionally, about the change in intellectual *mores* required to establish modern capitalist theory as the guiding principle of British economic activity.

A radical discontinuity

The economic views espoused by Swift were firmly grounded in longstanding theories of practice that had finally been codified in the seventeenth century, recapitulating ideas shaped in a different economic climate than that in which he lived and wrote. Though the word was unknown to him, arriving in English only in the early twentieth century as an import from German, Swift's economic understanding, such as it was, was distinctly in line with what we now recognise as mercantilism, the best summary of which is the title of a study of how that system functioned, *Mercantilism as a Rent-seeking Society* (Ekelund and Tollison, 1981). Mercantilism, Patrick Hyde Kelly writes, was in essence a combination of practical insights about economic phenomena expressed in a series of axioms justifying the control of economic activity in the interests of state power and well-being, rather than a formal analytic system ... Mercantilism was more a defensive system than a positive prescription for economic growth. (Kelly, 1991: 68)

For Swift, mercantilism was also a means to protect the moral underpinnings of civil society.

Of the more famous of Swift's near-contemporary commentators on economic theory one of the most prominent was John Locke, now best remembered for his political and philosophical treatises. But as Kelly elucidates in a series of introductory essays to *Locke on Money*, economic theory for Locke was part of an overall philosophical consideration of moral precepts. Modern readers of Locke, and, by implication, of Swift – who most certainly shared Locke's view of the contractual underpinnings of circulating money – would do well to remember that

the unquestioning assumption of earlier scholars that sixteenth-, seventeenth-, and early eighteenth-century writers were simply grasping with greater or lesser success after the categories which came to dominate [modern economic theory] ... has given way to a realization that there is a radical discontinuity between the two forms of discourse. (Kelly, 1991: 67)

The writers who were developing the fundamental assumptions that characterise modern economic theory found little they wished to preserve in mercantilist works. Indeed, 'in referring to Locke's pamphlets on money, [Joseph] Harris, [Joseph] Massie, and [James] Steuart all spoke of the incoherence and lack of organization in his work, despite flashes of insight' (Kelly, 1991: 67).[1] If Locke was deemed 'incoherent' by the advocates of the nascent science of economic theory, it is not surprising that the majority of contributors to popular debate on economic matters hardly began to understand the issues with which they were grappling and for which descriptive terminology had yet to be developed. A polemicist by inclination, Swift felt no great need to get his arguments straight, and where Locke was confusing while seeking clarity Swift preferred diatribe, a preference abetted by the inevitable murkiness of the intellectual waters.

Writing on the cusp of discontinuity, Swift instinctively looked back. Suspicious of new ideas, he shared a temperamental affinity with those who understood economic questions as a branch of moral philosophy and so as quite distinct from the emerging mathematics-based science of economics. Swift identified in Locke's writings on money, in particular in his *Second Treatise of Civil Government* (Locke, 1690), a connection between a fundamental concept of personal property (justified by natural law) and money. It was a connection that might make little sense to modern theorists, and which many of Swift's contemporaries either hadn't concerned themselves with understanding or did not find important, but which Swift held to be essential to the moral functioning of a well-ordered society. Linda Bomstad (2004), drawing on Karen Iversen Vaughn (1992) identifies that for Locke 'money provides the conceptual framework for civil society, thereby helping to set the rationale for both legitimate rule and revolution in its absence'. Bomstad (2004) notes that in Locke's analysis

> in a hypothesized state of nature ... God [gave] the Earth and its resources to humankind in common and, at the same time, endowed individuals with a natural right to private property ... On this basis, Locke develops a labor theory of practice, according to which each person is entitled to procure from the common anything with which he has mixed his labor ... But, as Locke observes, people naturally have the capacity and the desire to produce and accumulate more property than this. Thus people come to use money, 'some lasting thing that Men might keep without spoiling, and that by mutual consent Men would take in exchange for the truly useful, but perishable, Supports of Life'.

Swift shared this perspective, and for him two points were critical. The first is that Locke's theory justified a 'revolution' in the absence of a civil contract honoured by all parties. There is a complicated Anglican apology for the ouster of James II by William, Prince of Orange, behind this need for a means to circumvent the traditional Anglican requirement for 'passive obedience' in the face of exploitation by the crown, but there is also a social conservative's fear that change is inevitably destructive. So long as money is based on 'mutual consent' and is something that 'Men would take *in exchange for* the truly useful, but perishable, Supports of Life', Swift had no particular qualms, for that money must, ultimately, be secured by land, that property God gave 'humankind in common'. Swift's objection to the emerging modern concept of money was that it would undermine the social contract if that connection between natural resources and money were broken. As soon as money could beget money, as emerging financing practices appeared to promise, society was doomed.

Swift's sympathies might well have instinctively been conservative,[2] but he was also a cleric who identified the legacy of William III's devoted attention to the continental challenges faced by his fellow Dutch stadtholders, combined with a determined parliamentary commitment to secure the purse strings of state in such a way that a perpetual national debt was becoming a fact of national life, as essentially immoral. Such a debt brought with it a whole host of questions, metaphors and muddle-headed commentary. Combined with the rise of the daily and weekly print media, the stage was set by the reign of Queen Anne for an explosion of public discourse about money, wealth and status. Swift lived through a period of dramatic change in how the British economy functioned and through a quite remarkable period of public incomprehension of what the changes were, why they were happening, and whether or not they would be successful. These were the times that Swift the polemicist could only rejoice in, for when better to have a caustic, verdant scepticism than in a time when so much could be said?

In retrospect a variety of theories have been suggested to allow modern readers and thinkers to make sense of what happened. For some time, perhaps the dominant model has been that espoused by Jürgen Habermas (1989). He discusses three 'events occurring in 1694 and 1695' which enabled 'political conflict' to cross 'into the public sphere'. For Habermas, it was 'the end of the institution of censorship [which] made the influx of rational-critical arguments into the press possible and allowed the latter to evolve into an instrument with whose aid political decisions could be brought before the new forum of the public' (Habermas, 1989: 57). This reading of the emergence of the modern British state has been enabled at least in part by ignorance of the almost tectonic shift in matters fiscal that happened, as tectonic shifts are wont to do, slowly enough that almost no one noticed what was happening at the time. If, as Kelly (1991) reminds us, there was a 'radical discontinuity' between mercantilism and modern economic theory, that radical disconnect was not apparent at the time.[3]

The writers who were developing the fundamental assumptions that characterise modern economic theory found little they wished to preserve in mercantilist works. 'Mercantilism was far more a defensive system than a positive prescription for economic growth' dedicated to an 'apparently obsessive concern with increasing the national stock of precious metals', writes Kelly:

> Its assumptions ... had grown out of perception of the depressing effects of inadequate monetary circulation in times of crisis, manifested in collapsing prices, labourers laid off, bankruptcies amongst merchants, and resultant poverty and weakness in the state. (Kelly, 1991: 68–9)

In effect, mercantilists argued against change not because the existing system was perfect, or perhaps even perfectible, but because the alternatives were guaranteed to be catastrophic. Later commentators have sought to impose order upon these changes and clarity upon the debates, but these later arguments rely upon anachronistic interpretations of phenomena and of language unavailable to contemporary critics. Alan Downie notes that 'Habermas's unreconstructed Marxist account of English history requires a "bourgeois revolution" to have taken place in the seventeenth century' (2008: 134, n. 57). No such thing occurred.

Contemporary writers certainly offer no assistance when it comes to pinning down changes in attitude towards money, wealth and luxury. Perhaps the best exemplar of this maxim is Daniel Defoe. James Hartley (2008: 27)[4] offers a useful primer to Defoe the author:

> [Defoe's] first major book, *An Essay upon Projects,* had been published in 1687, and he wrote continuously for the rest of his life. The sheer volume of material written by Defoe is staggering. While nobody seems to doubt that the number of publications is large, there is extensive debate over just how large.[5] Peter Earle (1976) summed up the matter nicely when he observed that after he had signed a contract to write a book on Defoe, "To my horror I discovered that Defoe was probably the most prolific writer in the English language, a writer moreover who wrote on every conceivable topic from angels to annuities and from adultery to agriculture. But it was too late to back out" (Earle, 1976, p. vii). The variety of material is immense; the formats varied. As was customary in the day, much of the writing was anonymous, but less customary was the fact that Defoe was writing multiple anonymous journals, including anonymous commentaries on his own anonymously published works.

> So great was Defoe's presence on the English scene in the early eighteenth century that Earle would write, "It is possible to base a study of English society in the early eighteenth century almost entirely on the writings of Daniel Defoe ..." (Earle, 1976, p. viii).

The study which would result, however, would be, in Hartley's apt description, chameleonic, all things to all people. Which is appropriate, because that, in fact, was how matters appeared to those on the ground at the time. Unlike Defoe, Swift brought a reasonably consistent approach to his analyses of the state of affairs, but like Defoe, and like all the other denizens of Grub Street and beyond, Swift was able to pick and choose from a quite startling array of apparent evidence, omitting from his discussion inconvenient truths he was quite happy to address at another time should that suit his needs. In the end, Swift's work is more coherent than Defoe's not because of its intellectual rigour but because of the character of its author.[6] Defoe, writing for cash, was quite ready and willing to be all things to all people; Swift, writing with a Tacitian sense that affairs had not only declined for the worse since a historical period just outside living memory but that even if they improved that improvement would be temporary, at least had a defining self-perspective to guide his writing.

That said, Swift's writing can be almost as hard to pin down as Defoe's. One reason is that, as D. J. Enright observed, writers on irony 'can scarcely not say something about [Swift], even though everything has been said already' (Enright, 1986: 75). Consequently, many commentators upon Swift have taken the advice offered the younger cleric by William King, archbishop of Dublin:

> Say not, that most subjects in divinity are exhausted; for ... the most curious and difficult are in a manner untouched, and a good genius will not fail to produce something new and surprising on the most trite, much more on those that others have avoided. (Woolley, 1999: 377–8)

Swift had his own views on the appropriateness of 'produc[ing] something new and surprising on the most trite' topic, but that has not stopped modern critics doing something similar when it comes to Swift.

One trope of Swift's writing that is consistent is his suspicion of 'new and surprising' ideas about the appropriate functioning of an economy and, more specifically, of displays of wealth. Swift's consistency when it comes to how both public and private economies should function was informed by his own religious and philosophical inclinations. These instincts had guided Swift from the start of his publishing career and it does not take the type of close reading of *A Tale of a Tub* that the *Tale* itself mocks to identify the underpinnings of Swift's career opus on the matter of finance. Warren Montag most clearly articulates Swift's position when he notes that in the 'Digression Concerning Madness' Swift offers a demonstration of what happens when the mind fails to function in its '"natural position" ... indicated by [an] Anglican Aristotelian world in which nothing exists without a divinely ordained end' (Montag, 1994: 87). The author of the *Tale* is tellingly lucid while gloriously wrong-headed in his explanation that

> The two Senses, to which all Objects first address themselves, are the Sight and the Touch; These never examine farther than the Colour, the Shape, the Size, and whatever other Qualities dwell, or are drawn by Art upon the Outward of Bodies; and then comes Reason officiously, with Tools for cutting, and opening, and maligning, and piercing, offering to demonstrate, that they are not of the same consistence quite thro'. Now, I take all this to be the last Degree of perverting Nature; one of whose Eternal Laws it is, to put her best Furniture forward.[7]

Swift's satire consistently alludes to the preferred situation, to a functional Aristotelian balance; here, the allusion is in the recognition that it is nature's 'Eternal Law ... to put her best Furniture forward'. Madness lies in the failure of either the individual or the polity to honour this precept. From this, it follows that improving upon nature's furniture can be nothing more than vanity or delusion. The world may not be perfect in the eyes of man, but it has an eternal honesty to it. Both the rise in personal improvement and public initiatives to change the manner of doing business go against the fundamental precepts of 'eternal law'. Swift thus nicely conflates both the perspectives of Anglican theology and the emerging secular readings of philosophers such as Pierre Gassendi and Baruch Spinoza, readings which were informed by, but also informed, the developing suspicion that material – make-up, coinage, fashion – could have value in and of itself that need not be based upon security of 'real' value.

Here, Swift found himself allied with some apparently unlikely allies, among them Henry St. John, Viscount Bolingbroke, a theist of such remarkable secular bent that Samuel Johnson defined 'irony' in his dictionary thus: 'A mode of speech in which the meaning is contrary to the words: as Bolingbroke was a holy man' (1755). In his essay 'On Bribery and Corruption', Bolingbroke rails against public pensions and against a system that relies on money to sustain the political system. '[I]t is clearly evident', writes Bolingbroke, 'that an *unpension'd Subject* will give the wisest counsel to his *Prince*, and will always continue the most faithful to him' (Bolingbroke, 1740: 283). This is a summation of a lengthier argument Bolingbroke had long been articulating, that the increasing reliance of the state on public debt was inherently damaging to the natural order. For Bolingbroke, as for Swift, there is an inextricable interconnection between public and private greed. In the midst of a series of reflections upon England's long continental wars, Bolingbroke took time out to pen a reflection 'on Luxury'. His opening remarks that 'A discourse on *Operas*, and the gayer pleasures of the Town may seem to be too trifling for the important Scene of Affairs, in which we are at present engaged', permit an almost seamless segue into the consideration that

> A very little Reflection on History will suggest this Observation, that every Nation has made either a great or inconsiderable Figure in the World, as it has fallen into *Luxury* or resisted its Temptations ... When the Mind is enervated by *Luxury*, the Body soon falls an easy Victim to it; for how is it possible to imagine, that a Man can be capable of the great and the generous Sentiments, which Virtue inspires, whose Mind is fill'd with the soft Ideas and wanton Delicacies that Pleasure must infuse? (Bolingbroke, 1740: 72–3)

'*Operas* and *Masquerades*, with all the politer Elegancies of a wanton Age, are much less to be regarded for the Expence (great as it is) than for the Tendency, which they have to deprave our manners', Bolingbroke goes on, concluding the essay with the hope that 'What Effect *Italian* Musick might have on our polite Warriors at *Gibraltar*, I cannot take upon me to say; but I wish our *Luxury* at home may not influence our Courage abroad' (Bolingbroke, 1740: 76–8).

An increasingly intrusive state

That Swift and Bolingbroke could share such a cultural perspective while disagreeing on so much else – and disagree they did even while both sharing a 'Tory' perspective on party political matters – serves not only to remind modern readers of the dangers of labelling writers, but also to remind us of a common refrain among almost all thinkers of the period, a visceral resistance to the re-establishment of a powerful state presence. As John Brewer notes in his seminal work *The Sinews of Power*, 'between 1697 and 1701 it seemed as if the legislature would succeed in expunging many of the effects of nearly a decade of war [against France].

The standing army was decimated to a mere 7,000 ... The 1701 Act of Settlement – more properly entitled, "An Act for the further limitation of the crown and the better securing the rights of the subject" – ... removed placemen from the commons, made privy councilors more accountable to parliament ... [and] gave judges greater independence' (Brewer, 1990: 140–1). What went wrong soon after 1701 was, as Brewer puts it, that 'William [III]'s opponents had not reckoned with the behavior of Louis XIV' (Brewer, 1990: 141).

As the war continued, the need for the state to raise revenue rose with it, and the reductions in the power of the monarchy were replaced by an increasingly efficient and seemingly all-pervasive excise system. William Pulteney, later earl of Bath, would complain of the 'vast Bulk ... [of] our Statutes relating to Taxes, [which] have swelled since the Revolution ... It is monstrous, it is even frightful to look into the Indexes, where for several Columns together we see nothing but Taxes, Taxes, Taxes' (Chandler, 1742–4: 313). Most of these taxes took the form of excise taxes and excise officers increasingly criss-crossed the country taking notes wherever they went. An occasionally intrusive monarchy had, it seemed to many observers, been replaced by an increasingly intrusive state. It was not necessarily a deal to be welcomed. Excise taxes were preferred in England (and later in Britain) commentators such as Brewer note because the revenue was 'a comparatively discrete tax levied on a sizable but limited number of commodities ... whose producers and distributors paid the tax but passed on the cost of the duties by charging customers higher prices' (Brewer, 1990: 101). Swift and Pulteney enjoyed a friendship and respect for each other that crossed political boundaries precisely because their concerns about wealth, speculation and displacement were to be found throughout intellectual society.

The excise system, and the philosophy which justified it, was inherently offensive to Swift and kindred spirits for various reasons, none of them based on an economic argument as we would understand that term today. Swift's base objection was simple: taxes upon services violated fundamental precepts of sound fiscal policy. Wealth was to be found only in the land and those who worked on it to improve its value. Land, income generated from the land, and the people who worked the land as well as, importantly, ancillary related, drapers, weavers, etc., all not only contributed to the wealth of a nation but were the wealth of the nation itself. Thus, in his famous 1720 tract *Proposal for the Universal Use of Irish Manufacture* Swift addresses 'plain honest men', urging them to celebrate the forthcoming birthday of King George I by wearing clothing made in Ireland of Irish cloth. It was a custom Swift would have liked to see continue after the king's birthday, and he encourages this practice by making the point that 'I have, indeed, seen the Archbishop of *Dublin* clad from Head to Foot in our own Manufacture.' The next clause underscores that such practice should not be one of self-denial, though it implies that, at least as far as the quality of Irish clothing was concerned in 1720, it might well have required a certain sacrifice: '*his Grace deserves as good a Gown, as if he had not been born among us*' (Swift in Davis, 1948: 18). This clause is quite explicit in its objection to the habit of English-born residents of Ireland wearing clothing not made in Ireland, clothing of better quality but responsible for impoverishing Ireland by not employing Irish labour and by failing to use productively the land of Ireland. Excise taxes, which raised the price of finished articles, reduced the ability of people on incomes derived from land to attire themselves appropriately, for income from land came from one of two sources: from rents, which were relatively stable during this period, or from crops and animal husbandry, both notoriously dependent upon elements beyond the control of mere mortals. In Ireland there was the additional challenge that British trade regulation severely restricted the uses to which farmed goods could be put, further depressing the market. But here Swift's analysis diverged from a modern commentator's, for what Swift saw as the problem was that a system had been created which no longer permitted money to be exchanged for 'the truly useful, but perishable, Supports of Life'.

Archbishop King himself was startled by the conditions he saw around him, observing in a 1721 letter to archbishop Wake in Canterbury:

> Y^r South Sea [Bubble] ... has surely made us miserable to the highest degree, if starving be a misery ... I was of the opinion before that one Third of this City needed Charity; but [I find] that at least one Half are in this lamentable state ... & the cry of the whole People is loud for Bread. (William King in O'Regan, 2000: 291)

Notice how King connects speculative stock-market capitalism with destitution. The separation of land from money, of wealth from luxury, has inevitable social consequences. David Bindon would make the case quite clearly in a 1738 tract that was part of one of the ongoing debates about the status of the Irish economy:

> From Reason and Experience it is certain, that the power and Riches of a Nation depend not upon its having Mines of *Gold* and *Silver*, but

upon its having *a numerous and industrious People*. *Spain* and *Portugal* are rich in Mines of *Gold* and *Silver*, but thin of Inhabitants; and the few they have are idle or luxurious: Therefore neither of them has any great Power; and the Riches their Slaves dig from the Bowles of the Earth, are yearly sent out for Supporting the Idleness and Luxury of their people. On the contrary *Britain* and *France* have no mines of *Gold* and *Silver*; but they have Multitudes of People *usefully employed*, and consequently are rich and powerful. (Bindon, 1712: 4–5)

It is the 'luxurious' characteristic of the Spanish and Portuguese which reduces those nations' power and squanders their resources. Wealth is not a problem *per se* but, rather, the source of that wealth and the use to which it is put.

An ostentatious extravagance

The economic argument was irretrievably wrapped up in the political and the moral, and the decline in moral standards indicated by wanton displays of luxury reflected, even if it did not cause – and no one seemed quite sure of whether there was a cause-and-effect component – the increasing foreign involvement of the British state, a new country created by the 1707 union of Scotland and England which embarked upon adventures around the globe quite in contrast to the individual activities of the two countries since English interest in French territories that led to the Hundred Years War finally petered out around 1453. Thomas Cole, curate at St Paul's, London, complained in 1761 that 'an ostentatious extravagance is continually displaying itself in every part of this voluptuous city, and amongst all ranks and conditions of men ... There is scarce any one, but seems to be ashamed, as it were, of living within the compass of his own proper sphere, be it either great or small' (Cole in Brewer, 1997: 72). The British state, cried conservative Anglicans, opponents of public debt, critics of a standing army, and those generally distrustful of state power, was guilty of failing to 'live within the compass of its own proper sphere'. Not only personal but also civic integrity was doomed by an interest in luxury that was inevitably expansionist, exploitative and unsustainable. This was not a uniquely British point of view, and in the seventeenth century one of Blaise Pascal's *Pensées* had reflected on 'The Misery of Man Without God' and had 'discovered that all the unhappiness of men arises from one single fact, that they cannot stay quietly in their own chamber' (Pascal, 1910: 52). It was a sentiment with which clerics such as Swift and Cole agreed absolutely.

For them, one virtue of a mercantilist emphasis on wealth being inextricably linked to land was that it rendered it not only unnecessary but also unproductive to venture much beyond one's chamber.

Swift was consistent in this attitude throughout his professional life and it is in his poetry, almost always occasional, that it may be that we get a more honest glimpse of a notoriously difficult man to know than is otherwise available to us. Only Swift's early poetry was not occasional, but even in these extended panegyrics intended, presumably, to advance his career Swift is consistent. His 'Ode to the Honourable Sir William Temple' (c.1692–3) praises Temple for escaping the general hallucination that

> Taught us, like Spaniards, to be proud and poor,
> And fling our scraps before our door. (Swift in Rogers,
>   1983: ll. 56–7)[8]

Poverty itself is not honourable; indeed, Swift never in his writing even once suggests that he has any sympathy with the idea of hard work being its own reward, of poverty of the right kind being a guide to inner morality. Temple's virtue is indicated by his retirement to his home at Moor Park. But Moor Park is no dingy sanctuary:

> Sing (beloved muse) the pleasure of retreat,
> And in some untouched virgin strain
> Show the delights thy sister Nature yields,
> Sing of thy vales, sing of thy woods, sing of thy fields.
>   (Swift in Rogers, 1983: ll. 135–8)

Even allowing for youthful exuberance on Swift's part, and for his rather predictable efforts to mimic the accepted tropes of the day – efforts at mimicry that reportedly caused his cousin John Dryden to remark 'Cousin Swift, you will never be a poet'[9] – it is easy enough to recognize that Swift has a clear concept of the merits of land in contrast to cash.

Much has been written about Swift's views on the female wardrobe and the preparation of women to appear in public, the 'prepar[ing] a face to meet the faces that you meet', as J. Alfred Prufrock so memorably describes it (Eliot, 1917: 4–10). What has generally been overlooked is the quite clear distinction Swift makes between appropriate and inappropriate displays of wealth, a distinction that underscores his mercantilist sympathies (sympathies which bordered on the autarkic). In women's wardrobes, as for the nation at large, moderation and respect for the provenance of goods and services are the virtues that ensure a well-adjusted prosperous society. Wealth from the appropriate sources is good wealth, 'But gold defiles with frequent touch, / There's nothing fouls the hands so much' (Swift in Rogers, 1983: ll. 67–8).[10] This is a stance made clear in the longer poem 'Cadenus and Vanessa'. As the poem unfolds, Vanessa's unimproved beauty is subject to varieties of ridicule from those who would claim to be more sophisticated, more modern, than her. After various criticisms, most designed to highlight Vanessa's grace and purity in contrast to those who surround her, the poet reports that

> They rallied next Vanessa's dress
> 'That gown was made for old Queen Bess'.
> 'Dear madam, let me set your head:
> Don't you intend to put on red?' (Swift in Rogers,
>   1983: ll. 396–9)

Vanessa is mocked for wearing clothing that was suitable for that paragon of English womanhood, and regality, Queen Elizabeth, and then asked whether she will be wearing something red, a remark significant for the choice of colour, a colour based upon cochineal, first brought to Europe in 1519 by the Spanish, who encountered the pigment upon their contact with the Aztecs (Greenfield, 2005). Again, it is not the ornamentation that is at fault so much as the nature of the display. Red dye could not be produced domestically. To wear it was not only to show off one's wealth, but also to demonstrate one's collusion in lessening the wealth of England.

> Vanessa's detractors admit
> 'She's fair and clean, and that's the most;
> But why proclaim her for a toast?'
> ....
> Scarce knows what difference is between
> Rich Flanders lace, and colbertine,
> ....
> 'I own, that out-of-fashion stuff
> Becomes the creature well enough'.
> The girl might pass, if we could get her
> To know the world a little better.
> (*To know the world*, a modern phrase,
> For visits, ombre, balls and plays.) (Swift in Rogers, 1983: ll.
>   412–13, 416–17, 426–31)

Vanessa's virtues are clearly implied here in the criticisms levelled at her, one of which is that she knows so little of the world as to be unable to distinguish between expensive lace from Flanders and the French lace pattern, colbertine. Or, put another way, she is ignorant of two high-society fashion necessities that are each destructive of the local economy. Given her ignorance of foreign clothing fashions, it is safe to infer that Vanessa is another example of those few who understand that in a mercantilist world local manufacture, based upon local agriculture, is about more than just supporting local craftsmen.

Again, though, it is important to understand that Swift did not oppose displays of wealth on principle, simply the misuse of wealth to create the wrong display. In praising the recently deceased William King, whom he had earlier praised for appearing in Dublin wearing Irish clothing, Swift starts by noting that 'Virtue concealed within our breast / Is inactivity at best' (Swift in Rogers, 1983: ll. 1–2).[11] Or, in other words, by their works shall we know them. King is praised because

> Your hand alone from gold abstains,
> Which drags the slavish world in chains
>
> Him for a happy man I own,
> Whose fortune is not overgrown;
> And, happy he, who wisely knows
> To use the gifts, that heaven bestows. (Swift in Rogers,
>   1983: ll. 13–18)

'Gold' here is not a metaphor of wealth or luxury. It is, rather, exactly what it says it is: 'Gold', a metal imported from abroad, enriching those who trade in it but denuding both those who produce it and those who would buy it to varying states of slavery, literal in the case of those working the mines in South America and proverbial though barely less so in the case of economies such as that of Ireland denuded of its own wealth in pursuit of gold.

Lemuel Gulliver, not surprisingly, had something to say on this subject, to wit:

> England (the dear place of my nativity) was computed to produce three times the quantity of food more than its inhabitants are able to consume ... and the same proportion in every other convenience of life. But in order to feed the luxury and intemperance of the males, and the vanity of the females, we sent away the greatest part

of our necessary things to other countries, from whence in return we brought the materials of disease, folly, and vice ... Hence it follows of necessity, that vast numbers of our people are compelled to ... beg, rob, steal, cheat, pimp, forswear, flatter, suborn, forge, game, lie, fawn, hector, vote, scribble, star-gaze, poison, whore, cant, libel ... and the like. (Swift, 1726: 297)

It is both the 'luxury and intemperance of the males, and the vanity of the females' that is the root cause of the problem. Swift is an equal opportunity critic of needless extravagance. Terms such as 'luxury and intemperance', too, underscore the mercantilist foundations of Swift's critiques. Or, as he put it in 'A Short View of the State of Ireland':

The first cause of a Kingdom's thriving is the Fruitfulness of the Soil, to produce the Necessaries and Conveniencies of Life; not only sufficient for the Inhabitants, but for Exportation into other Countries. (Swift in Davis, 1971: 1)

You will notice here one inherent strain in mercantilist theory – imports tended to reduce the wealth of a nation, and yet one way for a nation to improve its own wealth was through the export of goods. Trade, in other words, was a zero-sum game: if there was a winner there had to be a loser, in contrast to modern economic theory which holds that it is possible for all parties in a trade to come out ahead of their initial starting position.

For Swift, such an apparent contradiction was not a problem: if other countries wished to import British goods (the export of Irish goods except to Britain was generally prohibited) that was their business (literally) and misguided though it might be, it was not for him, a loyal subject of the crown, to advise those misguided foreigners of the errors of their ways. If, on the other hand, the British (or Irish) wished to import products from abroad, that was a different matter.

It was luxuriousness, not wealth, to which Swift objected. And this attitude to clothing – to luxuriousness and also, in this instance, to miserliness that will also not offer employment to those that are the wealth of the nation – brings us back to *A Tale of a Tub*. The nature of the story need not be retold here, only the reminder offered that the three brothers (who represent Puritanism, Anglicanism and Catholicism) each have taken the original robes bequeathed them by their father (Christ) and made certain modifications. The initial modifications were adopted by all three brothers at the instigation of Peter. Over time, Jack and Martin come to doubt the validity of the adornments inspired by Peter. Jack works with some care to remove those ornaments that can be safely removed without destroying the fabric of the original cloth; Martin is so zealous in his puritanical enthusiasm that he rips and rends the clothing almost to destruction in removing even the slightest hint of Peter's additions, thereby rendering his own garment shoddy and unfunctional. While this parable is essentially a metaphor for religion, and a justification – albeit of a bizarre sort – for Church of England doctrine, it also serves to make the point that attire can be both practical and elegant (as Jack's ends up being).

Swift should be read, at least on the subject of money and displays of wealth, as indicative of his age. Money was, or should have been, nothing more, nor less, than a contractual mechanism based on a seamless blending of property, husbandry, and domestic manufacture. Swift sided absolutely with Alexander Pope's criticism of

> paper-credit! Last and best supply!
> That lends Corruption lighter wings to fly!
> Gold imp'd by thee, can compass hardest things,
> Can pocket States, can fetch or carry Kings;
> A single leaf shall waft an Army o'er,
> Or ship off Senates to a distant Shore. (Pope in Williams, 1969: 176–88, ll. 69–74)[12]

For Swift and those whose opinion he shared, displays of wealth and riches dependent upon anything other than local resources were not simply immoral in their own right, they facilitated (if not additionally required) immorality in others, eventually undermining society wholesale.

More than that, a society no longer based on land, or in which land was reduced simply to a means of leveraging disposable income, was ultimately doomed to economic collapse. In 1727 and 1728, Swift would make this argument when he joined a highly unlikely coalition of both Irish- and English-born bishops of the Church of Ireland in opposing a parliamentary bill designed to offer incumbent bishops immediately increased rents in return for reduced future income from land. Part of the argument used by the parliamentary faction in support of the bill, the majority of them minor landholders and renters of clerically held land, was that the increased initial income could be used to invest in the businesses of the new economy. In his tract *Against Enlarging the Powers of the Bishops*, Swift focused on the benefits accruing to those tenants who were the immediate renters of lands held by landlords who conducted themselves according to mercantilist theories of property management. As land was wealth, such landlords tended to invest in their property, looking to increase its long-term value. It was no coincidence that many such landlords happened to be clerics, but the analysis Swift offers is independent of the career of the landholders. Renters of such landlords, Swift argues, 'may [be] distinguish[ed] at first Sight, by their Habits and Horses; or if you go to their Houses, by their comfortable Way of living' (Swift in Davis, 1948: 54).

As such beneficial practices increasingly gave way to efforts to secure gold and silver coin to support extravagant lifestyles in Dublin, Bath or London, the consequences were significant and immediately felt at home: 'Within three Years past, the running Cash of the Nation, which was about five Hundred Thousand Pounds, is now less than two; and must daily diminish.'[13] This was the objection of Swift to displays of wealth and opulence. It was not that wealth in and of itself was harmful, but that it was increasingly built upon a system that was illusory and immoral. For Swift, these objections were conservative, nostalgic and moralistic.

Notes

1. Kelly (1991: I, 67). The tracts to which Kelly refers are Harris's *An Essay upon Money and Coins*, part ii (1758); Massie's *Observations Relating to the Coin of Great Britain; Consisting Partly of Extracts from Mr Locke's Treatise Concerning Money, but Chiefly of such Additions thereunto, as are Thought to be Very Necessary at this Juncture ...* (1760); and Steuart's *An Inquiry into the Principles of Political Economy. Being an Essay on the Science of Domestic Policy in Free Nations* (1767).
2. The word 'conservative' is almost as loaded when applied to Swift as is the word 'Tory'. In a full-length study of Swift as a churchman, I argue that Swift's instincts were more in line with a trope Isaac Kramnick identifies in the sub-title of his study of *Bolingbroke and His Circle: the Politics of Nostalgia* (1968). Significantly, Swift's nostalgia was for an imagined recent past that, in fact, had never really existed. See, if you are interested in such matters, Fauske (2002).
3. Incidental evidence of contemporary inability to recognise the sea-change in fiscal affairs is copious. Two examples will suffice: the first professor of economics was not appointed until the beginning of the nineteenth century, an appointment that went to the Rev. Thomas Robert Malthus. Even then, the new college at Haileybury combined the history professorship with that of political economy. Adam Smith and others whom we today think of as founders of modern economics held professorships in mathematics or philosophy, if they held any academic position at all. It was Malthus's *Essay on Population* (first published anonymously in 1798) that earned the field the sobriquet 'dismal science', a term coined by Thomas Carlyle. The second

example: the book that defined modern economics, Adam Smith's *An Inquiry into the Nature and Causes of the Wealth of Nations* was not published until 1776.
4. The paragraph which follows and the three notes below are all from Hartley (2008).
5. Maximillian Novak has a brief discussion of this debate in *Daniel Defoe: Master of Fictions* (2001: 3–5). The most inclusive list of publications, having 566 separate items, is found in John Robert Moore, *A Checklist of the Writings of Daniel Defoe* (1971).
6. Swift mentions Defoe in writing only twice, once anonymously, acknowledging him as 'One of these Authors (the Fellow that was pilloried, I have forgot his Name) [who] is so grave, sententious, dogmatical a Rogue, that there is no enduring him'. [Jonathan Swift], 'Letter from a Member of the House of Commons in Ireland to a Member of the House of Commons in England, Concerning the Sacramental Test' (London, 1708). In *The Prose Works of Jonathan Swift*, Vol. 2, *Bickerstaff Papers and Pamphlets on the Church*, ed. Herbert Davis (1957), pp. 109–26, p. 113.
7. Swift, *A Tale of a Tub*, p. 109.
8. All references to Swift's poetry are by line number to the version found in *Jonathan Swift: Complete Poems*, ed. Pat Rogers (1983).
9. The evidence would seem to be that this remark, first cited in Samuel Johnson's *Life of Swift*, most likely was never made. That it is apocryphal does not necessarily reduce the validity of the remark. See Johnson (1952).
10. 'The Fable of Midas', in *Jonathan Swift: Complete Poems*.
11. 'Part of the Ninth Ode of the Fourth Book of Horace', in *Jonathan Swift: Complete Poems*.
12. See also T. Jones (2004).
13. [Jonathan Swift], 'A Short View of the State of Ireland' (1728), p. 11.

4
Payments of Attention: Epitaphic Cash Flow in Gray and Wordsworth

György Fogarasi

Introduction

In the past decade, economic theory has shown a growing interest in the workings of attention, a concept whose importance, for many of its investigators, seems all the more obvious because of its idiomatic connectedness to the notion of payment, and thus to the workings of currencies and monetary systems in general. While the idea of an emerging 'attention economy' – as conceived by Richard A. Lanham (1994 and 1997), Michael H. Goldhaber (1997), or more recently, by Thomas H. Davenport and John C. Beck (2001), and again, by Lanham (2006) – certainly has its roots in previous views about the 'society of the spectacle' or the 'information society', the latter have been shown to be restrictive and ultimately inapplicable to the logic of current economic tendencies. In contrast to information or spectacle, attention is scarce, and since economies are governed by what is scarce, it is attention, rather than information or spectacle, that must provide the basis for the economy towards which we are moving.[1] This is how the attention economy appears as the 'natural economy of the net' (Goldhaber, 1997), or in a broader sense, as the 'new currency of business' in general (Davenport and Beck, 2001).

At a closer look, however, the notion of an attention economy appears, in most of its formulations, to be governed by the underlying narrative of a transition from 'material' to 'immaterial' production, from 'actual' to 'virtual' goods, from 'stuff' to 'fluff', from mechanical 'repetition' to intellectual 'originality', or from fame in 'death' to fame in 'life' – a narrative whose metaphysical conceptuality has been seriously shaken in recent years.[2] Interestingly enough, the proponents of this narrative hardly ever reflect on these distinctions themselves, so they are in danger of providing a simplified and highly questionable history of both economy and its theory. It is even more surprising that none of these researches has addressed the question of why and how the English language itself has come to think of acts of attention in terms of payment, well before the advent of 'post-industrial' capitalism, and its celebrated epitome, the Internet. If we take the example of the World Wide Web, and think of attention as a 'visiting' of 'sites' (that is, an act of attendance or frequentation), then the eighteenth- and nineteenth-century literature on the 'visiting' and 'revisiting' of memorials or memorable places might give us insight into the workings of this highly elusive currency. And since these earlier texts themselves speak of attention as the paradigmatic form of payment, their importance for any understanding of today's currency seems all the more obvious. It may turn out that the emergence of economics as an autonomous field of study in the second half of the eighteenth century is not entirely unrelated to a specific literary discourse, the British epitaphic tradition, which appears, in several respects, to be dealing with questions we today would call 'economic' but which at that time might have appeared to have an exclusively literary or moral character. What is more, the lexicon of graveyard poetry plays an essential role for the classics of economic theory: it permeates the writings of Adam Smith (as Esther Schor has lucidly shown), as well as the works of Karl Marx (whose 'graveyard rhetoric' has been minutely analysed by Jacques Derrida). So, it may turn out that 'economics' has never managed to get rid of its literary embedment, the poetic or figural birth of its concepts, and has in fact never reached the status of an autonomous discipline.

My selection of Thomas Gray and William Wordsworth as two of the most prominent representatives of the (pre)romantic epitaphic or elegiac tradition may seem a commonplace choice. But when it comes to revisiting texts that themselves meditate on the act of revisiting more or less common places, then the sense and value of the 'commonplace' may itself appear to be at stake. For the logic of attention *as* attendance, or of attention *as* payment (or again, of attendance *as* payment) seems to turn around this very act of visiting and revisiting places, of paying repeated visits to them, and my present goal is precisely to trace that logic – a logic of speculation and displacement, as we shall shortly see.

Elegy (Gray)

In his *Elegy Written in a Country Church-Yard* (1750), Gray occupies the attentive position of a visitor 'mindful of th' unhonour'd Dead', who ponders on the memory of those who are least likely to survive in the minds of future generations. The rural location as well as the poor construction of their monuments considerably lessens their chances of posthumous survival. Their merits are likened to 'unfathomed' pearls and 'unseen' flowers, because, for all their perfection, they are doomed to remain unrecognised. Their 'frail memorials' are hardly able to attract attention, even though that is precisely what they are for.

> Yet ev'n these bones from insult to protect
> Some frail memorial still erected nigh,
> With uncouth rhimes and shapeless sculpture deck'd,
> Implores the passing tribute of a sigh.
>
> Their name, their years, spelt by th' unletter'd muse,
> The place of fame and elegy supply:
> And many a holy text around she strews,
> That teach the rustic moralist to die. (Gray, 1977: 37, ll. 77–84)

As the above lines indicate, the ultimate function of a funeral monument and the inscription on it is to elicit a gesture of tribute (a 'sigh') from the passerby, and thereby to guarantee the ghostly survival of the deceased. But if it is located on a 'neglected spot' (as is the case here), there is little chance that it will ever catch the eye of a traveller. Yet, memorials must be attended to; they must be visited and read, in order to function as memorials. The ghosts of the dead will only visit us, if we visit them. Their survival depends upon our own ghostly habit of frequenting their habitations, and Gray's visitor does his best to meet that requirement. All this implies a chiasmic or mirror-like relationship between the living and the dead, and therein lies the speculative aspect of elegiac attention.[3]

But there is also another and perhaps even more important level to the speculative aspect of elegiac attention, related not so much to the logic of specularity but rather to that of calculation, an attempt to foresee the unforeseeable. Such an attempt occurs somewhat later in the poem, when the mind of the visitor turns from the past to the future. This redirection takes place through a complex set of displacements. On the one hand, the visitor places himself imaginatively in the position of the dead, and speculates on the future moment when another person will occupy his present place and will do for him what now he does for others. On the other hand, he also places himself in the position of his future substitute, from whose viewpoint he can look back upon his own death as if it were an event in the past. So it seems that we are dealing with a double figurative exchange. On the one hand, the visitor identifies with the dead, the 'forefathers' of the hamlet (who were once what he is now, and who are now what he will inevitably be in the future). But, on the other hand, he also identifies with the stranger, the 'kindred Spirit' or 'friend' (who is now what he was once, and who will hopefully be what he is now). There is a significant asymmetry between these two movements, for while the visitor's future substitution for the dead will occur inevitably (since he cannot escape death), his own substitution by another visitor is but a possibility desperately hoped for (since the future visit of a friend cannot be taken as certain). The poem's reference to 'chance' (and later to 'trembling hope') indicates a risk that should not be overlooked.

The shift from the past to the future, which is a shift from specular self-mirroring to speculative calculation, is curiously bound up with the idea of morality. As the poem suggests, the visitor is a rustic 'moralist' only in so far as he is able to make that shift, and see the past death of the forefathers as a prefiguration of his own future demise. The logic of this transition from retrospective mourning to prospective melancholy (or self-mourning) is in fact at the heart not only of the epitaphic tradition, but also of a broader philosophical discourse on the relation of humanity and morality. It was minutely explored by one of Gray's contemporaries, Adam Smith (often regarded as the father of economics), whose *Theory of Moral Sentiments* appeared in 1759, just a few years after the *Elegy* was completed. It might be useful to take a glimpse at Smith's argument, for it entwines morality with economy precisely through the activity of mourning and the consequent state of melancholy. Smith opens his treatise with a discussion of 'sympathy', presented as the fundamental sentiment of mourning, and thus the ultimate source of the melancholic state of poisoned happiness, which in turn is shown to be the basis for moral behaviour. And since sympathetic attentiveness is conceived as a 'payment' of honour, morality is bound up with economic relations between the dead and the living.

> We sympathize even with the dead [...] The tribute of our fellow-feeling seems doubly due to them now, when they are in danger of being forgot by every body; and, by the vain honours which we pay to their memory, we endeavour, for our own misery, artificially to keep alive our melancholy remembrance of their misfortune. [...] The idea of that dreary and endless melancholy [...] arises altogether from our joining to the change which has been produced upon them, our own consciousness of that change, from our putting ourselves in their

situation, and from our lodging, if I may be allowed to say so, our own living souls in their inanimated bodies, and thence conceiving what would be our emotions in this case. It is from this very illusion of the imagination, that the foresight of our own dissolution is so terrible to us, and that the idea of those circumstances, which undoubtedly can give us no pain when we are dead, makes us miserable while we are alive. And from thence arises one of the most important principles in human nature, the dread of death, the great poison to the happiness, but the great restraint upon the injustice of mankind, which, while it afflicts and mortifies the individual, guards and protects the society. (Smith, 1984: 12–13)

Sympathy implies an imaginary substitution, our putting ourselves in the situation of the dead.[4] According to Smith, this substitution creates the illusion of foresight. The price we must pay for this illusion is not only our 'honour' to the dead, however. According to the chiasmic structure of prosopopoeia (the trope of animation or personification so characteristic of graveyard poetry), to the extent that the dead come alive, the living must lose their vitality.[5] The survivors must pay with their very lives: they must lodge their 'living souls' in those inanimate bodies, a gesture which not only 'afflicts' but also 'mortifies' them, as Smith makes clear. The price we pay when we pay sympathetic attention to the dead is a painful price, but morality, for Smith, can come about only at the expense of such individual mortification.

This is equally true for the morality of Gray's visitor, who is a 'rustic moralist' only inasmuch as he pays due attention to the graves, risking that his expenses will never be returned. In a lucid book on the British culture of mourning, Esther Schor describes Smith's conception as a 'theory of moral *circulation*' (Schor, 1993: 36), and her literary example for such a view on morality is precisely Gray's *Elegy*. Schor argues that the eighteenth-century philosophical discourse on morality and its grounding in the notion of indebtedness towards the dead runs parallel with the evolving economic discourse on the value of paper money and its grounding in the establishment of a golden standard. Just as paper money gains its value from its reference to gold, the immensity of elegiac literature gains its seriousness from its connectedness to the dead whose corpses are 'deposited' into the grave just the way precious objects or materials are deposited into the safe of a bank. The physicality of gold or of the cadaver is to counterbalance the proliferation of texts (elegiac poems and paper currency alike), and thus to serve as the 'material basis' for both moral and monetary economy.[6] Schor also refers to Smith's seminal economic treatise on the *Wealth of Nations* (1776), in which he points to the revitalising power of paper money, its power to reactivate the 'dead stock' and put it in the service of production and profit-making: 'Just as sympathy transmutes the dead into a vital moral resource, paper money has the power to "convert this dead stock [of gold and silver currency] into active and productive stock"' (Schor, 1993: 37; the quotation is from Smith, 1976: II, 341).

We have just seen, however, that any effort to give life to the lifeless must risk losing its own vitality. If the revitalisation of the dead as a 'dead stock' can only be accomplished at the expense of the mortification of the living, then the moment of giving life is also necessarily a moment of loss, which in turn calls for a moment of salvation or recovery. Payments of attention, such as a 'sigh' or a 'tear', do not only imply the income of the dead but they also imply the grave expenditure of the living that needs to be compensated for. Hence, it is no surprise that the demand for recuperation is so essential for Gray's visitor. The closing epitaph of the *Elegy* describes exactly such an economy of loss and gain:

> Large was his bounty, and his soul sincere,
> Heav'n did a recompence as largely send:
> He gave to Mis'ry all he had, a tear,
> He gain'd from Heav'n ('twas all he wish'd) a friend.
> (Gray, 1977: 39, ll. 121–5)

The visitor pays attention to the past and awaits repayment ('recompence') from the future. This is not simply an economic system but a system of credit, or even more specifically, a system of social security. For just as in a pension scheme, for instance, one pays to people who were born before, while expecting repayment from the younger generation, here too, acts of payment are acts of loaning that follow one another successively, by a logic of constant displacement. The more or less implicit imagery of forefathers, fathers and sons, or somewhat differently, of the dead, the living and the unborn, can easily be associated with the more modern imagery of the no-longer-working, the working and the not-yet-working segments of society. This is not a binary system, a transaction between two figures, debtor and creditor, but a system of connections at the very least tripartite, one of endless displacements, a chain open at both ends, neither sufficiently established, nor having the potential ever to be closed off. Such an economy is always on the verge of going bankrupt, and as such, it is in fact both a-systemic and an-economic.[7] In a 'system' like that, the money you can spend is always money to be earned later on, therefore any payment is an expenditure for the account of the future. As the epitaph tells us, the visitor indeed has no capital to invest, except his tribute. His 'bounty' consists solely in his abundant attentiveness, but even that is something that he hopes to be attributed to him in death. Since all his payments (of attention) go to the debit of what is to come, he is spending in fact what he does not have.[8]

In order to conceal the absurdity of its own operation and preserve at least the illusion of being a system, this 'economy' has to appeal to an external authority that may guarantee the continuity of payments, the flow or 'liquidity' of the currency of attention. As the poem makes it clear, the credibility of the debtors, and thus the repayment of all debts, is sustained by 'Heav'n', a divine power whose function is that of the modern state, namely to serve as an external insurance for the operation of the system. This heavenly economy creates the illusion of permanence, whereby the tripartite process of transactions (between the dead, the living and the unborn) may appear to occur between two parties (between man and God), and thus may seem to form a closed system. This illusion may make us believe in the future repayment of all payments, and lay trust in what Schor has aptly termed 'moral liquidity' (1993: 39). But since the illusion of this permanence is produced by the figurative manoeuvres analysed above, there is little hope that it can ever attain the status of an autonomous and absolute guarantee.

In order to pursue this line of investigation, and further examine the relations between British epitaphic and economic thought, let us now turn to one of Gray's most enthusiastic readers, William Wordsworth, and see what his poetry and prose may add to this topic. I will examine three texts: his poem *Tintern Abbey*, his *Essays upon Epitaphs*, and Book VII of *The Prelude*.

Tintern Abbey (Wordsworth)

As for Wordsworth's lyrical poetry, the most obvious parallel to all that has been said of Gray's *Elegy* would probably be *Tintern Abbey* (1798), where one may find similar speculative displacements, this time not in the ghostly scenery of a cemetery but in the equally ghostly setting of a natural landscape. Geoffrey Hartman's remark about 'a general convergence of elegiac and nature poetry in the eighteenth century' (Hartman, 1987: 33), might be a good starting point in this transition from Gray to Wordsworth. Hartman gives an accurate description of the latter's stance, when he claims that 'The poet *reads* landscape as if it were a monument or grave' (Hartman, 1987: 40). This statement certainly holds for *Tintern Abbey*, even though, as Hartman himself points out, this time 'there is no actual corpse in the vicinity' (Hartman, 1987: 42). The contemplated scene still functions as an epitaph inscribed upon a tombstone.[9] The 'uncertain notice' of the smoke sent up from below by some 'vagrant dwellers' or a 'Hermit' is just like a message from the dead, and it turns the whole sight into an inscription whose uncertain readability is a correlate of the ghostly presence of the departed or the outcast. These spectral figures are the specular equivalent of the wanderer who is himself a *revenant*, revisiting the spot in an act of obsessive frequentation.

The speculative aspect of Wordsworth's piece, like that of the *Elegy*, does not consist solely in the specularity between visitor and visited. There is a turning point in the text, where the person visiting this funeral landscape suddenly changes perspective and speaks to his sister or friend from the position of the dead.[10] So, if the opening scene of *Tintern Abbey* presents us with a graveyard scene reminiscent of the *Elegy*, then the evolving triple constellation of the Hermit, the wanderer (William), and his sister or friend (Dorothy) might be equivalent to the sequence of the dead, the living and the unborn, and might once again confront us with the logic of speculative displacements whose quasi-economy proved to be so crucial in Gray's poem.

The motif of sleep is yet another point of convergence between the two texts, and it has a specific function in the attention economy they present. The imaginary figure of the 'Hermit', living in the total isolation of his cave, might remind us of the figure of the forefathers, each of whom 'in his narrow cell for ever laid' lives the reduced but not entirely extinguished life of 'sleep', ready to be invoked and reawakened when there is such a need. The mythical notion of death as a form of 'sleep' (cf. Ariès, 1981: 22–4) appears not only in the *Elegy* but also in the second section of *Tintern Abbey* where William himself (the Hermit's specular equivalent) seems to be 'laid asleep' in the isolated space of 'lonely rooms'. The trope of 'sleep' implies that the dead cannot be considered to be totally departed or non-existent. They are still among us, albeit in a reduced form, like ghosts, whose presence is all the more uncanny because it implies a certain level of absence. If death is a sleep, then the dead can be reawakened or reactivated, and as such, they are accessible to us as an energy resource (partly human, partly natural) that only waits for our attention and call in order to come alive again. The figure of 'sleep' runs parallel with the recently elaborated notion of the retired person as a 'reserve of labour' (Walker, 1996: 5), that is, as a labour force standing in stock, ready to be recalled and put to work when the market requires so.[11] In this respect, the poem speaks of the 'uncertain' presence of the homeless and unemployed, who are nevertheless always ready for reactivation or repositioning.

Essays upon Epitaphs (Wordsworth)

Wordsworth faces this problematic more explicitly, though from another angle, in his *Essays upon Epitaphs* (1810), focusing on a genre which can in fact be considered as the prototype for capitalist advertisements, which proclaim the names of products in much the same way epitaphs proclaim the names of humans.[12] In the *Essays*, Wordsworth pays special attention to the location of memorials. Unlike Gray, he foregrounds the ancient habit of erecting funeral monuments on the roadside, rather than on sacred places specifically designed for that purpose. While 'among the modern nations of Europe' the remains of the deceased 'are deposited within, or contiguous to, their places of worship' (Wordsworth, 1974: II, 53), in antiquity they were buried by busy roads, which contributed to the intimate relation between the dead and the living. 'In ancient times, as is well known, it was the custom to bury the dead beyond the walls of towns and cities; and among the Greeks and Romans they were frequently interred by the way-sides' (Wordsworth, 1974: II, 53). The roads leading out from ancient cities were centres of commerce, and more specifically, of the ancient attention economy, just as the huge advertising surfaces along the motorways of a modern metropolis are among the busiest places of attentive cash flow today. But while Wordsworth emphasises the advantage of heavy traffic, he is well aware that 'tombs lose their monitory virtue when thus obtruded upon the notice of men occupied with the cares of the world, and too often sullied and defiled by those cares' (Wordsworth, 1974: II, 54). The roadside location Wordsworth prefers is certainly much more frequented than the 'neglected spot' of the country churchyard described by Gray. But it is a place frequented by unheeding travellers, who pass by the monuments without due reverence, and whose attitude to the graves is fundamentally different from the respectfulness of the 'mindful' visitors who visit the sacred space of a cemetery with the specific purpose of commemoration and tribute. In a book on the changing customs of burial, Philippe Ariès draws a crucial distinction between the modern habit of *visiting* memorials and the ancient habit of *passing* by them. He elucidates the figure of the visitor through Gray's *Elegy*

(Ariès, 1981: 524), while about the passerby (the ancient figure highlighted by Wordsworth) he gives the following description:

> But who is this passerby? [...] The passerby is not [...] a relative, friend, or familiar of the deceased, someone who knew him, who misses him and mourns him, and who comes to visit his grave. This sentiment is absolutely unknown until the end of the eighteenth century. The person who is being addressed by the deceased is literally a passerby, someone who happens to pass by the grave, a stranger who is walking through the cemetery or has come into the church, either to say his prayers or because it is on his way, for, as we know, the church and the cemetery were public meeting places. Consequently the authors of wills no longer seek only the most *sacred* spots for their graves but also the most *frequented*; often the two qualities coincided.
> (Ariès, 1981: 220, my emphases)

By the end of the eighteenth century the spontaneous traversing of the places of worship has been superseded by the purposeful visit. So there is a significant difference between visitor and passerby, and this difference is closely related to the distinction between the 'sacred' and the 'frequented' spot, which appears at the end of the passage just quoted. For, while cemeteries attended by visitors are definitely sacred places, they are not as frequented as spots by the roadside. On the other hand, monuments erected along busy roads are certainly set up on frequented places, but their profane location may easily expose them to sacrilege. Wordsworth seems well aware of the tension between these, equally important aspects. Sanctity and frequentedness prove to be mutually exclusive criteria for the siting of a memorial. The double demand for both is indeed a double bind, an aporetic requirement that cannot be fulfilled. In the *Essays*, Wordsworth encounters this latent aporia but seems unwilling to face the underlying problem: the ambivalent workings of attention.[13]

The Prelude, Book VII (Wordsworth)

Just as the genre of the epitaph is a forerunner of the genre of the advertisement, the roads outside the walls of ancient cities (like the 'Strada dei Sepolcri' in Pompeii) were the cradle of metropolitan traffic and commerce. Following this logic, Wordsworth's description of the modern metropolis in Book VII of the *Prelude* (telling his Residence in London) may be still part of his meditation on the workings of epitaphs in the ancient necropolis, and the attention economy they presuppose. He depicts the figure of attention (the crowd) as an immense stream that overflows the network of streets:

> How often in the overflowing streets
> Have I gone forwards with the crowd, and said
> Unto myself, 'The face of every one
> That passes by me is a mystery.' (Wordsworth, 1979:
>   258, ll. 595–8)[14]

The succession of 'overflowing streets' appears as a winding riverbed unable to contain the massive current of the crowd. This image may recall in us the image of the 'overflowing Nile' from the previous book of the *Prelude*, so the ceaselessly moving crowd may implicitly appear in the guise of a magnificent river whose nourishing natural resource is also a power beyond human control, and as such, potentially lethal. The ambivalent work of the river is a recurrent image in the writings of Wordsworth. It also appears in his first essay upon epitaphs, when he speaks of hope as a poplar being simultaneously 'fed' and 'undermined' by the stream upon whose bank it grows (Wordsworth, 1974: II, 54).[15]

In another passage taken from the same book of the *Prelude*, Wordsworth speaks of this 'flow' as an 'endless stream of men and moving things' (Wordsworth, 1979: 235, ll. 150–1, quoted from the 1850 version). The juxtaposition of men and things suggests that for the poet, himself a member of the crowd, the realms of humans and objects, or of consumers and goods, radically intermingle. Men themselves become commodities. They go shopping not simply to buy some*thing* but to buy some*one*, and at the same time, to *be* bought. They try to sell themselves as goods, offering their own labour force for hire. This connection is affirmed in the following lines, where the rhythm of 'face after face' and 'shop after shop' suggests the same implication:

> The comers and the goers face to face –
> Face after face – the string of dazzling wares,
> Shop after shop, with symbols, blazoned names,
> And all the tradesman's honours overhead:
> Here, fronts of houses, like a title-page
> With letters huge inscribed from top to toe;
> Stationed above the door, like guardian saints,
> There, allegoric shapes, female or male,

> Or physiognomies of real men,
> Land-warriors, kings, or admirals of the sea,
> Boyle, Shakespear, Newton, or the attractive head
> Of some quack-doctor, famous in his day. (Wordsworth,
>   1979: 234, ll. 172–83)

'Faces' in the crowd are no longer just figures for attention (that is, for payment or purchase), they are also figures for 'shops' advertising and selling 'wares', that is, human labour force. To pay attention to them is tantamount to the act of hiring, employing or reactivating their bearers, just the way the dead had been shown to be ready for being hired, employed or reactivated through the revitalising attention of a passerby. Like the 'fronts of houses' or the 'title-page' of a book, faces are the external signs of something that lies beyond. Similarly, a funeral monument is the 'external sign' of the deposited body of the deceased, as the *Essays* tell us (Wordsworth, 1974: II, 49). Following this logic, the 'letters huge inscribed' upon the walls are not only analogous to the title on the front cover of a book, but more importantly, they are like the lineaments of a face, which in turn function precisely like the letters of an epitaph engraved on a tomb. In the streets of the modern metropolis, the attention paid to monuments and inscriptions is ceaselessly at work. The flow of this attention is the cash flow of capitalist economy, which has perhaps always been an economy of attention.

If the city of London is the miniaturised version of capitalism as a whole, and the picture of Bartholomew Fair presented later in Book VII is a picture of a 'city within the City', as Neil Hertz rightly notes (1985: 55), then the latter scene presents us the quintessence of modern commerce and economy. It is in this setting that the figure of the blind beggar enters the poem.

> ... 'twas my chance
> Abruptly to be smitten with the view
> Of a blind beggar, who, with upright face,
> Stood propped against a wall, upon his chest
> Wearing a written paper, to explain
> The story of the man, and who he was.
> My mind did at this spectacle turn round
> As with the might of waters, and it seemed
> To me that in this label was a type
> Or emblem of the utmost that we know
> Both of ourselves and of the universe,

> And on the shape of the unmoving man,
> His fixèd face and sightless eyes, I looked,
> As if admonished from another world. (Wordsworth, 1979: 260, ll. 610–23)

The frozen shape and stony gaze of the blind beggar make it hard to distinguish him from the wall he is leaning against. He is himself very much like a piece of stone, while the 'written paper' informing us about his fate is very much like an inscription upon a tomb, an epitaph whose reader might indeed feel 'as if admonished from another world'.[16] The lifeless image of the beggar points to the analogy between the dead, on the one hand, and the homeless or workless, on the other. His epitaphic mode is the mode of advertisements in the most literal sense: he *turns to us* in order to *turn us to* the thing he wants to sell. And this is indeed what takes place, for as soon as the poet happens to catch sight of the beggar, his attentive mind (itself allegorised as an immense flood moving 'with the might of waters') suddenly 'turns round', and flows right towards the blind man's figure.

The function of advertisements or epitaphs is to redirect or rechannel our attention, to make use of the power of its flow, and thereby to circulate the name of a personified product or a commodified person. All they want is to accumulate or capitalise this force, and then spend it on the mobilisation of a particular commodity. To the extent that they are designed to use the flow of attention for their own good, they are like power plants set in the way of a stream, 'implanted', as it were, in the current or currency of attention. They are supposed to reprogramme the flow of this current, to raise it to a higher power, just as power plants are supposed to produce electric current out of the current of rivers. In one of his essays on Baudelaire, Walter Benjamin notes that the crowd streaming through the streets of Paris, is indeed a 'stream of people' (*Menschenstrom*) to be understood as an electric current, or as a condensed form of such a current, 'a reservoir of electric energy' (*ein Reservoir elektrischer Energie*) (Benjamin, 1969: 167, 175; 1977: 198, 208). Wordsworth's own formulation is not far from this when near the end of Book VII he finally calls the whole scene of the fair (the countless tents and booths 'vomiting' and 'receiving' men, redirecting their attention without end) – when he calls this superhuman mechanism 'one vast mill' (Wordsworth, 1979: 264, ll. 692–5). Here once again, attention appears as an energy resource, as a reserve of power, which monuments and inscriptions try to entrap, accumulate and then spend for their own benefit.

Conclusion

Whether the Baudelairean picture of Paris derives in any way from Wordsworth's description of London (via Poe perhaps), is far from sure. It seems equally uncertain whether some of the post-romantic English novelists did follow, self-consciously or not, the steps of the *Prelude* in their treatments of the metropolis and the social issues it poses (even though some critics make that suggestion, see Williams, 1971: 17, for example). More important than such questions of genealogy and inheritance is perhaps the fact that *literary* representations of capital are not necessarily *literal* representations. As the examples of Gray or Wordsworth show, issues of economy may be posed and discussed implicitly on a figural level (in the imagery of attentive visitors, epitaphic texts, rivers, mills, and so on), and so the revisiting of commonplace works might result in readings that make us aware of the alien or uncanny nature of the 'common' place. To read them as figural speculations on economy (as a system of recuperation, that is, a secularised version of the Christian scheme of redemption) and at the same time as speculations on the quasi-economic logic of speculation itself is, however, just half of the work. What seems even more necessary is the recognition that such speculations cannot even be called figural, if the language of economy is itself full of tropes (as notions like 'currency', 'flow', 'liquidity', 'deposit', 'dead stock', or 'credit' demonstrate). One may conclude then that there is no other way we could speak of the history of economy and its theory. The language of literature remains the only medium for any such speculation.

Notes

1. What is usually called 'time management' derives precisely from the scarcity of attention, since to 'pay' attention is equivalent to the 'spending' of time. In this regard, Leigh Claire La Berge's claim (in this volume) that it is impossible to 'save time', since spare time is a time to be spent, runs parallel to my own claim below that accumulated attention operates as accumulated capital, whose ultimate function is to be spent or invested. (This also implies that the notion of the scarcity of attention is not be confused with the medical notion of Attention Deficit Disorder, the latter being understood as a developmental deficiency, while the former refers to a broader, non-pathological condition or necessity.)
2. Even Richard Lanham's lucid emphasis on the ancient tradition of rhetoric as an 'economics of attention' (Lanham, 2006: 21) seems to remain on the near side of a truly critical rethinking of his binaries ('substance'/'style', 'stuff'/'fluff'). While his investigations are very informative for any comparison of early and contemporary media, and his caution against a hasty

3. Geoffrey Hartman's remark on another poem by Gray (*Ode on a Distant Prospect of Eton College*) seems applicable here as well: 'The poet, like the other shades, seems a mere ghost in the landscape' (Hartman, 1970: 320).
4. It is worth noting that the concept of sympathy also plays an essential role in the eighteenth-century discourse on the sublime. In his famous aesthetic enquiry, published in the same decade as Gray's poem and Smith's treatise, Edmund Burke himself underlines the element of figural substitution in the notion of sympathy (even though he does not use the concept in an economic context), and claims that language is capable of evoking sublime affect precisely because it functions in a non-mimetic, figural mode, that is, according to the logic of sympathy: 'For sympathy must be considered as a sort of substitution, by which we are put in the place of another man, and affected in many respects as he is affected [...] It is by this principle chiefly that poetry, painting, and other affecting arts, transfuse their passions from one breast to another, and are often capable of grafting a delight on wretchedness, misery, and death itself'; 'In reality poetry and rhetoric do not succeed in exact description so well as painting does; their business is to affect rather by sympathy than imitation; to display rather the effect of things on the mind of the speaker, or of others, than to present a clear idea of the things themselves' (Burke, 1987: 44 and 172).
5. As Paul de Man demonstrated in an essay on Wordsworth, the chiasmic workings of prosopopoeia implies a latent threat: 'by making the death [*sic*] speak, the symmetrical structure of the trope implies, by the same token, that the living are struck dumb, frozen in their own death' (de Man, 1984: 78).
6. Because of its spectral (that is, animated, personified, fetishised) character, however, this 'material basis' is not simply material (physical or natural), therefore it can never function as a solid ground for the economic system which it is supposed to uphold. This non-natural aspect of the gold standard is highlighted in Ben Roberts's essay (in this volume) on Jean-Joseph Goux's reading of Adré Gide's novel *The Counterfeiters*.
7. The phrase 'an-economic' figures in Derrida's *Specters of Marx* within a set of related terms like 'adikia' or 'anachrony', and refers to a function that is not simply 'un-economic', but just as much 'pre-economic' or 'beyond' any economy, being utterly heterogenous to it (cf. Derrida, 1994: 23).
8. The notion of this paradoxical temporality also appears in Leigh Claire La Berge's essay on financial time (in this volume).
9. In this regard, we could legitimately call it, using Hartman's own expression, a 'nature-inscription' (1987: 39).
10. Hartman also calls attention to the displacements taking place near the end of the poem: 'The poet reads nature or his own feelings as if there were an ominous, admonitory relationship between this spot and himself. At the end of the poem, moreover, when Wordsworth foresees his death and urges Dorothy to perpetuate his trust in nature, he speaks as if he were one of the dead who exhort the living in the guise of the genius loci' (1987: 42).
11. The association of death and retirement also implies the association of life and labour (cf. Derrida, 1994: 187). If the dead have the potential to be

revived, retirement must equally be capable of a certain level of productivity. This is why it seems legitimate to claim that 'the relationship of retirement and productivity stands open to renegotiation, where until recently these had been mutually exclusive' (Walker, 1996: 13).
12. What distinguishes Wordsworth's treatment of epitaphs from that of earlier critics (William Camden, John Weever, or Samuel Johnson, cf. Scodel, 1991: 15–16, 362–6) is that, for him, the epitaph is not just one poetic genre among others but the 'epitome of poetic language' (Ferguson, 1977: 33).
13. He tries to get over this difficulty by associating the ancient with the rural (and accordingly, the modern with the urban) atmosphere, whereby the ancient wayside location is turned into a place as tranquil as a churchyard. This domesticating gesture is an attempt to turn the unheeding passerby into a reverent visitor and thus to save the memorial from being defiled or simply neglected.
14. All quotations from *The Prelude* are from the 1805 version, unless otherwise indicated.
15. Another example for such ambivalence can be found in one of Wordsworth's sonnets on the River Duddon, where he desperately faces the river's power not only to 'restore' but also to 'pollute' its environment (see Wordsworth, 1969: 298). The same duplicity prevails in Wordsworth's remarks on language (and more specifically, on the figure of prosopopoeia), as Paul de Man has shown in his analysis of the *Essays upon Epitaphs* (de Man, 1984: 80). The most famous post-romantic description of the double character of the stream (and, implicitly, of language or attention) would probably be George Eliot's novel *The Mill on the Floss* (1860), in which the river finally destroys the construct which it is supposed to uphold and energise. As the conclusive chapter of the novel remarks, the river also overturns a gravestone in the cemetery. The images of the mill and the gravestone are also linked metonymically in Book VII of the *Prelude*.
16. As far as the figure of the blind beggar is able to 'admonish' us, it functions similarly to monuments, whose 'monitory value' was so emphatic in the *Essays*.

5
Money, Manhood and Suffrage in *Our Mutual Friend*

Ruth Livesey

> 'If ever a good man were ruined by good fortune it is my benefactor. And yet, Pa, think how terrible the fascination of money is! I see this, and hate this, and dread this, and don't know but that money might make a much worse change in me. And yet I have money always in my thoughts and my desires; and the whole life I place before myself is money, money, money, and what money can make of life!' (Dickens, 1864–5: III. iv, 455)

Introduction

Almost precisely half-way through Charles Dickens's capacious and last complete novel, *Our Mutual Friend*, the mercenary beauty, Bella Wilfer comes to reflect on the power of the substance she has spent her short life pursuing. The example of her benefactor, the former dustman, Mr Boffin, who at this stage of the novel seems to have been turned into a vicious miser by an unexpected inheritance, confirms to Bella the troubling capacity of money to represent goods. Money is not a passive substance in this novel, awaiting transformation into carriages, fashionable clothes and smart dinner parties – the stuff of life – but has shaped the world in its own image. The future which Bella places 'before myself', before any autonomous sense of being, is one that is shaped by the agency of money; it is the circulation of money that has come to 'make' life itself in *Our Mutual Friend*, and threatens an end to all other modes of self-representation and social being.

The fascination with money, circulation and finance in *Our Mutual Friend* has received its due share of critical attention over the past decades. Dickens plays with the inheritance plot in the novel such that the legatee, John Harmon, stages his own death rather than submit to the conditions of his father's will and its prerequisite that he marry the unknown Bella Wilfer in order to inherit the mountainous dust heaps that are the family fortune. Humphrey House was but the first of many to explore the significance of that dust, its (debatable) status as a euphemism for human excrement, and the consequent psychic and material relations between the circulation of money and waste in the novel (House, 1961: 166–9; Gallagher, 2006). The manner in which Dickens rewrites familiar plots and genres, such as inheritance, to make them new in this work is something I will return to in the final section of this chapter; this rewriting of the old also serves to underline a second aspect of the text's uneasy interest in the power of money. *Our Mutual Friend* is a novel that, in comparison to Dickens's other works, is unusually engaged with the present of modernity, with the social and political life of the mid-nineteenth century, rather than inviting thoughts on the now through retrospect (Tambling, 1995: 211). I want to argue that, in part, the complex and uneven dual plots of *Our Mutual Friend* are a product of this strain of representing modernity; or, more particularly, of the representation of the people in modernity.

The two, relatively distinct, strands of the novel have been characterised as on the one hand a 'realist' plot revolving around the river, in which Eugene Wrayburn and Bradley Headstone pursue the love of Lizzie Hexham, and on the other a 'sentimental' plot, centred on wealth and dust, in the course of which Bella Wilfer is tutored out of her desire for money into conformable domesticity (Goodlad, 2003: 159–90; Poovey, 1995, 155–81). But both plots, I suggest, work through the systems of valuation and representation prevalent in debates on Parliamentary Reform and franchise extension during the mid-nineteenth century. In an era in which universal (male) suffrage promised (or threatened) to become a reality, the plots of *Our Mutual Friend* form a parallel to two competing systems of representation advanced within political debates during the late 1850s and 1860s. The founder of the Working Men's College, Frederick Denison Maurice, characterised the choice before Parliament during this period as lying between political representation on the broad basis of manhood, or on the narrow grounds of money (Maurice, 1866: 208). As we shall see in the latter part of this chapter, Dickens's narrative of the former pauper, Bradley Headstone, and his lethargic, gentlemanly rival, Eugene Wrayburn explores a democratic imaginary of universal (gentle)manhood and self-representation that can never quite be free from the revolutionary melodrama of class oppression and rage. The plot of Bella Wilfer and John Harmon, on the other hand, starts in a modernity in which money has ended representation and turned everything into a copy of itself.

This arraignment of modernity as simulacrum is most evident in Dickens's depiction of a culture of speculation which enables characters such as the 'Bran New' Mr and Mrs Veneering, the stock-jobbing Fledgeby and the fraudulent Lammles to gain social credit on the mere appearance and rumour of wealth.[1] Directly after their marriage, the Lammles discover that such false estimates have shackled them together for life, each believing that they were making a sound investment in a wealthy spouse. Mrs Lammle insists that her husband is to blame for her supposition that he was a creditable man of property and dares him to '"deny that you always presented yourself to me in that character"' (I. x, 128). Such play on credit, as Catherine Waters suggests, leads to a reflection on the status of narrative itself within the novel, and she concludes that 'the extraordinary signifying power of money [is] a power that resides in its circulation as a collective fiction' (Waters, 1997: 175).[2] But it is possible to push Waters's point further in relation to the modernity of this novel. After all, as Margot Finn's recent work has shown, the need to put on a lavish show of high living on credit to stop your tailor suspecting that you might not be able to pay his bill at the end of the quarter had been a popular financial (and fictional) strategy for decades prior to the publication of *Our Mutual Friend* in 1864–5 (Finn, 2003: 1–19).

Money, credit and representation

In the eighteenth and early nineteenth century, the granting of financial credit was largely grounded in a culture of mutual obligations based on long-standing familial and employment ties for the lower and middling orders, and on a perception of character, lineage and landed expectations for the upper classes.[3] Yet in Dickens's account of the modern financial market in *Our Mutual Friend*, valuation is formed in purely presentist cash terms with little regard to the past and less to the future apart from in the form of potential dividends. It is not that money is fiction in this novel, but rather that its pervasiveness threatens to denude established narratives of character, origin, family and identity of any significance. Dickens holds out the prospect of a world in which coherent stories are lost in the whirl of scraps of paper.

Money claims to be truth and value in *Our Mutual Friend*, whilst being, like a banknote, only a contingent signifier, always circulating in the present and without a beginning and an end. When the nefarious street stall-holder Silas Wegg first spies Mr Boffin wandering past he muses to himself:

> 'And what are you now? Are you in the Funns, or where are you? Have you lately come to this neighbourhood, or do you own to another neighbourhood? Are you in independent circumstances, or is it wasting the motions of a bow on you? Come, I'll speculate, I'll invest a bow in you.' (I. iv, 53)

Rather than let his motions go purely to waste, Wegg must judge whether Mr Boffin has money secured in the safest of investments, 'Funns': the national debt, or Government Funds.[4] Civil and political relations have here been reduced to purely monetary terms: Boffin's social standing is judged in relation to his ability to be a creditor to the nation; Wegg's deference in 'making a leg' or bow to Boffin is a similar investment for future dividend – and one that serves him rather better than the sale of his actual leg to Mr Venus. The granting of credit here is only on the basis of rapidly realisable cash value and not the mutual obligations of civility and trust that Dickens explores with all-too-intimate familiarity elsewhere in his works: credit relations in *Our Mutual Friend* are a world away from the assumption of social obligations (even when exploited) between, for example, Jarndyce and Skimpole or young David Copperfield and Mr Micawber.

This collapse of civic into monetary value and the habits of interested deference that accompany it had pressing political significance during the 1850s and 1860s. The 1850s witnessed a resurgence of parliamentary debate and bills in pursuit of further reforms to the electoral process in Britain, and this, in turn, provoked a wider consideration of voter qualifications.[5] In the years prior to the Second Reform Act of 1867 and 'shooting Niagara', as Thomas Carlyle termed it, into mass suffrage, the relation between property, money and political representation was a prevalent feature of political discourse (Carlyle, 1867). In 1832 the first Reform Act had extended the franchise such that male householders in urban boroughs occupying homes of £10 or more rateable value could vote, hence enfranchising the majority of middle-class men. The long-standing Whig notion that Parliament should represent the interests of different orders of society had thus ceded to a system of suffrage based on property. During the late 1850s and 1860s proponents of further franchise extension developed alternative criteria for the vote, ranging from the insistence on universal manhood suffrage on the part of former Chartists like Ernest Jones, to the desire to distinguish the mass of 'respectable working men' from the rough underclass voiced by the Radical MP John Bright, to franchise reforms establishing minimum educational or financial qualifications for prospective voters (McClelland, 2000: 89).

Dickens was sceptical about the capacity of franchise reform in itself to change the life of the nation. Writing to William Charles Macready in 1855 he concluded:

> As to the suffrage, I have lost hope even in the [proposal for a secret] Ballot. We appear to me to have proved the failure of Representative Institutions, without an educated and advanced people to support them. What with teaching people to 'keep in their stations' – what with bringing up the Soul and Body of the land to be a good child, or to go to the Beershop to go a-poaching and go to the Devil – what with having no such thing as a Middle Class (for, though we are perpetually bragging of it as our safety, it is nothing but a poor fringe on the mantle of the Upper) – what with our flunkeyism, toadyism, letting the most contemptible of Lords come in for all manner of places – making asses of ourselves for Prince Albert to saddle – reading the Court Circular for the New Testament ... I do reluctantly believe that the English people are, habitually, consenting parties to the miserable imbecility into which we have fallen, and will never help themselves out of it ... at present we are on the down-hill road to being conquered, and the people *will* be content to hear incapable and insolent Premiers sing Rule Britannia, and *will not* be saved. (Dickens, 1965–2002: vii, 715)

A successful extension of the franchise, could, for Dickens, only be possible if the working-class 'Soul and Body' country were educated into independent manhood and the middle classes lost their fascination with the glamour of upper-class doings. Excessive deference, or 'toadyism', infantilising education and the power of money threatened an end to 'Representative Institutions'.

Dickens's contempt for middle-class deference to the aristocracy put him at odds with a major contributor to the wider Reform debates and a later critic of his own works, Walter Bagehot.[6] For Bagehot, whose essays on the English Constitution appeared in the *Fortnightly Review* in 1865 just as the serial issue of *Our Mutual Friend* came to an end, the English political system was formed by custom and tradition and protected by that culture of deference anathematised by Dickens.[7] The 'pomp' and 'spectacle' of court and aristocracy 'coerced' the masses into acceptance of the existing Constitution, Bagehot argued: 'their imagination is bowed down; they feel they are not equal to the life revealed to them' (Bagehot, 1867: 51). He concluded that the numerical majority of the population were therefore eager to hand over electoral responsibilities to the chosen, educated middle- and upper-class few and marvel at the spectacle of power at a distance. The immense political trust vested in elected representatives thus functioned like 'the best mercantile credit' in England. The system of 'political credit' meant that 'we trust our fellow countrymen without remembering that we trust them' (Bagehot, 1867: 40). Bagehot's analogy was, perhaps, rather ill-chosen given the massive financial crisis triggered by the collapse of the discount bank, Overend, Gurney & Co. in 1866, but it built on an increasing identification of financial investment with political representation during the reform debates of the mid-nineteenth century.

A few years prior to the composition of Dickens's *Our Mutual Friend* and Bagehot's *English Constitution*, the Chancellor of the Exchequer, Benjamin Disraeli, presented a Reform Bill to Parliament that made this connection between money, credit and political representation explicit. Disraeli, who was, of course, to extend radically the borough franchise to all male householders and £10 lodgers in 1867, proposed a conservative model of franchise extension in 1859 aimed at preserving the Constitution from radical arguments for manhood suffrage. Disraeli's Reform Bill dismissed democracy as a dangerous theory that valued numbers over quality. The object of his Bill was rather to reconstruct the constituent body of the country 'with no mere view of increasing its numerical amount, but solely with the object of improving it, by the addition of various classes and individuals to whom the privilege of the franchise may be trusted with safety to the State and benefit of the community' (Corry, 1867: 196). In pursuit of such reconstruction, Disraeli proposed that the residential property-based franchise of 1832 be supplemented by a new form of property qualification. Men who had had over £60 in a savings bank for over two years and those in possession of East India Stock or Bank of England Funds yielding over £10 per annum had demonstrated their manly foresight, and such a form of portable property qualification, Disraeli argued, opened an 'avenue to the mechanic, whose virtue, prudence, intelligence and frugality entitle him to enter into the privileged pale of the constituent body of the country' (Corry, 1867: 192). Money was to become the sign of respectable citizenry for the working man, whilst being a creditor to the national debt ('in the Funns' as Silas Wegg has it) would bring the dividend of an extra vote in elections. In addition to such financial signifiers of virtue, Disraeli also tabled a 'fancy franchise' in which members of certain professions, including barristers, lawyers and board certified schoolmasters, should be entitled to a vote regardless of their property qualifications. Money, credit and the professions were to improve the make up of the electorate and enable a slow evolution in the customary British Constitution.

Corruption, custom and the Constitution

The portable property that Disraeli's 1859 Reform Bill claimed as a sign of virtue and citizenship is, as I have suggested, at the heart of a crisis of representation in *Our Mutual Friend*. Property of any sort, the social reformer Frederick Denison Maurice argued, could only be a legitimate basis for franchise qualification if it stood as proof of a 'man's dealings with the world' (Maurice, 1866: 208). And yet money, throughout the first two-thirds of *Our Mutual Friend*, is capable only of proving itself and displacing all other systems of representation. Even the solid-seeming Government Funds approved by Disraeli are part of the wild speculation, plots and misrepresentations of Silas Wegg. Perhaps most telling though, in his narrative of Mr Veneering's election as Member of Parliament for the rotten borough of 'Pocket Breaches' Dickens explicitly connects the question of political corruption and parliamentary reform to the contingent nature of money as a form of representation:

> Britannia, sitting meditating one fine day (perhaps in the attitude in which she is presented on the copper coinage), discovers all of a sudden that she wants Veneering in Parliament. It occurs to her that Veneering is a 'representative man' – who cannot in these times be doubted – and that Her Majesty's faithful Commons are incomplete without him. So, Britannia mentions to a legal gentleman of her acquaintance that if Veneering will 'put down' five thousand pounds, he may write a couple of initial letters [MP] after his name at the extremely cheap rate of two thousand five hundred per letter. (II. iii, 243)

The proud emblem of national identity, Britannia, has come to mimic her two-dimensional representation on coins: the currency no longer serves the nation; rather the nation has been turned into the image of cash. It follows accordingly that Mr Veneering, who exists only, as his name suggests, as a thin reflective surface, has become a 'representative man' for these times. As Veneering careers around his 'bran new' dearest best friends, securing their support for his election and insisting on the identity of his political opinions, 'not previously having been aware of having any', with potential aristocratic patrons, Dickens emblematises a world in which the reflection of money has displaced representation and manhood (II. iii, 244).

In his speech introducing the 1859 Reform Bill, Disraeli argued for the continuance of tiny pocket boroughs like 'Pocket Breaches', with its 'feeble little town hall on crutches' (II. iii, 251). The type of electoral corruption summarised by a reporter for Dickens's *All the Year Round* in 1859 as 'marvellous revelations of systematic bribery', was, for Disraeli, a small price to pay for the ability of such boroughs to return MPs who could never get in by other means and yet represented important interests: the tiny borough of Arundel, for example, had been swung in such a manner in order to return the only Roman Catholic MP in the House (Anon. 1859: 53; Corry, 1867: 198).[8] In the logic of *Our Mutual Friend*, however, buying, selling and deference in elections strip that process of any representative function. Mr Veneering's speech to the electors of Pocket Breaches contains 'two remarkably good points' (II. iii, 252). The first is an appeal to his honourable friend Mr Podsnap, indicating to the electorate that this intimate is the 'greatest and most respected' among the merchant princes of Marine Insurance and hence a man of wealth; the second, that he is connected through his friend Twemlow, with the noble Lord Snigsworth and the 'exalted sphere' of the aristocracy (II. iii, 252). Veneering is 'brought in' by the borough on the strength of his pale reflection of these two figures.

The British Constitution was in the mid-nineteenth century, as it remains today, an unwritten accumulation of ancient customs and convenient innovations, which, according to Bagehot, 'guide by an insensible but an omnipotent influence the association of its subjects' (Bagehot, 1867: 11). Yet in *Our Mutual Friend* Dickens associates such complacency about custom and representation with the smug world of Podsnappery, closed to any thought of change. Quizzing a visiting Frenchman on his impressions of the city, the self-satisfied patriot Mr Podsnap asks '"Do You Find, Sir ... Many Evidences that Strike You, of our British Constitution in the Streets of the World's Metropolis, London, Londres, London?"' (I. xi, 136). Podsnap might, rather like Bagehot, insist that '"We Englishmen are Very Proud of our Constitution, Sir. It Was Bestowed Upon Us By Providence. No Other Country is so Favoured as This Country."' But when he clarifies his question regarding the visibility to an outsider of '"any Tokens ... Signs ... Appearances – Traces"' of such greatness, the poor visitor scrambles for the only marks he has seen on the street: '"Ah! Of a Orse?"' (I. xi, 136). The proud boast of a customary Constitution has been displaced by the visible tokens of piles of shit – and money – in this text and Dickens satirises the notion that the safety of the British representative system lay in its illegibility. When the historical narrative of custom cannot be read by the people, the circulation of money fills the void of representation.

Property and trust

In addition to its attack on political corruption and the ability of money to displace representation, *Our Mutual Friend* is also a novel that probes at a seemingly more straightforward association implicit in constitutional debate in the mid-nineteenth century: that the occupation of a certain sort of household was a legible marker of a certain sort of man. The second chapter of the novel, with its title 'The Man from Somewhere', introduces this unfixing of place and social identity: the ostensible subject in question is the missing John Harmon, whose mysterious disappearance is charted to a dinner party by the lawyer Mortimer Lightwood in fewer words than it takes for them all to speculate on his point of origin. Eventually Lightwood concludes '"Sorry to destroy romance by fixing him with a local habitation, but he comes from the place, the name of which escapes me, but will suggest itself to everybody else here, where they make the wine"' (I. ii, 23). This lack of definitiveness about where exactly John Harmon can be located, other than on an export route, is mirrored in his reappearance as the Wilfers' 'suspicious lodger', John Rokesmith (I. iv, 51). Ushered in by the austere Mrs Wilfer's 'Act-of-Parliament' manner, the mysterious lodger refuses to supply references and agitates 'the bosom of [the Wilfer] family': '"Pa," said Bella, "We have got a Murderer for a tenant." "Pa," said Lavinia, "we have got a Robber"' (I. iv, 47). Mr Wilfer's insistence that '"Money and goods are certainly the best of references"' emphasises the commercialisation of the home through the practice of taking in lodgers; but the irony of this statement being uttered by the least mercenary character in the novel merits some further attention.[9]

Despite Mrs Wilfer's 'Act-of-Parliament' welcome to Rokesmith, no lodger could vote for members of that Parliament prior to the 1867 Reform Act, and even that achievement was hard-won in the teeth of arguments that lodgers were necessarily shiftless men who had not proved their respectable dealings with the world. Rokesmith's apparent lack of a past and of creditable references seems to confirm the unfitness of such a class of men for the business of representation. Yet the novel works to contrast the humble, concrete contributions Rokesmith's presence makes to the domestic and moral economy of the Wilfers to the social being of the Veneerings. Rokesmith pays eight sovereigns in advance for his rent (swiftly converted in part into a veal and ham supper) and offers to 'trust' his own furniture to the Wilfers' home. Mr and Mrs Veneering's 'bran-new' home, with its interior composed entirely of reflective surfaces, recently invented heraldry, new oldest friends, on the other hand, is founded on credit and speculation, and founders into bankruptcy at the end of the novel. The Veneerings' property is not proof of Mr Veneering's dealings with the world, but rather, it is implied, his dealing in shares; and Shares, in this novel, are the antitype of narrative representation:

> Have no antecedents, no established character, no cultivation, no ideas, no manners; have Shares. Have Shares enough to be on Boards of Direction in capital letters, oscillate on mysterious business between London and Paris and be great. Where does he come from? Shares. Where is he going to? Shares. What are his tastes? Shares. Has he any principles? Shares. What squeezes him into Parliament? Shares. Perhaps he never of himself achieved success in anything, never produced anything? Sufficient answer to all; Shares. O mighty Shares! (I. x, 118)

When property is based on the insubstantiality of shares – a mere sign without a referent – how can the home itself represent anything more solid than 'a state of high varnish' (I. ii, 17)? The common consent of 'society', from the scions of nobility to languid gentlemanly professionals, to dine with the Veneerings and thus reflect credit upon them, is a critique both of this new plutocracy and the eagerness of the propertied upper-middle-classes and indebted aristocracy to take them to their bosom.

Occupying a certain sort of property in this novel is no longer a solid sign of distinction and social place. Indeed, the Lammles play the game so well that they continue to be considered very wealthy and gifted with exquisitely refined taste by merely putting out that they remain in Alfred's bachelor chambers whilst waiting for their perfect home to appear on the market. Property and homes on a grand scale are associated with financial credit in the novel and such credit is stripped of social instantiation and mutuality and undermines customary values. The modest living of the lodger, John Rokesmith, on the other hand, demands time for mutual trust, building on eight solid sovereigns paid in advance, rather than instant credit. Trust, even blind trust, such as Bella Wilfer must demonstrate to prove her love for the mysterious Rokesmith, is the antidote to money in this novel, bringing back to life those histories, identities and characters, like John Harmon, killed off by its powers. By this means Dickens restores a sense of faith in indirect representation through the liminal figure of the lodger: once removed from the mercenary world of credit, Bella must trust John to be her agent in the world. This paternalist model of family works to settle the fears raised in the first three books of the novel that money not only trumps all other systems of value, but threatens an end to representation itself; where national government has succumbed, household government remains a site in which manhood, rather than money, legislates on behalf of others.

Manhood and melodramatic narrative

If the John Harmon/Rokesmith narrative of *Our Mutual Friend* plays out the political melodrama of the socially deracinated lodger with a light touch, then Eugene Wrayburn and Bradley Headstone's competition for Lizzie Hexham plots the unpredictability of lower-middle-class manhood in far darker tones. As we have seen, Disraeli's proposals for a professional suffrage in 1859 aimed at broadening the franchise on the basis of secure standing in a chosen field of work and specifically foregrounded the advantages this would bring to members of the legal profession and the relatively new, socially indeterminate category of board certified schoolmasters.[10] Despite this potential political validation of the power of work to make a man in the mid-nineteenth century, *Our Mutual Friend* is an anxious rewriting of the joys of professionalisation, self-improvement and *Bildung* evident in Dickens's earlier works like *David Copperfield*. Here the lethargic, upper-middle-class barrister Eugene Wrayburn has never represented a client in his life whilst the former pauper and certified schoolmaster, Bradley Headstone, progresses across the threshold Disraeli proposed for suffrage only at the cost of a fatal suppression of his self which bursts out in a murderous attack on Wrayburn himself.

Headstone's melodramatic plot is the limit of the democratic imaginary in *Our Mutual Friend*. Whilst the eventual marriage of Eugene Wrayburn and the working-class Lizzie Hexham seems to hold out a fantasy of classlessness and universal gentility, Headstone's implacable rage against Wrayburn marks Dickens's retreat from social mobility. Despite his carefully stored education and dedicated self-improvement, the schoolmaster still has 'a certain stiffness ... as if there were a want of adaptation' to his respectable suit 'recalling some mechanics in their holiday clothes' (II. i, 218). Headstone's stiffness and his retentiveness of his 'mental warehouse' is representative of his inability to convert his carefully fashioned self into any other social goods, unlike the languid gentleman, Wrayburn, who can wander between social worlds and turn things and people to his own ends.[11] If, in 1855, Dickens believed that the right sort of education would equip the working-class 'Soul and Body' of the nation to take part in political representation, then by the mid-1860s the schoolmaster had come to exemplify the wrong sort of tutelage in civic life: Headstone contains the rage of the revolutionary mob in a 'decent black coat'.

The complex plotting of *Our Mutual Friend* and its play with established generic conventions is in part an attempt to re-contain the threat of Headstone. Much as Dickens was attracted by the democratic ideal in many respects, it seems to have been for him an ideal in which distinctions of class – or, at least, class consciousness – needed to be wiped away.[12] Headstone represents the danger of retaining that sense of class-bound shame and anger in an era of democratisation. It is no coincidence, therefore, that in *Our Mutual Friend* Dickens rewrites the class dynamics of the melodrama. Juliet John has recently observed that the novel subverts the stock plot in which the respectable daughter of the poor is seduced by the rapacious, cool aristocrat (a plot, of course, that Dickens worked with quite comfortably in *David Copperfield*) (John, 2001: 188–96). For the first three books of the novel Eugene Wrayburn's pursuit of the waterman's daughter, Lizzie Hexham, seems to promise an end in nothing but her seduction and abandonment by this upper-class dilettante. Headstone, on the other hand, stands in precisely the position of the approved, respectable lover who is her social equal, destined to avenge and rescue his beloved from the clutches of her would-be seducer. Yet Dickens collapses that conventional triangulation of melodrama in the final book of the novel: Headstone's very respectability becomes the forcing-house that brings out his violence against the gentleman he can never be; conversely, Wrayburn's rescue by, and marriage of Lizzie is an attempt to resolve both the novel and the problem of the representation of class.

In the light of the franchise debates of the 1850s and 1860s I have outlined, this rewriting of the melodramatic plot gains a sharp political inflection. In the nineteenth century that conventional cross-class love triangle, amongst other attributes, made melodrama a popular vehicle for the expression of working-class radical dissent (Brooks, 1976: 84–6). Such melodramatic narrative formations seeped into broader political rhetoric during the mid-nineteenth century. For Frederick Denison Maurice, for example, schemes such as Disraeli's franchise bill of 1859, and further suggestions of a professional franchise, were forms of 'money suffrage' that failed to acknowledge the proud true history of the English Constitution and risked undermining that education in citizenry to which he was devoted. Limiting the franchise to those working men who had proven themselves 'decent' through cash savings or professional advancement was part of a 'miserable theory of numbers' that would soon lead to nothing but

> a series of plots and counterplots: plots to gain admission into a narrow, exclusive circle; counterplots to keep the circle more narrow, to devise precautions against intruders. Thence arise perpetual suspicions of the few against the many, and of the many against the few; of the few against each other, of each one in the many against his neighbours; ending in the domination of one who reduces all to the condition of corpses, and then boasts that by destroying freedom he has secured equality. (Maurice, 1866: 208)

Representation on the basis of money alone would, in short, provoke a melodrama of conspiracy, revenge and revolution.

In order to 'repudiate mob force' and recover 'the old maxims of the constitution', Maurice argued, it was necessary to understand that English constitutional history was the history of 'the growth of a people' and widening political representation in an Anglo-Saxon golden age, prior to the Norman conquest (Maurice, 1866: xii). If those campaigning for the extension of the franchise could be taught to see themselves as part of an earlier, pre-modern, story – the organic Romance of the growth of 'a people', rather than this revolutionary melodrama of the many and the few – then the representation of manhood through the suffrage would at the same time instil an ethos of manhood in these prospective voters. The one thing needful, Denison argued, was a return to this true 'manhood suffrage' practised in the medieval period. This would enable the newly enfranchised male population to recognise their part in a narrative of conservative populism: that all were 'freeborn Englishmen' before the imposition of that infamous 'Norman yoke' and could return to their proud Yeoman roots even in the midst of modernity.

The social historian Patrick Joyce argues that such appeals to a golden age of democracy prior to the 'Norman yoke' were common in the era of the Second Reform Act. Such narratives served, he suggests, to legitimate a 'sense of political identity' for those working men anticipating enfranchisement (Joyce, 1996: 188).[13] Yet this collective Romance of a lost universal manhood – this sense of a freedom waiting to be recovered – is precisely what Headstone is represented as lacking in *Our Mutual Friend*. If the anaphoric passage on Shares enacts the foreclosure of narrative representation by money, then anaphora, once again, demonstrates the limits to Headstone's self-representation:

> Bradley Headstone, in his decent black coat and waistcoat, and decent white shirt, and decent formal black tie, and decent pantaloons of pepper and salt, with his decent silver watch in his pocket and its decent hair guard round his neck, looked a thoroughly decent young man of six-and-twenty. (II. i, 218)

Headstone's route from workhouse to schoolhouse is constrained by the test of decency, rather than the presumption of innate manliness; that is, his livelihood, property and putative vote rest on his narrowly crawling his way out of the 'jumble' of the pauper school into the restricted order of the professions.

Such progress is no longer virtue in the world of *Our Mutual Friend*. The confrontations between Wrayburn and Headstone replay the melodrama of class antagonism consequent on a world of democratisation in which the schoolmaster feels entitled to claim equality with the gentlemanly barrister, but is constantly reminded that that claim is, as he is, illegitimate under the rule of money. In response to Headstone's assertion that '"You think me of no more value than the dirt under your feet"', Wrayburn replies, '"I assure you, Schoolmaster ... I don't think about you"' (II. vi, 289). Headstone's rage that his 'value' will never be above that of dirt in the world of money is thus stoked by the complacency of Wrayburn. Dickens's inversion of the melodrama might restate the revolutionary potential of the lower classes, even when on the move upwards, but it also serves to implicate the casual violence of upper-middle-class snobbery in such disorder. Headstone's maiming of

Wrayburn strips the latter of such self-possessed superiority and hence his part in the melodrama of class antagonism and enables the novel to end in a very different narrative mode: a romance in which the people can be united by transcendent values of virtue.

Early on in the novel, Mortimer Lightwood drawls to his newly enriched clients the Boffins that their independence of mind is evidence of 'Vigorous Saxon spirit – Mrs Boffin's ancestors – bowmen – Agincourt and Cressy' (I. viii, 95). This tracing of the dustman's wife to a line that endured the 'Norman yoke' undaunted reads at first glance as an instance of Lightwood's habitual cool humour. But it also ties the deracinated Boffins into the populist rhetoric of the 'freeborn Englishman' prevalent in discussions of the suffrage in 1850s and 1860s: the Boffins' virtue lies precisely in the fact that money and modernity, like the Norman invasion, cannot alter their vigorous independent spirit of self-representation. Mr Boffin thus might seem to be corrupted by money into becoming a copy of all the stories of famous misers he collects, but in fact he sets himself up as the '"kindest fingerpost that ever was ... pointing out the road"' and end that Bella needs to be steered from (IV. iii, 755). The apparent melodrama of Boffin's corruption, the expulsion of Rokesmith and flight of Bella is instead a reassertion of the status of character and narrative as legible signs with an ethical content against the world of money.

Whilst the Boffins entirely lack the sense of entitlement and resentment of a Bradley Headstone (or a Silas Wegg or Rogue Riderhood) it is worth noting that Dickens's resolution to the putative melodrama of the golden dustman requires Mr Boffin to return his fortune to the patrilineal inheritor, John Harmon. The Boffins' narrative might draw to a close with a scene of mutual recognition in which they are revealed as agents of virtue, uniting all people in a common cause; but they also resume their place as, in effect, family retainers to Bella and John. Eugene Wrayburn's eventual marriage to, rather than seduction of, Lizzie Hexham provides a resolution that treads a parallel path of conservative populist Romance. Headstone's failed murder attempt leads to Wrayburn renouncing his languid leisured status to become Lizzie Hexham's husband: a true man of '"purpose and energy"' who will turn all to '"the best account"' (IV. xi, 735). Conversely, Bradley Headstone, who in the conventional triangulations of melodrama would be the respectable lower-class love rival here becomes the villain and sinks in death into the river mud. Dickens thus invokes and eventually displaces the antagonistic radicalism of melodrama with a conservative populist Romance in which Wrayburn's drowning and rebirth – in itself a Romance trope – erases all sense of insurmountable class distinctions between himself and Lizzie. Headstone's fatal and implacable resentment of and desire to claim the identity of gentleman means that he, however, remains impelled in the melodramatic imaginary of excess; of persecution, class consciousness, shame and anger.

In the final chapter of the novel, Dickens brings together this inversion of conventional plot and the question of political representation. Mortimer Lightwood revisits the Veneerings' house for dinner to discover what 'the voice of society' has to say about Wrayburn's marriage. The irrepressible dowager, Lady Tippins, commands, '"let us resolve ourselves into a Committee of the whole House on this subject"' and votes are cast by the guests (IV. xvii, 795). As each person present offers an opinion on the matter – '"Madness and moonshine"' to contract the match for less than twenty thousand pounds – the nervous poor relation of a peer, Twemlow, is finally asked for his vote in the matter and he concludes '"that this is a question of the feelings of a gentleman"':

> 'if such feelings on the part of this gentleman induced this gentleman to marry this lady, I think he is the greater gentleman for the action, and makes her the greater lady. I beg to say when I use the word, gentleman, I use it in the sense in which the degree may be attained by any man. The feelings of a gentleman I hold sacred.' (IV. xvii, 796)

This language of democratic gentility becomes the 'voice of society' itself at the close of the novel as Twemlow and Lightwood walk home arm in arm, leaving the Veneerings' House of Parliament behind. The re-entry of the Wrayburn and Lizzie Hexham plot into the world of the Veneerings at this point seems to proffer a closure in which the simulacrum of money – and the plots spawned by it – is displaced by the universal value of feeling. With the marriages that end the dual plots, an alternative narrative of 'the people' and the virtues which unite them comes to displace the language of class and difference which characterised the first three books of the novel. But the moments of melodrama, shame and rage in the text remain an excess that cannot be recuperated by this assertion of cohesion and democracy: the ending remains haunted by Bradley Headstone and the all-too-convincing performance of Boffin's corruption by wealth unsuited to his station. If Dickens attempts to close the novel by depicting a world of common values and customs in which democracy might succeed, it is a world that, like Headstone himself, can scarcely repress the passions of class-consciousness it needs to keep down in order to function.

Notes

1. On *Our Mutual Friend* in relation to financial legislation and speculation in the 1850s and 1860s see Poovey (1995).
2. For similar arguments about different texts see Brantlinger (1994: 144); James (2003: 1–9).
3. Finn (1993: 63) suggests that an early modern culture of reciprocity and gifts gave way only gradually and late to individualist conceptions of contract and property during the period covered by her study.
4. For Dickens's editorial interest in the meaning of Government Funds as civic representation see 'A Great Meeting of Creditors', *All the Year Round* 1(7) (1859): 153–6.
5. See Finn (1993) and Taylor (1995) for two contrasting historical analyses of this period of political debate.
6. Here Dickens's debt to early nineteenth-century Radicalism remains clear. On the part this played in Dickens's earlier writings see Ledger (2007).
7. Bagehot (1867) was originally published in the *Fortnightly Review*, 15 May 1865–1 January 1867. The monthly serial parts of *Our Mutual Friend* were also published by Chapman from May 1864 to November 1865.
8. Taylor (1995: 173) suggests that Disraeli's 1859 Bill succeeded in uniting Liberals on the question of suffrage extension by moving away from the divisive issue of the redistribution of seats and abolition of pocket boroughs.
9. See Waters (1997: 183–4) for an examination of the challenge to the ideology of domesticity presented by lodgers.
10. For contemporary debate on the social identity of the schoolmaster in relation to Headstone see Goodlad (2003: 167–82).
11. Goodlad (2003: 177) points out that this retentiveness due to class deracination is the social explanation of the anality that Eve Sedgwick famously identifies with Headstone: see Sedgwick ([1985] 1993: 161–80).
12. Dickens's encounter with the American republic in the 1840s is significant in this respect: see Sanders (1999: 111–53).
13. See also Joyce (1991) for the argument that the 'Norman yoke' represents a melodramatic narrative: it is clear, however, that its structure is far more akin to that of Romance as I argue here.

6
Feverish Speculation: the Railway Across the Isthmus of Panama

Marian Aguiar

Introduction

> From the moment of their arrival at Aspinwall an Isthmus fever floats before them tangibly in the air. It hangs a yellow veil before every object. Their sight is jaundiced. They hurry over a railroad, laid, as they have been told, on human sleepers. The rich luxuriance of the forest along its course, now first opened to the eye of man, seems only rank, unwholesome vegetation. Instead of appreciating the almost superhuman enterprise that has placed such a trophy of civilization in the very home of unchanging repose, they growl because the prudent trains do not despatch them speedily enough to the discomforts of the next stage of their journey. (Winthrop, 1863: 306)

The passage above from Theodore Winthrop's 1863 travel narrative *Isthmiana* describes the fever that greeted Americans arriving on the Isthmus of Panama *en route* to gold mines in California. Yellow Fever seemed to float in the air and sleep in the vegetation, but it is the men who have jaundiced sight. Their vision is tinted the colour of both the disease and gold, and the yellow veil of greed prevents them from seeing that they race over a track laid upon the dead bodies of workers struck down by fever. Moreover, the men and women cannot even see the 'trophy of civilization', a railroad through a dense jungle, bought for this terrible price. Winthrop's text was one of a number of travel narratives in the mid-nineteenth-century United States, part of a surge in popular renditions depicting Latin and Central America that defined the public sphere of the day (Frenkel, 1996: 321). His language was typical of these memoirs and journalistic renderings that used the word 'fever' to bind together descriptions of a foreign space, an economic cultural milieu, and a physical illness with a common linguistic term and a shared image of excess. In this chapter, I analyse the notion of fever that recurs in narratives about the Panamanian railroad and argue that the pervasive image became a cultural referent that simultaneously suggested both a lived reality of disease and, symbolically, an attitude towards the transformation of the United States. Specifically, the image of fever indicated a cultural ambivalence within the United States at a defining moment in national history, a period that included an expansion of finance capital, growing imperial ambitions, and increasingly fluid relations between the races in Central America.

Door of the seas

The Isthmus of Panama is a small neck of land interrupting a continuous sea passage between the Atlantic and Pacific oceans. As the shortest distance across the continental mass, the fifty miles offered a tempting alternative trade route to the six-month sea voyage around Cape Horn at the tip of South America. The possibility of a route across the Isthmus, either in Panama or Nicaragua, attracted at different times the attention of Spanish, British, French and American investors. As early as the sixteenth century, Spanish King Charles V dreamed of a sea passage cutting through the land; in the late seventeenth century William Patterson, founder of the Bank of England, funded an ill-fated colony at the future 'door of the seas' (McCullough, 1977: 21). By the nineteenth century, the territory formed a nexus in a trade complex connecting Europe to Asia, East- to West-Coast North America, and the Caribbean to Central and South America. British, French and American governments at different points during the century pursued plans for a path across the Isthmus. Many in the financial world were able to see profit in a faster route to Asia and, later, to the western coasts of North and South America. In the early nineteenth century, for example, Alexander von Humboldt promoted a canal scheme to Thomas Jefferson; an English company, meanwhile, raised vast sums to support a canal based on an evidently fictional map (McCullough, 1977: 21). The idea appeared in the American popular press as well; an 1850 article entitled 'Short Cuts Across the Globe' in *Harper's New Monthly Magazine* (Volume 1, Issue 1) describes the possibilities of trade with Chile, the development of Costa Rica, Oregon and the Sandwich Islands, and commerce with China, Russia, Tahiti and Australia that would all be advanced by a canal. Although a sea route was always the dream for foreign powers looking at a passage through Central America, a railroad at first proved the more viable option.

During the nineteenth century, private investors in the United States were putting money into railroads and plantations throughout the Central American region (Frenkel, 1996: 321). Many nineteenth-century railway investments did not pan out for those who bought bonds floated in the speculation market or stocks traded on the New York exchange, but the Panama railroad was an exception. Ironically, given the history of interest in a trade route through Central America, investors initially had modest plans for a passage to connect mail routes between East and West Coasts, until events on the West Coast altered their view of the strategic role of the Central American region.

When the United States acquired Oregon and then California, it subsidised a steamship mail service to the Pacific. Shortly after William Aspinwall and George Law bought the rights to Atlantic and Pacific steamship routes to Central America in 1850, rumours of gold began to circulate. Gold was so plentiful, the New York *Journal of Commerce* reported, 'People are picking gold out of the earth just like a thousand hogs let loose in a forest would root up ground nuts!' (Schott, 1967: 15). In the 1850s, steamship passengers and their porters hastened down to travel on foot through the Central American jungle to access the West Coast. The gold rush to California added new life to the efforts to build a short transcontinental route across Central America. Merchant Aspinwall, banker Henry Chauncy and developer John Lloyd Stephens joined together to create a short railway to ferry prospectors from coast to coast, creating the Panama Railroad Company that would play an important role in the American stock market for the next twenty years, until the 1869 completion of the first transcontinental railway in North America. The Panama railway began construction in 1850, with the terminus located in a swampy, snake-filled island called Manzanillo, now known as Colon.

When the railway was completed six years later, it became, per mile, the most expensive ever built, totalling eight million US dollars. At twenty-five dollars a ticket, the railway also became the most expensive of its time to travel. Investors saw extraordinary profits; in the first six years the profits were seven million dollars and the stock was at one point the highest priced listed on the New York exchange (McCullough, 1977: 35). By 1859, the railway reaped six million dollars for a group of large investors that included William H. Aspinwall, Lloyd Aspinwall, Samuel Comstock, Henry Chauncey and John Lloyd Stephens (Manthorne, 1989: 46). In addition to the bankers and shareholders investing in this development project to bring gold speculators to their destinations, the pyramid of profit around the Panama railroad also contained gold diggers gambling on unheard of riches in the West Coast, hotel owners and salespeople capitalising on the travellers' expectations, and the American government underwriting these financial interests through international manoeuvres of state.

The Panamanian passage was crucial to the development of the United States. The passageway offered an important route to connect the flow of information and people between East Coast financial centres and the growing settlements in California and the Pacific Northwest. It also linked North America to investment and commercial interests in Latin America. As well as being an important economic site, Panama played a key role in American ambitions for expansion, and the nation secured these economic and military interests with military occupation. As Michael LaRosa and Germán R. Mejía put it: 'the Panama Railroad was the first result in the United States of a historical necessity turned into state policy and carried out via private capital' (2004: 1). The Panama Railroad Company brought labourers from China, India, Jamaica and Ireland to work under near-slave conditions; these workers fell under the jurisdiction of American laws. New Granada (Columbia/ Panama) sold the United States government exclusive rights to build transit across the Isthmus in exchange for an American guarantee of New Granada's rights of sovereignty and assurances of neutrality in the Isthmus (McCullough, 1977: 33). Despite this agreement the United States became an occupying power in the Central American region, a right they wielded when in 1856 they sent in soldiers after a riot in which Americans were killed. By the early twentieth century the construction of an American canal became a milestone in Theodore Roosevelt's policy that saw America's expansionism as its destiny. The development of a Panamanian passage routed United States economic interests for West Coast development and military interests to unite the Navy through an international territory, securing its national security through international manoeuvres of state.

The culture of international investment

Travel narratives made the extended territory of United States – and the nation's imperial ambitions – known to a popular audience. One nineteenth-century writer went so far as to say 'To describe Panama to North American readers would be like describing New York or Boston, or any other city with which we are familiar' (Merwin, 1966: 16; cited in Frenkel, 1996: 321). News of the Isthmus was disseminated in the United States by published economic and political proposals, as well as by travellers' accounts and sketches. Newspapers made frequent mention of Panama as a site of financial and military interest (Frenkel, 1996: 321). *The New York Times* carried stories and book reviews as well as stock information. *Harper's New Monthly Magazine* and *Harper's Weekly* illustrated newspaper gave a fuller forum, publishing regular stories and engravings on Panama and the Panamanian railroad. The publications played a key role in educating the North American public on the strategic importance of the Isthmus (LaRosa and Mejía, 2004: xv). *Harper's Weekly* and *Harper's New Monthly Magazine* provided a continual forum for both travel writing and for economic proposals concerning the region. In 1857, for example, *Harper's Weekly* mentioned Panama in nearly every issue, covering everything from discussions of the Panama Riot (Issue 08/08) to stock information (Issue 05/09), and offered opinion pieces on the strategic importance of Panama to American national interests (Issue 02/21). The newspaper specifically mentioned both military and financial interests in the 'occupation of the Isthmus of Panama by United States troops in the interest of the commerce of the world' (Issue 05/30). The first issue of *Harper's New Monthly Magazine* in 1850 promoted a passage across the Isthmus, and five years later the magazine began publishing accounts of exploration and the new railway, with more than ten articles appearing over the next four years, including J. T. Headley's 'Darien Exploring Expedition' (1855: 60), the anonymously published 'Panama Railroad' (1859), and Oran's 'Tropical Journeyings' (1859).

Some travel narratives were penned by luminous figures, such as Mark Twain, who wrote a series of journalistic accounts in 1868. Mary Seacole, the intrepid Scottish-Jamaican doctor, wrote about her time in the Isthmus of Panama in the years before and during railway construction. Most accounts were written by little-known journalists, or unknown individuals who published their memoirs and correspondences after their return. Lesser-known writers such as Robert Tomes, Bayard Taylor, Ida Pfeiffer and Carrie Stevens Walter described their journeys in recollections that were often published in serial form in American newspapers and magazines. The first-hand (and sometimes second-hand) accounts brought distant market spaces in to the American cultural context in a period of economic and imperial expansion.

Personal accounts carried the added weight of investment news, including literal renditions of developments such as the railroad or proposed port cities. As opposed to company reports, the testimony of a traveller seemed both objective and accessible. Many of the accounts offered themselves as 'A plain statement of fact for the perusal of those interested' (Cash, 1872), the title of one memoir. Reviewers promoted this notion of impartiality. A book review appearing in the *New York Daily Times* on 26 October 1855 described Robert Tomes's depiction of the railway line as 'not at all like the *couleur de rose* linings of Wall Street speculations who "bull" the stock' ('Notice of new books', 1855: 2); this impartiality is all the more remarkable, the review goes on to note, since Tomes's trip was financed by the directors of the new railroad.

Yet despite this overt appeal to transparency and neutrality, these renditions were part of a cultural imagination that shaped as well as represented the international financial arena and echo discussions by Fauske and Goodacre in previous chapters concerning labour, product and speculated value. The nineteenth-century Panama chronicles described an emotional climate that was itself both an indicator and object of speculation. Audrey Jaffe writes of the stock market: 'The line's trajectory is assimilated to a narrative of feeling: universally apprehended as a picture of emotions – a snapshot of the national (or global) mood – it is understood as swinging between (for example) elation and depression, optimism and alarm' (Jaffe, 2002: 44). The narrative relevant to the market does not simply register development, such as the construction of the railroad. Rather, the narrative describes the emotions around the financial transformations, emotions that themselves become an intrinsic part of speculation and their analysis a key part of financial dealings. Speculators reading about Panama wanted to understand mood, for speculation was built upon the shifting sands of emotion. Literary representations provided a key arena to develop the affective aspect of finance. Literature could carry sentiment, and sentiment lay as the key register between what was perceived as rational investment and what was deemed feverish speculation.

Travel memoirs were popular narratives with a particular audience; the nineteenth-century American reading public comprising a growing middle class had a voracious appetite for literary and pictorial renditions of the tropics (Manthorne, 1989). Accounts of the occupation and development of Panama contributed to the establishment of a nineteenth-century American national culture composed of this middle class. Michael LaRosa and Germán R. Mejía point out that renewed American interest in the Panamanian crossing coincided with the new publication of *Harper's Monthly Magazine* in 1850, a journal that reshaped American culture at a time when readerships were expanding (LaRosa and Mejía, 2004: xiv). Mid-nineteenth-century

Europeans and Americans were learning about their own financial systems by reading literature (Schmitt, Henry and Arondekar, 2002). Travel literature served a particular role in this process, for in the context of international speculation, even narratives that did not directly relate information about developments such as the railway were ultimately works with financial themes. The images presented in the travel literature depicted a pervasive cultural response to the social and economic processes that linked the United States to the distant tropical location.

Journalism and travel narratives participated in working out new economies, revealing cultural interests and anxieties as the expansion of European and American markets through colonialism and commerce brought different parts of the globe into relation. The literary representations offered in travel narratives were different from the stock reports that appeared in *The New York Times* or *Harper's Weekly*, however. These journalist accounts and published memoirs both promoted American commercial and military interests, and more subtly, revealed a cultural anxiety about these very changes transforming the United States.

Borderless states

Speaking of the nineteenth-century British representations of Latin America, Kristine L. Jones argues that economic expansionism and the growth of foreign trade 'had directly contributed to the development and standardization of a stylized form of travel accounts' (Jones, 1986: 200). The same may be said of American travel narratives of Panama, which uniformly celebrated American might. The Panamanian railway in particular caught the imagination of citizens of what was then a growing global power. Travel writers represented a victory over the Isthmus as the American success of industry over previous European failures to conquer 'the door to the seas'. Joseph W. Fabens wrote in his 1852 memoir 'where but recently the slow boat toiled up against the swift current of the river, or the languid mule dragged his weary feet over the rough mountain passes, the iron horse snorts defiantly as he rushes on his undeviating course' (Fabens, 1852: viii). In fact, it was America rushing on an undeviating course to expand, driven by the power of investors travelling lines of state policy. Business correspondence explicitly connected the Panamanian railroad to strategies for securing for the United States new markets in the territory of California as well as in China and other parts of Asia (King, 1850: 232). British developer Bedford Pim wrote in 1869 that the railroad was 'a noble monument of American enterprise' (Pim, 1869: 11). The caption to an engraving of the railroad in *Harper's Weekly* described the starting train of the Panama railroad: 'The railroad was constructed by an American Company and is one of the most striking examples of American energy and perseverance.' After enumerating the statistics of the train and fare, the caption went on to note: 'The fortunate shareholders receive a dividend of 20 per cent, but much more is earned' ('Aspinwall and the Panama Railroad', 1866: 0062bc) The 'much more ... earned' here presumably referred to the benefit of the development project to the American economy and, furthermore, to America's emerging role as a world power.

Despite statements overtly testifying to American victories of progress, many of the detailed descriptions that made up the Panamanian travel narratives offered a cautionary tale about the horrors of the Isthmus. Panama was almost uniformly presented as a muddy place where previously upright citizens joined local thieves as outlaws. The most famous example representing this climate was coverage of the case of the watermelon riot in 1856, when a drunken gold speculator refused to pay for his watermelon slice and was shot, prompting an American military occupation (Walter, 1897). In travel narratives, Panama was counterpoised to America, with the foreign space seen as corrupt and corrupting. Most consistently, accounts presented the space of the Isthmus as infected by the terrifying 'Panama fever'.

Travellers returning from Panama repeatedly used the word 'fever' to describe colonial Panama. Literally they were describing the high recurrence of disease, including malaria and cholera. Travellers and workers feared 'Yellow Jack', the Yellow Fever carried by mosquitoes that every summer ravaged areas in Central and North America well into the twentieth century. Fever was a real threat and travellers' representations portrayed recurring epidemics that affected everyone in the territory: indigenous peoples living in the mountains, railroad labourers and local merchants, and travellers who passed quickly through to California. Of these, it was the labourers who most often died of the fever. A rumour had it there was a railroad tie for every dead body. Although disease was a very real experience, its meaning was constructed within a system of representation. 'Illnesses have always been used as metaphors to enliven charges that a society was corrupt or unjust', Susan Sontag writes (1978: 72). The idea of fever operated as a trope in the Panamanian travel narratives, symbolically presenting a set of cultural interests and anxieties regarding the American presence in Panama and transformations within the United States itself.

In travel narratives, fever became the invisible force associated with the environment of Panama. Writing in 1855, Robert Tomes called it a 'pestilential climate, with which no race of men and no strength of constitution can contend; and against which no measure of precaution and no process of acclimation is a safeguard' (LaRosa and Mejía, 2004: 13). Ida Pfeiffer described a 'malignant fever' caused by 'the uncultivated state of the land' (Pfeiffer, 1856: 224). Fever appeared to lie in the atmosphere, a hidden threat borne by foreign air. The notion was certainly consistent with the epidemiological theory of miasmas, or 'bad air', that marked popular notions of infection, but the language also suggested a specific character ascribed to this foreign space. The pestilence was invisible, pervasive and vengeful. 'No man could hope to escape the terrible "Panama fever" for more than a few weeks, or months at most,' Tomes wrote in his 1855 memoir (LaRosa and Mejía, 2004: 13).

The fever appeared to nest in the dense, luxuriant and gigantic proportions of vegetation. A self-described 'California tramp' depicted, 'The surface of the fever-breeding slope [...] covered with a matting of creeping vines above which rose a growth of mammoth plants' (Kenderdine, 1888: 292). Fever caught unsuspecting travellers who wandered into the jungle. In one narrative, the allegorical character Mrs Prudence sat on the train and suddenly worried that 'the atmosphere appeared heavy, and that she'd better take another pill – and she did' (Cash, 1872). The land, with its 'splendid overplus of vegetable life' (Taylor, 1850: 14), became an environmental corollary for the bodily excess of fever. In fact, at times the passion for the beauty of the land (another recurring motif in the literature) seemed to produce the very mental agitation associated with fever. Bayard Taylor described with wonder how, 'You gaze upon the scene before you with a never-sated delight till your brain aches with the sensation' (Taylor, 1850: 15). Contemporary critic David Miller comments on this representation of the jungle, and suggests a broader cultural preoccupation with social deterioration and the unleashed energies of the unconscious (Miller, 1989: 196). Although the representations do suggest such a social and psychoanalytic reading, it is important to also note that the fever was identified with a land critical to the visitors' plans for development.

The disease appeared to be indigenous rather than a product of the conditions of development by the outside world – extreme labour, crowded areas filled with travellers, for example. It is not surprising, then, that fever came to be identified with another indigenous force: 'the natives', a group that actually included a mix of indigenous, Spanish, Asian and Caribbean peoples. Writing in 1868, Thomas M. Cash described the

Panamanian soldiers who protected the travellers from mobs: 'These natives are themselves quite sufficient to give one an attack of Panama fever, even if there was no malaria or other exciting cause in the place; and yet they remain the same all the time, and will, until some other power rules the country' (Cash, 1872). Fever represented the natives' ungovernability, as the excess ascribed to the land was transferred onto the inhabitants themselves.

With the fever-ridden climate and the agitated natives, it seemed to many travel writers that nature had set itself against commerce. Fever was seen fighting against efforts for the railway; yet in another sense the trope functioned as a foil in the argument for development. When the railway broke a path through the jungle, it was 'a wonderful triumph of man's indomitable will over the hostile powers of nature, visible and invisible' (LaRosa and Mejía, 2004: 13). Nicolas King connects epidemiological discourse to past colonial and present post-colonial economic strategies. He argues that public health has long been interlinked with international commerce, notably when eighteenth- and nineteenth-century mercantilism 'provided the impetus and, in many cases, the ideological underpinnings, for the creation and extension of public health practices in Western Europe' (King, 2002: 764). As Europeans and Americans opened new markets and sought to control trade routes, they focused on public health. These policies were concerned with the safety of Europeans, but also the native and imported workers. The anxieties about imminent infection appeared as these networks of trade expanded. Thus the discourse of disease justified the investment projects to develop Panama.

Within the context of the 1850s, the portrayals of a degenerate Panama certainly made the case for development. Taken as a whole, however, the representations connecting the speculation space of the United States to Panama presented a more ambivalent picture of both regions as possible sources of infection. The prevalence of these images suggested certain reservations: a conflict with the narrative of progress that lay at the core of an American national narrative. The image of diseased natives haunted writers. Travellers literally feared the bodies of natives as unsafe, though it was often the visitor who carried devastating diseases to new territories. Yet it would be a mistake to consider disease as solely a physical threat in these representations. The idea of the land or native as reservoir of disease may be viewed as part of a larger discourse about a perceived threat of physical and moral degeneration.

One of the consequences of speculation and the spread of market space was new relations between the races. This was particularly true in the Caribbean and parts of Central America. The idea of fever embodied the fears felt by whites in these locations where racial lines became blurred. King argues that Western science has viewed particular places or populations as sources of infection. Public health policy thus became a form of border control: 'Unhealthy (non-Western) places or populations posed a threat to healthy (Western) individuals when the borders between them were transgressed, either by colonials in foreign lands, or by immigrants contaminating home countries' (King, 2002: 764). Global movements produced this anxiety over increased contact and mixture between the races, and the travel narratives from Panama reveal this anxiety even as there is an insistence on an original foreign source for the disease.

In the contemporary system of racial representation, the 'primitive' suggested the passionate and the bodily. Both notions were associated with fever, so that the onset of fever meant a kind of cultural and racial regression. Several writers made a point of talking about how fever did not distinguish between its victims. Robert Tomes wrote: 'The people of all countries, and of all races and colour, whom the call of duty, the stimulus of enterprise, and the hard necessities of labour have gathered together in Aspinwall, are equally forced to pay the fatal tribute' (Tomes, 1855: 68). Here fever acted as more than an impartial equaliser. The Caribbean was a location where whites, blacks, indigenous peoples and Asians mixed in ways unthinkable in North America or Europe. A fever that moved across race represented the transgression of all boundaries.

The trope of fever revealed concerns about the degeneration of European races through global relations expanded by commercial enterprises. In the Theodore Winthrop passage that opened this chapter, the image of Panama fever doubled and reversed its orientation from outside to inside, going from a 'yellow veil' to 'jaundiced' sight. On the one hand, fever was depicted as an external threat. This fear of infection revealed concerns about proximity to foreign lands and bodies, as well as apprehensions about the sanctity of bodily boundaries, including racial boundaries. On the other hand, fever was presented as the symptom of an already present disease. This representation of fever showed an internal state of passion manifested as a physical symptom. Although distinct, both representations of fever presented through a bodily metaphor fears about dangerous passions. Fever, associated with both agitation and degeneration, symbolised the antithesis of reason and civilisation; images of fever functioned as warnings against a seductive return to the primitive that could take place in a climate of speculation. Together, the portrayals of external and internal fever drew a line connecting a nineteenth-century discourse on hierarchies of race to social commentary on the morality of investment.

Feverish speculation

The idea of speculation was compatible with mid-nineteenth-century American ideals, and it was promoted as such. An article dated 7 May 1853 in the *New York Daily Times* suggested, 'Speculation ... is commercial sagacity, shrewdness, the way to wealth. Men grow rich by it; some stake incautiously and at unfortunate moments and lose. But Speculation is the great business engine of the age' (*New York Daily Times*, 1853: 4). During the mid-nineteenth century, the United States was entering a period of expanding international finance capital. Transnational investment in Panama was a precursor to the explosion of foreign investment that grew from the Civil War to 1897 from 75 million dollars to 685 million dollars (Lebergott, 1980). Yet despite its centrality to an emerging national identity in the United States, speculation was viewed culturally as irrational – and thus dangerous – excitement. The discussion of speculation in the public sphere was frequently married to a moralistic discourse about greed and irrationality. The above tribute to speculation, for example, was followed in the article by praise for those who give their profits to charity. By 1860, the *New York Daily Times* was warning its readers against 'the sudden fever of speculation in railway securities' (31 August 1860).

Speculation has often been understood as passion over reason. The line between speculation and investment has been heavily patrolled, suggesting a kind of symptomatic preoccupation with a permeable boundary. Audrey Jaffe comments on how American Federal Reserve chairman Alan Greenspan has attempted to excise the 'irrational exuberance' of the market as the way to remove instability. Jaffe argues the emotions provide a determining factor for the market, but that the logic of rationality remains pervasive:

> Indeed, from Trollope to Greenspan, discussions about investment and the market have repeatedly sought to draw similar lines: between the solid and the ephemeral, between safety and risk – between, in general, value securely located in companies or commodities and value that is only imagined to be there – as a means of countering the uncertainty and unpredictability – indeed, the sheer uninterpretability – of the fluctuating value of shares. In seeking to fix such lines, they merely point toward the uncertainties, and the

movements of the heart with which we register them, that tie our identities to the market. (Jaffe, 2002: 45–6)

Thus there is a kind of double move, in which the market is repeatedly shown to be erratic and driven by emotion, at the same time that these fluctuations are presented as aberrations from a 'normal' rational model of the market. The ideal of market rationality performs a disciplinary function, continuing to order a narrative of the market even as it advances its antithesis. Lines are drawn by this master narrative to regulate unseemly exuberance in the market by providing a tableau of what is correct and incorrect market behaviour. Jaffe illustrates the way this process functions in literary narratives, as authors such as Anthony Trollope create characters whose immediately recognisable treachery extends beyond the confines of the market. The characters act as a kind of foil in which the morality of market behaviour is ordered by the portrayal of emotion-driven financial behaviour as transgressive.

In mid-nineteenth-century American travelogues, the trope of fever, another representation of agitation, played a similar role to this depiction of villainy. The narrative about feverish delirium that came out of travelogues from Central America reached as far as the investment circles of North America. Fever became a manifestation of an internal state of passion that threatened the rational order. When fever appeared as a trope, it marked the affective excess within the context of investment, what Jaffe above calls 'the movements of the heart'. That excess appeared metaphorically as bodily fever and infectious passion. The recurrence of fever as a trope in travel narratives alongside literary discussions of speculation revealed anxieties about expanding economic and military territories of the United States and a changing American culture.

The travellers might have feared catching Yellow Jack, malaria or cholera in Central America, but they carried another disease that plagued much of North America and Europe – speculation fever. Travel narratives about the Isthmus represented the excess of both the speculators and the speculation itself. In this way, the narratives presented a moral discourse about the kinds of foreign investments that were reshaping the American national identity. One may see this cautionary message against 'sudden fever' in the descriptions of the Panamanian railroad. Speculation fever showed its first sign in the desire to move, to get to the Californian and Oregon coasts where rumour had it gold could be swept up off the saloon floor. According the British travel writer Lady Emmeline Stuart Wortley, the Panamanians thought the Americans to be mad and imitated them shouting '*vamos*! Go-ahead! Ho! *Poco tiempo*, *poco tiemp!'* (Wortley, 1851: 312). In her memoir, Carrie Stevens Walter remembered how agitated speculators enabled disease-promoting conditions on the journey to Panama. Steamship captains, working on behalf of investors, took advantage of the 'California fever' to pack as many travellers onto the boats with 'dirt, crowed berths, foul air, food unfit for human beings, and many other horrors' (Walter, 1897). In her representation, a feverish greed appeared to beget the literal diseased conditions. The gold itself became a source of infection as well. Bayard Taylor described how at the sight of a returning Californian with a box of gold-dust: 'Men ran up and down the beach, shouting, gesticulating and getting feverishly impatient at the deliberate habits of the natives' (Taylor, 1850: 12).

As is often the case, great expectations gave rise to advance spending. Visitors passing through Panama bought their way through the journey with the prospect of imminent wealth. One particularly critical commentator wrote: 'This desire to purchase everything the natives on the Isthmus offer for sale, is another description of Panama fever that quinine will not reach' (Cash, 1872). The *sensibility* of travellers was thus affected as well as their bodies. The same travelogue depicts an exemplary character that, even after she returns home 'in her daily habits and tastes is a remarkable example of the insidious character, which no precaution can avert, of the Panama fever' (Cash, 1872). Here fever was identified with consumption, specifically unseemly purchase habits acquired in the degenerate environment of colonial Panama. Travel writers thus used the trope of fever to represent a physical and social condition. The mind-altering nature of bodily fever found its cultural counterpart in the intense speculation that fuelled the economy in the same colonial location. As in the theory of miasmas, or bad air, from which it borrowed its symbolic lexicon, the individual 'caught' speculation fever from a general culture of speculation.

Speculation fever was denounced in letters with a moralistic tone. Travellers complained of exorbitant prices for even the smallest necessity as speculators anticipated an urgent demand for subsistence and superfluous products that would appeal to would-be miners with great expectations of wealth. In a letter dated 13 March 1853, William B. Johnson wrote: 'Starting from Aspinwall you will begin to experience the effects of Gold' (cited in Moore, 2000: 212). Later, Johnson noted one of the most striking costs to the railroad: 'we are pained by the frequent sight of small graveyards along the whole line of the road, of those laborers who had so far built the line and more to follow for the foundation yet to be laid. Ah! Gold what misery doth thou cause!'

(cited in Moore, 2000: 212) The observer might have been even more pained if he had known of a ghoulish business in Panama: so many died constructing the railroad that the Panama Railroad Company entered the business of supplying cadavers, pickled in large barrels, to medical schools around the world (McCullough, 1977: 37).

Travel writers associated investment with disease for didactic purposes. They used the trope of fever to warn that elements of increased investment might lead to a destructive delirium. At the same time, they wrote their way to a new economy. Even those who viewed Panama as an Eden under siege by modernisation saw an unbending road to progress. Early on, Lady Emmeline Stuart Wortley wrote: 'One almost foolishly shrinks from the idea of a railroad coming through such a lovely, idle, flower crowned, unsophisticated place ... by careful precautions and perseverance, I dare say its difficulties will be overcome' (Wortley, 1851: 297). In the literature, images resolved the development of the railway with the seeming excess of Panama's nature. Traveller Albert Webster wrote in 1876 about the land that witnessed the new railroad:

> The tall reeds bent over toward the ground, the ferns sank listlessly upon each other, and the pendent vines and creepers seemed cast in metal, so motionless were they. The green was a dead and gloomy green, a shade that yielded no rest or solace to the eye, tired like the rest of the body with so much warmth. Had the whole landscape been cut in begreened copper, had it been carved out with a knife and chisel, and had it been wedged, riveted, and bolted, it could not have seemed more rigid nor could it have been less inspiring. (Webster, 1876)

Webster turned the land itself into a railroad, naturalising the new technologies that speculation had brought to the Isthmus. Development in the form of railway construction offered itself as an organic consequence. As medicine tamed the body, so too would the construction of the railway order the excesses of nature.

Imaginatively, the Isthmus was an extension of United States territory, occupying the same but different liminal place that characterises colonial space (Bhabha, 1994: 86). Material ties, such as military occupation, partial sovereignty of United States law, and the physical presence of travellers, bonded the Central American region to its powerful neighbour. Prolific travel writing made the Isthmus of Panama seemingly familiar to North Americans. Yet even as this writing cast the occupied location as like 'any other city with which we are familiar' (Merwin,

1966: 16; cited in Frenkel, 1996: 321), these works also represented Panama as a place where both the land and the people threatened infection. Reading these contradictory depictions within their historical context of international imperialism and speculation, one may perceive a broader cultural ambivalence within the United States about certain transformations taking place in the nineteenth century. These changes, which were justified by a narrative of progress, included more fluid contact between races, a financial capitalism increasingly central to the nation, and international military and commercial imperialism that was part of this new economy. The setting of Panama offered North American travel writers an arena in which they might work out through representation the shifts taking place within the United States.

The trope of fever was a specific way writers registered the contradictions inside this narrative of progress, as development and fever become one and the same. Nature and industry were usually presented as opposites in the effort to promote the railroad; yet in the images of fever, nature and capital frequently seem perfectly aligned. On one side, infectious land and natives harboured Yellow Jack, a mysterious fever that attacked the traveller. On the other side, the speculator caught the fever back home and carried it to the Isthmus. In accounts of the Isthmus, body, land and economy were linked by this shared image of excess – after all, fever denotes an excess of the body. Travel writers linked the fevered visitor to the tropics to a delirious case of speculation. In doing so, they showed evidence of a systemic cultural anxiety about a transforming nation. The trope of fever revealed the ambivalence of a United States that was caught up with commercial and imperial expansion; at the same time it was preoccupied with the perceived moral dangers of such expansion. Yet despite how the image of fever offered evidence of conflict, the trope ultimately allowed writers to validate a narrative positing progress through imperial development and enabled them to author a new global economy.

7
Reading Finance Capital

Leigh Claire La Berge

Introduction

Marx famously introduces *Capital* with the claim that 'the wealth of societies in which the capitalist mode of production prevails appears as an "immense collection of commodities"; the individual commodity appears as its elementary form' (Marx, 1976: 125). As he explains in the first chapter of *Capital*, the unique and historical power of the commodity stems from its ability to efface any trace, content or history of its own production. Production is the temporal category of object formation and human labour; it provides the active history of a commodity. Without knowledge of the production of a commodity, one loses the ability to have a temporal relationship with that commodity, a historical relationship to it and, most importantly, the human labour that produced it is obscured. Herein lies the possibility for the creation and extraction of surplus value. Due to cooperation, technology and coercion, workers are able to produce a commodity in less time than is 'socially necessary' for its production, and out of this temporal discrepancy surplus value is born.[1] Thus – already to recapitulate – wealth in capitalism *appears* in the form of commodities, which veils productive time, yet the value extracted from commodity production is not in the object but rather in the time itself. As Moishe Postone says of surplus value, the fundamental category of capitalist exploitation and progress, 'its essential quality is temporal' (Postone, 1993: 283).

In this chapter I explore this temporal nature of capital accumulation, and I hope to do so in such a way as to elucidate representations of capital in literary as well as cultural texts. It is my belief that finance, in addition to the more commonly cited commodity form, offers an optic for such criticism. Marx claims that finance capital is 'the form of [capital] devoid of content', as well as capital 'elaborated into pure form' (Marx, 1981: 516). And what is form for Marx? Alfred Sohn-Rethel convincingly argues that 'for Marx, form is time-bound' (Sohn-Rethel, 1978: 17). By this, he means that time is the privileged category of capital accumulation and historical materialism. Marx's sense of form is time-bound and finance is capital which has been elaborated into pure form; finance and time are, then, related. Finance produces and represents the production of time under capitalism.

This co-constitutive relationship between time and finance is evident in instruments of finance like the credit card, whose major disciplining and productive operation is lending through time-cycles, as well as finance capital, which famously 'annihilates space with time' (Marx in Harvey, 1982: 442), a phrase I will have occasion to consider in some detail. This financial-temporal link also appears in the etymology of our daily financial lexicon: the word 'mortgage', for example, literally translates as 'death wage' while the word 'finance' itself derives from the French *finir* (to end, to finish off).[2] Finally, cultural critics might transform finance's co-constitutive relationship with temporality into an optic for criticism, or a 'financial form' similar to that of the commodity form, and in doing so offer a novel strategy of literary interpretation. Recent attempts by Mary Poovey, Walter Benn Michaels and Fredric Jameson, among others, to use finance as a hermeneutic device all neglect this most formative and distinctive property: finance's unique, productive and contested relationship to time.[3]

Finance is dependent upon demarcations of manifest, structured time, in that its operations 'refer to activities relating to the provision (or transfer) of liquid capital in expectation of future interest, dividends, or capital gains' (Krippner, 2005: 174). The temporal possibilities of financial practices are used to bridge the real temporal disjuncture between intention, production and consumption and make the credit-based 'time aspect crucial to economic activity' (Guttman, 1996: 12). These conceptions of finance are opposed to commodity production and trade. Financial activities, often referred to as 'abstract', are not employment intensive and their 'products do not show up in transparent ways in national economic statistics' (Krippner, 2005: 174), or, we might add, in literature. How, then, does one represent logics or practices which could be subsumed under the rubric of the financial, whether in their theoretical manifestations as financial capital, or in their quotidian manifestations as financial instruments?

The most popular approaches to the representation of finance typically centre on either the person of the financier or on the concept of social risk as it becomes embodied in the financial transaction. Indeed, this can be a very generative strategy as Alison Shonkwiler demonstrates in her reading of *The Financier*.[4] Yet the definition which I have cited claims that financial operations are 'in expectation of future' profit, while Theodore Dreiser understands finance capital to 'release the source of social action' (Dreiser, 1995: 182). David Harvey suggests that finance capital operates through its 'link to future labour as a counter-value' (Harvey, 1982: 265). How, then, is one to represent something not yet fully in existence? It is here that I take recourse to the link between finance and time in capital accumulation, and to a similar relationship between finance and narrative in literature. My reading of Dreiser's 1912 *The Financier*, a text written four years after Austrian political economist Rudolf Hilferding introduced the term 'finance capital', demonstrates how time itself may serve as a mediating category between financial accumulation and the literary representation thereof. This reading of *The Financier* is also a challenge to the overly simplified production/consumption dyad in cultural criticism that emerged in the mid-1980s in response to post-1973 economic restructuring and is still with us today. In correctly responding to the waning of production as an organising economic trope, scholars interested in the representation of capitalism incorrectly located consumption in its place. Commodity consumption, however, does not replace commodity production as a purveyor, store or representation of value; finance does. In order to understand why this is the case, and why it matters to representation, I introduce recent work in political economy to understand the financial form in the next section, and I show its ability to be employed heuristically in section three.

Producing time

The value form of capital has two forms of storage, or two ways of being represented: the commodity and money; finance is a sub-set of the latter. Finance is to money what a factory is to commodity production – the place of its process. Capital is both an object and a process, wherein the commodity assumes the role of the former, and finance the role of the latter. The commodity is a present object ready for sale, but that exchange requires a malleable matrix of time and space, usually in the form of credit, in order to reach completion. Think, for example, of a futures market in wheat: the objective referent 'wheat' concretises an economy of risk and displaces it into an uncertain and uneven future, a future which this transaction also aids in producing. In this section I approach the differences between finance and the commodity from a number of angles, including the epistemological, the ontological and the historical. Underscoring all of these categorical distinctions is the manner in which finance and the commodity each produce, occupy and represent temporality and spatiality.

Marx himself does not use the term finance capital, and 'financing' as a defined category of activity is not operative in his texts.[5] However, in *Capital, Volume 3* he does investigate the forms that money and capital take (commercial, industrial, merchant, banking, as well as credit and fictitious), and many of these distinctions may be characterised as financial, especially those of banking capital, credit distribution, fictitious capital and interest-bearing capital in general. What he does provide is the general formula of capital: M-C-M', whereby money (M) acquires a commodity (C), which commodity is subsequently sold for more money (M') in the form of profit. At the fetishised apex of this cycle, the material object 'C' disappears entirely so that accumulation may be represented: M-M', money producing more of itself through financial transactions. This formula may be explicated so that in addition to providing the form of capital expansion, it may also be seen to provide the very content of historical materialism. I will trace how value in the form of finance capital has been represented in recent political economy as producing the material content of time and space and indeed, according to some theorists, producing time and space as well. In doing so, I focus specifically on how finance reconfigures the time/space horizon of capital, and how the representation of capital in literature is altered (and may be reapproached) in response to this financial form itself.

Three theoretical texts are crucial for developing a concept of financial temporality, out of which a financial form may be derived: David Harvey's *The Limits to Capital* (1982), Moishe Postone's *Time, Labor and Social Domination* (1993), and Giovanni Arrighi's *The Long Twentieth Century* (1994). In each text value is represented as a materialised movement both in and of time and space, although the times and spaces that are produced differ. Furthermore, each text offers a specific representation of the relationship between time and finance, which I want ultimately to translate back into a literary context. In Arrighi's work I locate cyclical phases of accumulation which metabolise cumulatively *more* geographical space in progressively *less* historical time; for Harvey the central bank interest-rate is the empirical regulator of time/space production; and for Postone, time itself is the material that is produced and metabolised in every cycle of capitalist accumulation, what he calls 'the intrinsically temporal nature of value' (Postone, 1993: 269).

All of these approaches, while different in object and scale, build on Marx's description of finance capital as the purest form of capital. He claims that interest-bearing activities represent the fetish character of capital 'elaborated into pure form'; 'the mystification of capital in the most flagrant form'; and the 'form of [capital] devoid of content' (Marx, 1981: 516). Such transactions are not limited to a steadily increasing numerical balance on one's monthly stock portfolio statement. Rather these financial transactions both represent and configure the productive geography of capitalism; they shape its development, orientation and representation. Giovanni Arrighi suggests that, 'coercion implies the use of force, or a credible threat of force; consent implies moral leadership. In this dichotomy there is no room for the most distinctive instrument of capitalist power: control over the means of payment' (Arrighi, 1994: 17).

It is precisely this narrative of power through payment that Arrighi provides in *The Long Twentieth Century* by using finance as an optic to read history. In his model, finance is used as the representation of an empirical, temporal duration; it is represented as a reflexive, proto-temporal and non-spatial investment of capital in itself which has real material and temporal effects. Arrighi rejects the common periodisation of the emergence of finance capitalism to the early twentieth century and opts for, instead, a structural formula of capital in which the ascension of finance capital is one phase of a Braudelian *longue durée* of capital expansion, a cycle that he traces as far back as the fourteenth century. He presents history as a cyclical repetition composed of two types of capitalist accumulation: territorial and capitalist (financial), which are dialectically entwined, and should be viewed here as the historical abstractions of the commodity as object (C), and finance as process (M).[6] Thus the formula M-C-M' is the heuristic of capitalist history in addition to that of capitalist logic. For Arrighi these structural cycles of capitalist accumulation form hegemonies in temporal durations of 'long centuries', i.e. hegemony is transformed from a spatial into a temporal category and becomes dependent upon the money form. And, as a result of the cumulative development of capital, these temporal durations have become empirically shorter, a process which renders the 'long twentieth century' the shortest yet. My interest here is in the homology formed between the financial transaction (M-M') and history itself: just as the financial transaction strives to minimise its own temporal component in order to produce more money in a shorter time span, history has quickened by metabolising more space in less time.

David Harvey specifically foregrounds the problem of the representation of capital by focusing on the interest rate as the central coordinator of time/space production in his *The Limits to Capital*. The interest rate, or the cost of employing finance capital, determines whether investment will be in the built environment of commodities or the financial environment of money. A high interest rate will draw money out of commodity circulation and into financial circulation; a low interest rate will draw money out of finance and into commodities. Again, the former is co-constitutive with the production of space, and the latter co-constitutive with the production of time. 'The effect is to reduce time and space to a common socially determined metric – the rate of interest, *itself a representation of value* in motion. Temporal and geographical horizons of capital flow are simultaneously redefined ... As rates of interest fluctuate ... so the temporal and geographical horizons of capital flow pulse outwards or contract' (Harvey, 1982: 396–7, my italics). The representation of capital, then, is implicated in its materialisation. Thus Harvey uses a model similar to Arrighi's, and from Harvey I want to isolate a similar, co-constitutive link between finance, representation and temporality: the metric of time/space production is represented in the interest rate, and the interest rate then determines time/space production. Out of this matrix, time (and by extension finance) emerges as the privileged category of capital: 'Spatial distance then reduces itself to time because the important thing is not the market's distance in space but the speed with which it can be reached ... Capital must strive to tear down every spatial barrier to exchange ... it must annihilate space with time' (Harvey, 1982: 377).

Finally, Moishe Postone in *Time, Labor and Social Domination* does not critique 'finance capital' by name as a system of the abstract allocation of future-oriented labour-power. Rather Postone focuses on the temporal nature of value *per se*. If Harvey emphasises spatial production as an effect of capitalist time, and Arrighi emphasises historical hegemonies as materialisations of different forms of capital, then Postone reads temporal production as the *sine qua non* of capital itself.

> The movement of capital is without limit, without end. As self-valorizing value, it appears as pure process. In dealing with the category of capital, then, one is dealing with a central category of a society that becomes characterized by a constant directional movement with no determinate external telos, a society driven by production for the sake of production, by process that exists for the sake of process. *This expansion, this ceaseless motion is, within the framework of*

> Marx's analysis, intrinsically related to the temporal dimension of value ... this alienated form [capital] constitutes an immanent logic of history. (Postone, 1993: 269–70, author's italics)

Capital accumulates by producing its own 'ceaseless motion' (i.e. value in motion) which Postone labels 'abstract time'. Abstract time is time freed from social content and devoted to the increase of value. It is an accumulative time which renders all other times commensurable and thus available for production and consumption. The process of producing and metabolising abstract time is an ultimately asymptotic endeavour in that capital produces a form of time for the sole purpose of attempting to overcome it, of metabolising it: the fantasy is to have M-M' transpire instantaneously, to make money in 'no time at all'. And yet time cannot be eliminated, since value itself is 'intrinsically temporal'. With gains in productivity through labour subversion or technological advancement, abstract time renews the baseline standard of its own measure. Not only does this process ensure that time will not be overcome, but it ensures that it will be continuously reproduced as qualitatively similar, an outcome with decisive historical and political effects. If this process seems opaque on a theoretical level, on an everyday level it will be immediately recognised: why can one never seem to 'save time' under capitalism, especially with the aid of technology: email for example? The answer is, quite simply, that time under capitalism exists not to be 'saved' but to be produced and then metabolised as profit – the process that increases value and that continues to reproduce a society dedicated to the production of value.

Reading finance capital

How might such a theoretical understanding of the dimensions and possibilities of finance capital as a measure and producer of temporality be translated into a textual, literary field? Just as finance represents and produces time within capital accumulation, we can locate a similar trajectory of its representation in narrative accumulation. The form of finance is temporal, as is the form of narrative, and these two instances of accumulation can be read dialectically together. In order to demonstrate how this connection may be realised in literary criticism, I will use the foregoing theory of the financial form as an optic to read Dreiser's *The Financier* (1912). Dreiser's text is an exercise in the problems and possibilities of representing not just the finance capitalist himself, but rather the temporal process of financial accumulation.

My reading of finance as one of temporal dynamics both breaks with and critiques perhaps the most widely used approach to reading the representation of finance, which is to employ the social category of risk. This strategy is followed by Walter Benn Michaels (1987) in his reading of Dreiser's *The Financier* and Howard Horwitz (1982) in his reading of Frank Norris's stock-exchange novel, *The Pit*.[7] In both of these readings of Naturalist texts, the financial pole of value is associated with probable danger, located on the border of social legitimacy via the actions of the financier/protagonist, and posited as homologous to the surreptitious, extramarital affairs of the financier. According to Horwitz and Michaels, the opposite of financial risk is found in the corporeal and objective stability of the commodity and its accompanying social institutions, i.e. marriage. These readings are not uninvited by their textual objects of study. Perhaps the most apt example of this dichotomy (the commodity as foundational/finance as aleatory) is found in Frank Norris's first 'Trilogy of Wheat' instalment, *The Octopus*, whose last page contains the line, 'But the WHEAT remained. Untouched, unassailable, undefiled, that mighty world force, gigantic, resistless' (Norris, 1958: 448). Comparatively, Norris describes the surreptitious financial cartel, or Trust, which controls the railroad, in the following terms:

> The League [of soon to be disenfranchised ranchers] was clamorous, ubiquitous, its objects known to every urchin on the streets, but the [financial] Trust was silent, its ways inscrutable, the public saw only the results. It worked on in the dark, calm, disciplined, irresistible. Abruptly, Dyke received the impression of the multitudinous colossus. (Norris, 1958: 237)

Thus wheat as a commodity is omnipresent, while the financiers who operate the railroad lack the corporeality of presence. Norris's distinction is both suggestive and neat, and yet to view an object as a commodity is to understand it *already* as dependent upon the contingencies of capitalist accumulation, even if these contingencies are repressed in the understanding and representation of the commodity as concrete materiality and extolled in the understanding and representation of finance as abstract, uncertain and socially unnecessary.

Although the categories of risk, abstraction and the instruments that produce and manage their dissemination are both popular and structural components of financial transactions (as they are of all capitalist activity), I want to stay with the political economic uses of finance as they were presented in the last section; that is, to look at finance as a representation and production of temporality, as the time-measure of capital accumulation. If a commodity is objectified human labour, then finance is not yet actualised human labour; if a commodity is human labour time subsumed into the past, then finance is potential labour time able to create, form and reify the future. As such, my critical approach to the representation of finance differs from the two predominant methods of analysing literary representations of capital (whether as finance or its more common variant, money): much of Marxist criticism with its focus on class consciousness on the one hand, and much New Historicist criticism, as we have just seen in the Michaels and Horowitz readings, with its focus on categorical transubstantiations between economic and literary texts, on the other. As Fredric Jameson says of the first, Marxist criticism 'has less often tried to analyze its objects in terms of capital and value ... than it has in terms of class, and most often of one class in particular, namely the bourgeoisie ... Money enters the picture here insofar as only exchange, merchant activity and the like, and, later on, nascent capitalism, determine the coming into being of ... bourgeois class life' (Jameson, 1998: 145).[8]

The New Historicists, however, have examined money, including finance, in literary and other representational contexts.[9] Yet, within the New Historical approach money is often treated as a problem of semiotics: how is it that paper money as a textual symbol comes to represent value, understood as purchasing power? What is the import of that symbolic economy, with its representational arbitrariness when compared to gold, a material object understood to have 'intrinsic' value? While this approach to money has been salient in establishing formal relations *between* literary and economic realms, to understand money as a signifier of value is already problematic. Much as wealth within capitalism *appears* as 'an immense collection of commodities', money *appears* as a symbol of value. Postone suggests that 'the very existence of value as a social mediation, whether located in the commodity or its expression as money is veiled by this contingent surface relationship between signifier and signified. This real process of obfuscation is reinforced ... by credit money [among other forms]' (Postone, 1993: 265). In other words, money does not appear to be a bearer of value because its form of appearance, circulating paper money, invites investigation as a sign of value instead of a form of value. Finance, in many cases, does not possess even a paper trail. But, as we have seen, money and finance are forms and not simply signs, although these forms are notoriously elusive – Norris was correct in claiming that we cannot observe the process but only the results.

Therefore I will use finance's chief component, time, to arrive at a more nuanced representation of its form. I will read finance through time, and time through finance as they obtain in Dreiser's text – the story of protagonist Frank Cowperwood's rise to financial heights in Philadelphia, his collusion with the city treasurer in embezzlement, and his eventual imprisonment, release, ascension and departure for the 'manufacturing city' of Chicago.[10] We have seen Harvey make a useful distinction between finance capitalists as a group, who are commonly understood as a dominating power bloc within the bourgeoisie, and finance capital as a process. I read Dreiser's novel as manifestly concerned with the former, the finance capitalist, who metonymically stands in for the latter, the process of finance capital, what Alison Shonkwiler has called 'the text's preoccupation with the system itself'.[11] Indeed, we might see the reduction of process to person, so common in representations of finance as well as capital in general, as an exemplary instance of what Jameson labels a 'strategy of containment', whereby the historical and social context of the Real is evacuated in order that its remainder might be consumed in a socially palatable form (Jameson, 1981: 53 and 102).

I will use the financial form to maintain this distinction between process and person and in doing so I will hold open a space to distinguish between time as a social category of accumulation, derivative of finance capital, and time as a phenomenological category of perception. Thus I hope to avoid criticism that is too monadic, as is so often the case in the criticism of commodity-induced desire, of which much of the criticism of Dreiser's *Sister Carrie* is a prime example.[12] Of course to read *The Financier* for process over subject is to read against much of the manifest content of the text, which is concerned with Cowperwood's incessant desire for women and money, control and power. Dreiser supports such a reading by offering plenty of moralistic commentary on the individual himself. 'If only the great financial and political giants would for once accurately reveal the details of their lives!' he exclaims, immediately before Cowperwood's indictment (Dreiser, [1912] 1995: 200).[13]

Dreiser employs a similar strategy to distinguish between different stores of value, referring to Cowperwood's 'perpetual material *and* financial calculations' (p. 120, my italics). He states further that, 'Business was engrossing him so. Finance was his master' (p. 216), and that 'few people have the sense of financial individuality strongly developed', as Cowperwood had (p. 182). What is the import of these distinctions of value? Is it to underscore the social relationships between abstraction, speculation and finance on the one hand, and corporeality, fact and stability, on the other? This is a common reading, not only of Dreiser but of all who would make such value (and values) distinctions. 'The vision of value that emerges here might almost be called agrarian, an economy shielded from fluctuation by the joint facts of marriage and commodities' (Michaels, 1986: 63).

If we accept that one of Dreiser's narrative threads is to draw our attention to varying representations of value both through a representation of financial activities ('money, represented by stocks and bonds') and through sexual entanglements, then we should then ask *how* the representation is registered. Michaels's reading of the twin plot lines of *The Financier* (romance/finance) as essentially reinforcing each other as kinds of value seems to be correct. And yet to focus on the relationship between these two representations of value is to cut off the text from a more political economic reading. The crucial point is not the homology that obtains between commodity/wife and finance/mistress, but that both are underpinned by 'financial individuality'.[14] The organising narrative locus of *The Financier* is 'financial individuality', and this may be expressed through either Cowperwood's financial or sexual endeavours. Indeed, when the first begins to disintegrate in the wake of market panic is precisely the point at which the second, Cowperwood's extra-marital liaison with Aileen, becomes enjoined with his finances since it is Aileen's father who could help Cowperwood survive financially but who chooses not to after learning of the affair. All of these distinctions place finance solely in the frame of Cowperwood as individual and they result from a conception of finance as risky, abstract, surreptitious, etc., which is of course how finance is seen and experienced individually. But if we look at finance instead as representation of temporality, the text of *The Financier*, and the role of finance in it, does not appear to be so binary. Rather finance becomes co-constitutively linked with narrative itself, much as in political economic work finance becomes linked with history and historical processes.

Financial accumulation is especially rich for narrative representation because like the detective story, it is structurally predicated on gaps in information, representation and a kind of temporal unevenness, all of which occur over time. The narrative trajectory of *The Financier* is essentially accumulative. Socio-symbolic meaning accrues over time by representing capital, which accrues over time.[15] Our interest is in the relationship between the two. As long as the accumulation of capital through financial transactions is secure, the narrative progresses evenly. Finance is both representing and producing time, in the content of Cowperwood's accumulative life and in the form of narrative development. Subsequently, when Cowperwood's access to accumulation is threatened as a result of a fire-induced stock market panic, the elapse of narrative time is threatened as well. This financial panic is the narrative crux of the novel – its ultimate effect is that Cowperwood goes from controlling time via his financial apparatus to serving time in the state penitentiary. In the prose that governs this transition, Cowperwood's relationship to 'time' becomes of central and manifest importance.

Time is contested, overvalued, devalued and narrated simultaneously. This is represented on a number of levels: literal in the repeated use of the word 'time'; referential in the sense that when someone is in debt, they negotiate time in order to reconcile their accounts; but beyond these thematic readings, or perhaps *between* these thematic readings, there emerge pieces of a social sub-text in which the production and metabolisation of time through finance is rendered 'visible'. It is precisely when the structural relationship between temporality and finance is threatened that its connection becomes manifest. Here, we join the narrative *in medias res*, with the protagonist beginning the ultimately futile process of reorganising his debts.

Cowperwood begins his negotiations for time in a literal manner. 'In three months, or less, I can fix it so that you can put [the money] back. As a matter of fact, I can do it in fifteen days … *Time* is all I want', he tells the city treasurer, George Stener (p. 182). This desire for time is soon repeated. '"Well George", [Cowperwood] said earnestly, "I wish you'd tell me. Time's short. We haven't a moment to lose"' (p. 183). '"I can't, Frank", said [George] finally, very weakly, his sense of his own financial future overcome for the time being' (p. 183). The chapter ends with Girard National Bank 'refusing an hour's grace' (p. 184). Here we see Cowperwood pleading for time, so as to correct his finances, and not getting it; essentially we are being shown the form of financial time, which had thus far propelled the narrative, devoid of its content. This empty financial time has real formal implications.

The next chapter cuts from Cowperwood's financial to personal life, and from financial to personal time, beginning with 'For the first time in his life Cowperwood felt conscious of having been in the presence of an interesting social phenomenon' (p. 195). The phrase is repeated twice, 'it was the first time in his life that Cowperwood had ever shown the least sign of weakening or despair' (p. 206). Again, after he tells his lawyer 'I only want a little time, that's all', Dreiser tells us that 'for the first time in his life [Cowperwood] was a little depressed' (p. 221). The juxtaposition between financial and personal time allows us to begin to disaggregate these two forms of time which have been thus far inextricably bound in the course of *The Financier*: the temporal process of finance capital, and Cowperwood's individual life as a financier.

The narrative climax of this episode shows Cowperwood unable to settle his affairs and so surreptitiously lifting more money from the city treasury, though not nearly enough to cover the margin calls on his loans. 'If he could only get time! If he could just get a week!' (p. 208) the narrator exclaims. After Cowperwood has made the transaction for which he will soon be sentenced, we are told that 'Time was not a thing to be had in this emergency' (p. 208). In response, Cowperwood explains that he has 'decided to call a meeting of [his] creditors ... and ask for time' (p. 213). To his creditors he pleads: 'It's the time I want. Time is the only significant factor in this situation. I want to know if you can give me fifteen or twenty days – a month if you can' (p. 218). The creditors refuse, and again Cowperwood struggles for a way to regain control of financial time, which had previously directed both the trajectory of his life and the form of the novel's narrative. He fails, and both the narrative and the dialogue, the accretion of value – whether verbal or capitalist – over time is gradually rendered static. Cowperwood has 'temporarily suspended' his financial operations on the stock exchange, and the narrative flow of the novel has been temporally suspended too as Dreiser issues one repetition after another.

With financial time suspended, the narrative takes on a circular, spatial quality. Cowperwood navigates Philadelphia in an effort to extricate himself from an increasingly circumscribed financial panic – his circulation follows the layout of the city streetcars from which he has derived his fortune – encountering one creditor after another, having the same conversation, and receiving the same negative response. The repetition of the word 'time', frequently three or four instances a paragraph – in personal, financial and, as we will see, antagonistic forms – has the effect of slowing time down, and making it visible. But it also has the effect of revealing time to be a social category, one which is able to move out of the claustrophobic perception of Cowperwood and into the realm of contestation.

While Cowperwood is unsuccessfully attempting to reorganise time around his debts, members of the opposing financial group attempt the organisation of an antagonistic time, one which would supersede Cowperwood's own and guide the remainder of much of the narrative. 'After a time' Senator Simpson spoke, urging that they 'begin a prosecution [of Cowperwood] in a reasonable time'; that they 'act in such a way as we had been planning to do so all the time'; that 'the thing to do is gain time'; that 'we have no time to lose'; and that they 'suspend the [city] treasurer for the time being' (p. 227). Finally, 'The senator rose. His time was always valuable' (p. 230). 'The time was not far off', when Cowperwood would be indicted and sentenced. Thus by gaining control over time in all its social facets, the coalition that opposes Cowperwood is able to take control of his finances (his railroad stocks are especially coveted). Conversely, the reason he has lost control of his time is that he has lost control of his finances which, in true naturalist fashion, was ostensibly the result of fire, a natural force beyond any social intervention. This relationship, however, is only ascertainable through the form of finance itself. And by employing its most distinctive structural property – its relationship to time – we are able to understand the representation of finance as a representation of time, and vice versa.

Concluding remarks

If cultural criticism intends to take seriously the problem of economic representation, signification or determination, it must approach the multiple facets of economic value including its financial form. This problematic has taken on a new urgency after the finance-based economic reorganisation in the mid-1970s and particularly since the most recent spate of financial speculation otherwise known as the 'dotcom' stock market bubble of the late 1990s. These events have been well theorised by political economy, but their translation into literary and cultural studies has been uneven. My chapter has demonstrated that, once isolated and understood, the financial form of value is not unique to the post-Bretton Woods economy; rather it may be employed wherever capitalism is the context out of which a text has derived. And this is a substantial historical scope indeed. As Patrick Brantlinger has claimed, 'from Defoe forward, realistic fiction, at least, is always in some sense about money' (Brantlinger, 1996: 144). While Brantlinger's claim is no doubt true, work on the financial form of value remains in a technical state.[16] I have suggested one way to move beyond this difficulty by linking one formal property of both finance and narrative: time. However, time is certainly not the only mediation between finance and literature, and it is the strength of this volume and the essays contained herein, that finance-based activity, whether seen in the work of Swift or DeLillo, is given specific consideration.

Notes

1. The reference is to 'socially necessary labour time', the mean production time of any given commodity (Marx, 1976: 303).
2. The relationship between time and finance is hardly confined to the examples I have provided. The entire stock market, on whose floor paper certificates (or the electronic equivalent) of joint-stock companies are traded, are in a sense built on fictitious capital. 'Investors hold titles of ownership and receive interest. The titles are simply marketable claims to a share in the future surplus value production' (Harvey, 1982: 276).
3. Mary Poovey, forthcoming, provided by the author, and 'Writing About Finance in Victorian England' (2002); Walter Benn Michaels, 'The Man of Business as the Man of Letters', in *The Gold Standard and the Logic of American Naturalism* (1986); Fredric Jameson, 'Finance Capital and Cultural Criticism', in *The Cultural Turn* (1998). More recently still, see Renata R. Mautner Wasserman (2001).
4. See Shonkwiler (2005). Cited with permission of the author.
5. For early work on finance capital, including the introduction of the term, see Rudolf Hilferding, *Finance Capital* (1981) and Vladimir Lenin, *Imperialism, the Highest Stage of Capitalism* (1939). Hilferding, who defines finance capital as the unification of bank and industrial capital, an occurrence he dates to the late nineteenth and early twentieth centuries, explains that, 'finance capital signifies the unification of capital. The previously separate spheres of industrial, commercial and bank capital are now placed jointly under the direction of high finance' (Hilferding, 1981: 409). For more contemporary work see Harvey, *The Limits to Capital* (1982); Ernest Mandel, *Late Capitalism* (1975); and Arrighi, *The Long Twentieth Century* (1994). For its specifically American context see Michel Aglietta, *A Theory of Capitalist Regulation* (1979) and P. Baran and P. Sweezy, *Monopoly Capital* (1963).
6. Arrighi's terms for this division are, more precisely, 'Territorial' and 'Capitalist'. For clarity and to emphasise the financial nature of capital, I have here labelled the capitalist form as 'financial'.
7. See *American Realism: New Essays*, ed. Eric Sundquist (1982).
8. Jameson is referring to a long tradition in orthodox literary criticism that has taken class consciousness as its formal vantage point for the basis of aesthetic criticism, particularly of realism. For the most canonical example see, Georg Lukács, *History and Class Consciousness* (1971a). But see also Sohn-Rethel *Intellectual and Manual Labor: a Critique of Epistemology* (1978) for a critique of the relationship between the commodity *form* and the Kantian *a priori* categories. See also Jameson's interesting discussion of these texts in *The Political Unconscious* (1981). One would need to do much more theoretical work to move from the commodity form to the form of capital, however, and we may debate whether Jameson's stagiest historical progression from *The Political Unconscious* to *Postmodernism, or the Cultural Logic of Late Capitalism* (1991) and, finally, to *The Cultural Turn* (1998) accomplishes this.
9. Walter Benn Michaels in his *The Gold Standard and the Logic of American Naturalism* (1986) set the standard for this approach to texts. See also Marc Shell, *Money, Language, Thought* (1982). There are, of course, exceptions to

the binary I have set up between New Historical and Marxist approaches to economic representation in literature. See, for example, Richard Godden, *Fictions of Capital* (1997) and see also Jean-Joseph Goux's *Symbolic Economies: After Marx and Freud* (1990) for an attempt to relate the psychoanalytic categories of value and fetish to their Marxian, economic counterparts.
10. All references to *The Financier* are to the 1995 Meridian edition. One could undertake a similar reading of *The Titan*, Dreiser's narrative of Cowperwood's construction of a fresh financial empire in Chicago, replete with the same business machinations and philandering as found in *The Financier*.
11. Shonkwiler (2005).
12. *Sister Carrie* is an obvious choice for representation of consumer desire both textually, in its representation of feminine desire for commodities, and historically; it was one of the first American texts to present mass consumption thematically. Furthermore, it juxtaposes that consumption with a representation of the factory system in which those same commodities were being produced. See, for example, Rachael Bowlby, *Just Looking: Consumer Desire in Dreiser, Gissing and Zola* (1985). My larger concern is with consumption studies in that it assumes a stable monadic subject who can then become a subject of desire. With that monadic subject, then, comes a phenomenology of perception and experience that is individual rather than collective or social.
13. Hereafter cited by page number only.
14. In my PhD dissertation, I develop this theme more fully as a problem of 'financial masculinity'. See Leigh Claire La Berge, 'Scandals and Abstractions: 1980s Finance and the Revaluation of American Culture', New York University, May 2008.
15. See Jameson's concept of narrative meaning accumulated over time as an ideological form in *The Political Unconscious*.
16. I am referring to works on finance in the humanities that are devoted to trying to decipher the techniques of financial transactions, quite literally. See, for example, Edward LiPuma and Benjamin Lee, *Derivatives and the Globalization of Risk* (2003). In presenting those technical aspects, this work is, of course, quite important for future readings of finance and representation like the one I have presented here.

8
The Gold Standard and Literature: Money and Language in the Work of Jean-Joseph Goux

Ben Roberts

Introduction

It has been commonplace for critics to read André Gide's 1925 novel *Les Faux-Monnayeurs* (*The Counterfeiters*), as being concerned with the theme of sincerity. Yet, as the novel's very title suggests, this is also a novel preoccupied with something like the opposite of the sincere, that is, with the insincere, the inauthentic and the fake. Indeed, in a certain sense, the title of Gide's novel is itself fraudulent. For only a handful of the novel's three hundred or so pages are directly concerned with the matter of counterfeit money. Moreover, the actual sub-plot concerning the passing of fake gold coins by schoolboys is somewhat tangential to the main thread of the novel. Since *Les Faux-Monnayeurs* is a novel about a novelist, Edouard, who is himself writing a novel called *Les Faux-Monnayeurs*, it is perhaps not surprising that the forgers are at one step remove from the narrative. Yet it is possible to argue that whilst the real counterfeiters and actual counterfeit money are somewhat marginal within Gide's narrative, counterfeit money remains symbolically central to the novel. Indeed this is very much the argument of the French critic and philosopher Jean-Joseph Goux in his influential reading of Gide's novel *Les Monnayeurs du Langage* (*The Coiners of Language*).

Goux takes as his starting point a brief scene in the novel where Gide's novelist, Edouard, is explaining what his unwritten novel is about and why he is so interested in the idea of counterfeit money:

> '... imagine a false ten-franc gold piece. In reality it's not worth two sous. But it will be worth ten francs as long as no one recognizes it to be false. So I start from the idea that ...'

'But why start from an idea?' interrupted Bernard impatiently. 'If you were to start from a fact and make a good exposition of it, the idea would come of its own accord to inhabit it. If I were writing *The Counterfeiters* I should begin by showing the counterfeit coin – the little ten-franc piece you were speaking of just now.'

So saying, he pulled out of his pocket a small coin which he flung on the table.

'Just hear how true it rings. Almost the same sound as the real one. One would swear it was gold. I was taken in this morning, just as the grocer who passed it on to me had been taken in himself, he told me. It isn't quite the same weight, I think; but it has the brightness and the sound of a real piece; it is coated with gold, so that, all the same, it is worth a little more than two sous; but it's made of glass. It'll wear transparent. No; don't rub it: you'll spoil it. One can almost see through it, as it is.' (Gide, 1925: 172–3 [189]).

For Goux the 'monetary metaphor' provided by this fake coin not only represents the key idea of the fictional novelist Edouard, but also comes to inhabit the entirety of Gide's text. This is because, for Goux, Gide's novel in its entirety is something of a false coin: a novel which while adhering on the surface to the conventions of realist fiction continuously undermines them from within. As he puts it:

The only novel that Gide managed to write is a trick novel, a counterfeit of the real thing. It is a work with all the external trappings of the genre, one that 'passes itself off as' the real thing ... but whose substance and internal composition make it something other than a novel: it is a challenge to the novelistic form, a critical essay disguised as a novel by the brilliant depiction of pathetic themes woven or engraved in it; a true novel, but one consumed from the inside by critical reflection, by a perspicacity that wears through (*abîme*) its fine appearance and discredits its face value, until it is devalued to a mere cheat of a token devoid of opacity and colour, a clear crystal of no account among the circulating money that the authentic writer must mint. (Goux, 1994: 10)

Goux's point here is not, of course, that Gide fails as a novelist in *Les Faux-Monnayeurs*. Rather it is that the speculative nature and reflexive form that the novel adopts serve not so much to undermine its own status as novel, but to challenge the novelistic form itself. If *Les Faux-Monnayeurs* is not an 'authentic' novel, it is because it problematises the very 'authenticity' of the novel form. Here the particular form of counterfeit money (a crystal coin re-covered in gold) that Bernard tosses in front of Edouard in the scene above is particularly pertinent for Goux. The *mise en abîme* which places Edouard's novel within Gide's own itself results in a wearing away (*abîme*) of the realist facade of the novel, revealing underneath the crystal of a pure construction. For Goux the actual monetary metaphors of Gide's novel are in a sense secondary to a formal construction which serves to make it an example of a much wider homology between literature and money.[1] For what is at stake in *Les Faux-Monnayeurs* is really a crisis of literary representation, one which for Goux is inextricably linked to a crisis of financial representation or of currency.

How does Goux make this comparison between literary and financial currency? The financial crisis that Goux has in mind is that of the decline of gold money, the disappearance of a currency that is backed by gold and its replacement by a purely representative paper money. The historical event of the replacement of gold money in France precedes the writing of Gide's novel yet – and this is crucial for Goux's reading – the events depicted within it take place before the First World War, when gold money is still in force. Goux comments:

> ... the novel is conceived precisely at the time of a qualitative rupture in the mode of economic exchange, but is fictionally set at a moment in history when gold money is still in force. Gide's fiction is therefore influenced by the disjunction between past and present, between the vanishing order and the emerging order of the monetary object. Even if the action internal to the novel necessarily takes place before the war, at a time when gold coins are still in circulation, it is profoundly haunted by the disappearance of gold money and advent of the regime of inconvertibility. (Goux, 1994: 21)

For Goux the disappearance of gold money, while not being registered directly in the text, is paralleled by a crisis in literary or representational language that he locates in Gide's novel. In short Gide's novel registers a struggle between the 'gold language' of literary realism and the 'inconvertible' language of modern literature:

> The type of language that could be compared to *gold money* would be a full, adequate language [*un langage plein*]. In it and through it, the real would be conveyed without mediation, both as the objective reality of the external world and as the subjective reality of the internal

world. This type of language would be *expressive* in its subjective aspect, relating to the soul and to others, and it would be *descriptive* in its aspect of relation to the external world. Such a gold language formulates truth *immediately*, thus dispensing those who avail themselves of it from questioning the linguistic *medium*. [...]

If we now consider a system in which language is compared to *representative paper currency*, we encounter another situation. In this case, the relationship between language and being begins to be problematic. Just as in the economic sphere there arises the question of *convertibility*, that is, the existence or not of a deposit serving to back the tokens in circulation, likewise in the domain of signification the truth value of language will become a crucial concern. Language will no longer be conceived as fully expressing (or as being *capable* of expressing) reality or being; it will necessarily be conceived as a means, a relatively autonomous instrument, by which it is possible to represent reality to varying degrees of exactitude. (Goux, 1994: 17)

Goux therefore associates 'gold language' with nineteenth-century realism and 'token language' with an emergent modern writing. The understanding of language as a 'token' rather than rooted like gold in reality will find its culmination, for Goux, in the work of Saussure whose conception of a 'system of differences without positive terms' – comprehending language as arbitrary and conventional – corresponds to representative paper currency.

In the course of his own reading of Baudelaire's much earlier short essay 'The Counterfeiters', Derrida refers in a footnote to Goux's analysis and comments as follows:

[In Goux's analysis] Gide's novel would mark, both as a symptom and a writing that records the event, the degradation or fictionalization of a literary language that (after World War I and the transition to non-convertible money and to a fixed rate) is no longer 'comparable to gold money' [Goux, 1984, p. 29]. Without questioning either the interest of this hypothesis or the necessity of trying to pinpoint the greatest possible historical differentiation, one wonders how far one can credit the proposed break (between 'gold-language' and 'token-language') and its *analogy* with an historical *rupture* in a literary periodization ('romantic realism', Zola, Hugo, on one side, Mallarmé, Valéry, Gide, and a few others on the other side) of a 'fundamental crisis' of 'the language of literature, in its relation to being'. Does not this hypothesis tend to naturalize and de-fictionalize gold-money, that is, to confirm an old and stable convention, the very one that [Baudelaire's] 'Counterfeit Money' interrogates obliquely? And above all: where would one situate [Baudelaire's] 'Counterfeit Money' in this historical schema? And its author? (Derrida, 1993: 110 n.1)

However interesting the links that Goux is making between money and literary language may be, they seem to result in a rather neat and at the same time rather violent historicisation of literature. As Derrida points out, if the homology between the two 'currencies' carries the kind of analytic force that Goux tends to associate with it, there arises a compelling question about what to do with texts such as Baudelaire's which do not seem to fit into the historical relationship being asserted here. For Derrida it also seems as if the association between gold-money and realism that Goux makes in *The Coiners of Language* might result, as he puts it here, in a naturalisation and defictionalisation of gold-money. Indeed on a certain reading (although Goux resists this) it might seem as if Goux is mourning the decline of both gold-money and the 'full, adequate' language of literary realism. However that this is not in fact the argument Goux is advancing becomes clear when one places *The Coiners of Language* in the context of his earlier work.

For in some ways Goux's arguments in *The Coiners of Language* simply develop those he has laid out in the earlier *Économie et Symbolique*. In *Économie et Symbolique* Goux sets out a thesis about the fundamental 'isomorphism' between various different symbolic economies (language, objects and subjects) and commodity exchange. The evolution of the money form as what Marx calls the 'general equivalent form' of commodity exchange would find its correlative in the field of objects and subjects: 'the phallus is the general equivalent of objects; the father is the general equivalent of subjects, in the same way that gold is the general equivalent of products'.[2] All these different value systems ('distant registers of the general social body')[3] display this remarkable isomorphism: 'Every genesis of a major symbol ... is isomorphic to that of the discontinuous elaboration of the monetary form.'[4] In each case, in each evolution or genesis, the disappearance or effacement of the history of that genesis is marked by the appearance of a fetishised equivalent form. The genesis of the money form is demonstrated by Marx in the transition from simple commodity exchange, where one commodity determines its value in relation to another commodity which stands in relation to the first as the *equivalent form* of its value, to the situation where all commodities measure their value in relation to one commodity alone, the general equivalent form or gold (Marx, 1976: 183–4, 188). Once it has achieved this status of general equivalent in which all commodities determine their value, gold becomes in effect the *fetishised* form of value itself.

In a similar way, as Goux attempts to show with reference to Freudian–Lacanian psychoanalysis, the child first finds its own value as a subject, the *moi*, by identification with another, its mother: Lacan's mirror stage (Goux, 1973: 58). In a manner analogous to that by which for Marx the commodity can only find its exchange-value in the use-value of *another* commodity, for Lacan it is 'in the *other* that the subject identifies and even experiences itself first of all'.[5] After finding its identity first in the mother, in a second stage, like a commodity in a bustling market place, the child finds itself standing in a series of relations to diverse 'others': brothers, sisters and father. Goux comments that, 'the subject – newly born into the commerce of humans – reflects bit by bit its value (its soul) in the body of its numerous likenesses, [quoting Marx] "the total (or developed) form of relative value puts a commodity in social relation with everything"'.[6] But, just as a market without money form suffers from numerous practical difficulties, the child's relations to these diverse others is ultimately unsatisfactory:

> What is it [for the child], this being always relative to others as different as they are numerous? They all reflect his soul only fragmentarily. What should he do in order to really know what he is in appealing to each one? To make himself recognized by each one? ... But moreover, here, at the same time that he appeals, specularly, to the image of such and such other, he also plays himself the role of the mirror: the inextricable relations of domination and subordination find themselves linked, activity and simultaneous passivity, antagonism, reversible polarity, or, better said, ambi-*valence*.[7]

Like the commodity which, in what Marx calls the 'total' or 'developed' form of value, finds its value reflected in the form of diverse other commodities – as well as itself reflecting their value back to them – the child finds itself making a diverse series of identifications, but can secure its identity as subject in no particular identification or equation, only in the total system. In effect this series of diverse and *ambivalent* relations is unsatisfactory to the child and poses a problem: a problem that is, Goux comments, 'quasi-algebraic' – it amounts to the need to reduce the diverse relations or 'equations' in which the child finds himself situated, or the need for a common denominator (1973: 60). Just as gold answers this demand in the realm of commodity exchange, the father fills this role in the development of the subject:

> What is it about, if not that the father becomes the reflective and unique image of all subjects in search of their price? What is it about, if not that access to their reciprocal autonomy, at the same time as their social status, conferred by the assumption of the norm, passes through this mediation? The passage from the developed form of value (Form II) to the general form of value (Form III) – which is effected on the basis of a 'return', of a 'reciprocity' – is isomorphic to the denouement of the Oedipal crisis: the image of the father functioning in this economy as general equivalent and the image of particular others (and of the *moi*) as relative form.[8]

Identification as a subject can only take place on the basis of the murder of the 'real' father, who henceforth is fetishised as paternal totem, the abstract general equivalent value of subjectivity (Goux, 1973: 62). In the same way that one commodity, gold, emerges as the form of value for commodities in general, identification with the father here becomes the standard for subjectivity and replaces a complex series of identifications with diverse others. The resolution of the Oedipal crisis is thus the installation of the 'father' as the prototype or measure of the subject.

Moreover, for Goux, in psychical organisation, as it is for the 'subject' so it is for the object: Goux goes on to sketch, with reference to Freud's *Three Essays on Sexuality* and Lacan's reading of Freud in *Écrits*, how the phallus emerges from a series of partial objects (breast, excrement, etc.) with their own libidinal investments as the privileged object for the child, concluding that 'castration, "the elision of the phallus", whatever the more or less bloody dramatisation that decides the scenario be, is nothing other than the syntactical exclusion of the general equivalent from the world of relative values (partial objects)'.[9]

In each case, then, Goux is able to map Marx's thesis about the commodity onto psychical systems of value. In each case the four stages in the evolution of the money form – that is, the simple or accidental form of value (Form I), the total and developed form of value (Form II), the general form of value (Form III) and the money form itself (Form IV) – are found to have corresponding phases in the evolution of psychical value systems. It is, therefore, according to Goux, no accident that Freud finds four stages in the developmental organisation of sexuality (the oral, anal, phallic and genital phases), for it is 'the same genetic process, the same principle of discontinuous and progressive structuration that orders the accession to normative sovereignty of gold, the father and the phallus'.[10] Moreover, in both cases, it is the forgetting of the evolutionary process that is responsible for the fetishised form of the general equivalent.[11] Here Goux refers explicitly both to Marx's remarks in *Capital* on the way in which the money form fetishises the qualities of precious metals and Lacan's analysis of the fetishisation of the phallus being derived from its status as a privileged signifier (Lacan, 1977: 311–22). What they have in common is that, for Goux, 'it is from *the effacement of a genesis* that fetishism is born ... From the effacement of a history. And only an *analysis* can lift that illusion.'[12] Goux underlines here the word 'analysis' in order to point out the fundamental homology between the *analysis* Marx sees as being called for by the fetishisation of gold and *psychoanalysis* itself. Gold in effect is here the 'symptom' of the capitalist mode of production.

Goux attempts to show that Marx's 'science of money' can be extended to any system of symbolic value that regulates social exchange (1973: 79), and thus inform a critique of those systems. The moment where any symbolic system has recourse to a general equivalent, whether it be gold, father or phallus, playing the role of the universal intermediary, assumes a legal or legislative significance. The point that Goux seems to want to underline is that this process of legislated equivalence – be it numerative or nominative – has the status not merely of a *convention*, or *convenience* by which reciprocal needs (for example, for food or clothing) can be satisfied, or an individual subject can communicate or relate to others, but carries with it the force of law, the force of compulsion or interdiction:

> So, in the same way that 'it is courtesy of the Name-of-the-Father that man does not remain attached to the sexual service of the mother [...] and that the Law is at the service of a desire which it institutes by the interdiction of incest' [Lacan], it is courtesy of money (to the numerary [*numéraire*], to the name of gold) that the commodity, (1) defers its immediate *usage*, (2) defers its immediate *exchange*, – and desires to relate its price to coinage [*monnaie frappée*], entering into the detour of exchange founded by the law.[13]

Just as the price of partaking in a human community, according to the Oedipal scenario, is abiding by the law that prohibits incest, the price of the entry of the commodity into the community of commodities is that it assume its 'price', or its value in the equivalent form of gold. What is at stake in both is the assumption of what Goux calls the 'common denominator'. Here denomination carries both its numerate sense and the string of meanings tied to its Greek root of *nomos*, that is, of *naming* and of *law*.

> The general equivalent is the place of a law, the place from where one names. If the father is the common denominator of particular subjects – and the transmission of the proper name is made through the father – if the signs of language, by their very function of denomination, of articulation of *names*, are the common denominators *par excellence*, similarly *money is the 'common denominator of all commodities [Marx]'*, in the same way that the phallus is 'the smallest common denominator of what is object [Lacan]'.[14]

The equivalent form, then, announces the law by legislating and normalising value (one might think here of Marx's comparison of money with weights and other measures). Since there is nothing natural *per se* about the fact that, for example, the equivalent form of monetary value should be gold, it comes not from nature but from law.

> In a general fashion the institution of money obliges relations between 'commodities' to make a legislative detour. Aristotle writes, 'Money becomes, by convention, the sole means of exchange with a view to satisfying reciprocal needs. It bears also the name of NUMISMA because it proceeds not from nature but from law (nomos).' The monetary detour is therefore the assumption of the law. If one thinks about the role (isomorphic to the whole of this process) of linguistic signs, if one thinks about *denomination*, a *numismatic* chain is brought to light – a legislative and juridic chain which reunites the name, the number, numeration, nomination and denomination.[15]

As the Greek word 'nomos' here might make one suspect – Goux is quoting here from just before the section of the *Nicomachean Ethics* Marx cites in his commodity analysis[16] – this process of legislation is analogous to that of *naming* and thus also to the whole process of signification which Goux will turn to in the following chapters. The point here for Goux is to lay out the manner in which the emergence of a general equivalent – gold, for example – is in effect an event of naming *and* of legislation. On the one hand, then, Goux simply reiterates the force of the critiques he is drawing on: commodity exchange is no more 'natural' for Marx than subjectivity and desire are for Lacan;

for both writers they are contingent on the symbolic institutions (general equivalents) that make them possible. On the other hand, what Goux seems to want to underline is that the development of the general equivalent *in general*, if one can say that (though the inextricable relationship between the possibility of general equivalents and the possibility of a *general* analysis or critique of general equivalents may be exactly what is at stake here), the process of nomination or denomination, has an intrinsic legislative and political significance. For Goux is engaged on a project with a much wider scope, that is, to link the development of the 'numismatics' he has outlined with respect to the father, the phallus and money – the formation of general equivalents *in general* – with the political centralisation characteristic of modernity (Goux, 1973: 85). Thus Goux's concern here is not with the effacement of a *particular* symbolic genesis, or *numismatique*, like that of money, but the *general* process by which general equivalents are produced, which Goux links more widely to the history and ideology of the West.

Thus even if in later work Goux will concern himself directly with the historical moment of 'money', where paper money and the 'virtualisation' of gold will be tied to the emergence at the end of the nineteenth century of whole new cultural and specifically literary forms, what concerns Goux in *Économie et Symbolique* is to trace, somewhat sketchily, with reference to Hegel's remarks in the *Encyclopedia* and the *Philosophy of Right*, the development of the monarch as a kind of symbolic general equivalent of the law. The development of the modern constitutional monarchy would represent in effect the triumph of the monarch as a *symbol* in which competing *particular* interest groups, such as the aristocracy, would recognise the universality of justice. Both individuals and interest groups give way to the instituted general equivalence of the monarch as symbol of law, which is their condition of access to the community represented by the law. An access which requires, as a sort of law of general equivalence, an alienation from their immediate needs and interests: 'There is therefore, as we see, a strict homology between the alienation from individual work in the process of exchange, as a correlative of the *a priori* legislation of all exchange in the field of commodity circulation, and the total alienation of individuals as the *a priori* condition of all exchange (between rights and duties).'[17] Just as the producers of commodities, as we have seen, must become alienated from the immediate use-value of their work – making products not to satisfy their own needs but purely with a view to their marketable value – the individual, in order to become a citizen of the state, must alienate his or her own needs and interests into an identification with the rights and duties of a subject of the law:

> In each case (economics, politics, sexuality) it is alienation which permits, obliges, the accession to the social norm and to the exchanges that it regulates following a certain common evaluation. In this way it appears that the general equivalent, as measure of values and standard of prices, comes to precisely occupy and *occult* this previously transcendent place – where it functions as the sensible delegate. In the same way that the Name-of-the-Father comes to occupy the place of the Other and represents the law that the latter institutes, *gold* comes to occupy the place of the regulative law of commodity values, and the *monarch*, in order for justice to be made to reign, comes to occupy the place of the 'original contract' (which would be nothing other than, as extreme point of philosophical mystery from Plato to Hegel, that of the *unwritten laws of the city*).[18]

The general equivalent – monarch or gold – then comes to both represent and conceal (the structure of maintenance and disavowal characteristic of the fetish for Freud)[19] a self-alienating structure which gives access to the social norm, whether that norm be 'price' or 'subject under the law'. And thus the appearance of general equivalents of this kind are the driving force of the historical process of alienation and centralisation characteristic of Western modernity. Indeed for Goux, what one might call 'the West' is constituted by this very process: 'Western civilisation defines itself formally as that which has pushed to the extreme limits, and in every register, this solution of the organisation of social elements by [their] subordination to an equivalent.'[20] As the term 'subordination' here implies, Goux seems to view this process of Western civilisation as a kind of suppression or repression of what he calls 'vital activities' (*'activités vitales'*, p. 113) or 'concrete and particular forces' (p. 110).

> The sphere of production puts in play *forces* (libido, labour power ... individual and collective social forces) which find themselves occulted by the sphere of circulation – founded on the detour of exchange. But the forces put in play *reestablish* themselves in the world of exchange in the form of *values* of which they are the unrecognized *substance*.[21]

The 'subordination' to general equivalents is therefore an 'antagonistic circuit between diversified and productive investments [substantial forces] and counter-investments [idealised values] which repress and universalise them'.[22] The suppression represented by the geneses of 'general equivalents' is that of an historical ongoing process of abstraction and idealisation or, as Goux puts it, a 'reduction of the material' (1973: 112). What is required in response to this suppression therefore, for Goux, is a 'materialist overturning'. For Goux, '[the] materialist overturning [*renversement matérialiste*], dialectically restores meaning and value in a direct material continuation of vital social activity. It is the profound meaning, generalised, of a triple critique: philosophical – of *idealism*; economic – of *fetishism*; political – of *capitalism*.'[23] For Goux, the main model for such a critique, overturning or reversal is, of course, Marx. A Marx who, in his critique of political economy would have demonstrated that the root of the abstract and *idealised* system of monetary value was in fact to be found in the *material* world, in a finite expenditure of *concrete* labour. And thus also a Marx who would have made *conscious* the hitherto unconscious laws governing economic exchange (Goux, 1973: 112):

> Marx is therefore really the place of a radical break, in that his movement inaugurates and prefigures all those who will set out their themes after him. Be it Nietzsche or Freud, this is the struggle against *the hypostasised result of an effaced genesis*. The battle against the outcome of a history which, in establishing values in their current abstract and idealised role, is the very effacement of its material base.[24]

It is these analyses in *Économie et Symbolique* that will lead Goux in the later *The Coiners of Language* to concern himself directly with the historical moment of 'money', where – as we have seen – paper money and the 'virtualisation' of gold will be tied to the emergence at the end of the nineteenth century of whole new cultural and specifically literary forms. Moreover, Goux's arguments about the conventional and 'numismatic' nature of gold in his earlier text serve to contest the criticism that his reading of Gide somehow naturalises or normalises either 'gold money' or the 'gold language' of realism to which it is compared. This criticism is not confined to Derrida's reading. Michael Lucey has argued, for example:

> [Goux's] discussion of a suspiciously sudden disappearance of a universal equivalent ... recasts the sincerity game into economic terms, which Goux then applies homologically to diverse realms. In these

applications we can begin to sense how easily the sincerity game (a.k.a. the universal equivalent game) leads into both misogynistic and homophobic assertions of the valued stability of what is nonetheless a clearly imaginary normativity against which free-floating and spuriously subsequent perversions will be measured and found wanting ... the apparently 'rigorous' system Goux uncovers in *Les Faux-Monnayeurs* need not be seen as such, unless one has a stake in inauthenticity versus sincerity, in standards versus an unanchored system of desires. (Lucey, 1995: 110–11)

Lucey may well be justified in the general criticism that Goux fails to pay sufficient attention to the question of the overt homosexuality present in the novel. But he is certainly mistaken in the view he presents of Goux as a sort of anti-postmodernist, mourning the loss of the authenticity and 'standards' of the universal equivalent in the face of a desire that is as free-floating as the circulation of paper money. For as we have seen in our reading of Goux's earlier *Économie et Symbolique*, Goux's work in fact maintains a consistent critique of the general or universal equivalent in all its forms. It is never a question of regarding one particular form of value as more authentic than another, but rather of developing a theory of the historical development of value systems as being 'isomorphic' to that of the money form.

It is perhaps understandable that, if one confines oneself to reading Goux's *Les Monnayeurs du Langage* in isolation, one might come to the conclusion that Goux is valorising 'gold' – in both its literary and financial forms – over its replacements. In voicing this suspicion Lucey echoes Derrida's remark (cited above) that Goux's analysis tends to 'naturalise' and 'defictionalise' gold money. But when these remarks are set in the context of Goux's earlier work it becomes clear that this is not at all Goux's project. Goux's aim, rather, is to demonstrate a homology between the historical evolution of different forms of symbolic value. It is quite clear from *Économie et Symbolique* that it is demonstrating the four-stage evolution of the symbolic form that is at stake for Goux and not the superiority of one stage of evolution over another.

On the other hand, having placed Goux's analysis of Gide in the context of his earlier work, it is quite clear that Derrida's second criticism of Goux stands. That is to say, whatever the similarity between different forms of symbolic value, Goux's historicisation of their co-evolution, his desire to 'locate a historical turning point', seems problematic (Goux, 1994: 4). The idea that one could locate a particular point in time where realistic representational forms give way to modernist representational forms – analogous to the point at which currency breaks with the gold standard – would raise the question, as we have seen Derrida observe, of what to do with works either side of the break that don't fit into the schema. It is perhaps finally on the question of historicity that Goux's homology between literary and financial representation breaks down.

Notes

1. 'The themes of Gide's novel, then, bear witness to a crisis of representation, since the general equivalents he illustrates are *Representatives*. At the same time, his literary devices are *formally* in the grip of a challenge to the representational system similar to the challenge already experienced in the field of painting' (Goux, 1994: 11).
2. 'Le phallus est l'équivalent général des *objets*; le père est l'équivalent général des *sujets*, de même que l'or est l'équivalent général des produits' (Goux, 1973: 69, his emphasis).
3. 'registres distants du corps social général' (Goux, 1973: 65).
4. 'Toute genèse des symboles majeurs ... est isomorphe à celle de l'élaboration discontinue de la forme monétaire' (Goux, 1973: 65).
5. 'C'est dans l'autre que le sujet s'identifie et même s'éprouve tout d'abord' (Lacan, 1966: 181, my emphasis).
6. 'le sujet – nouveau né dans le commerce des humains – reflète peu à peu sa valeur (son âme) dans le corps de nombreux de ses semblables, "la forme totale (ou développée) de la valeur relative met une marchandise en rapport social avec toutes"' (Goux, 1973: 59).
7. 'Quel-est il, cet être toujours relatif à des autruis aussi différents que nombreux? Tous ne lui réfléchissent son âme que fragmentairement. Devrait-il pour savoir réellement ce qu'il est en appeler à chacun? se faire reconnaître pas chacun? ... Mais davantage encore: voici qu'en même temps qu'il en appelle, spéculairement, à l'image de tel ou tel autre, il joue aussi bien, lui-même, le rôle de miroir: – des rapports inextricables de domination et de subordination se trouvent ainsi noués, d'activité et de passivité simultanée, d'antagonisme, de polarité renversable, ou pour mieux dire d'ambi-*valence*' (Goux, 1973: 60).
8. 'Qu'en est-il sinon que le père devient l'image réfléchissante et unique de tous les sujets en quête de leur prix? Qu'en est-il, sinon que l'accès à leur autonomie réciproque en même temps qu'à leur statut social, entériné par l'assomption de la norme, passe par cette médiation? Le passage de la forme valeur développée (Forme II) à la forme valeur générale (Forme III) – qui s'effectue sur la base d'un "retournement", d'une "réciproque", est isomorphe au dénouement de la crise œdipienne: l'image du père fonctionnant dans cette économie comme équivalent général et l'image des autruis particuliers (et du moi) comme forme relative' (Goux, 1973: 61).
9. 'La castration "l'élision du phallus", quelle que soit la dramatisation plus ou moins sanglante qui en décide le scénario, n'est pas autre chose que l'exclusion syntaxique de l'équivalent général du monde des valeurs relatives (des objets partiels)' (Goux, 1973: 68).

10. 'C'est un même processus génétique, c'est le même principe de structuration discontinue et progressive qui commande l'accession à la souveraineté normative de l'or, du père et du phallus' (Goux, 1973: 69).
11. 'C'est "le caractère *fétiche* que la forme monnaie imprime aux métaux précieux". De même dans le registre du sexe, et de sa "fonction signifiante" privilégiée, "l'organe qui en est revêtu prend valeur de fétiche"' (Goux, 1973: 78; quoting Marx (1976), Lacan (1977)).
12. '... c'est de *l'effacement d'une genèse* que naît le fétichisme ... De l'effacement d'une histoire. Et seule une *analyse* peut lever cette illusion' (Goux, 1973: 79).
13. 'Ainsi de même que "c'est grâce au Nom-du-père que l'homme ne reste pas attaché au service sexuel de la mère [...] et que la Loi est au service du désir qu'elle institue par l'interdiction de l'inceste", c'est grâce à la monnaie (au numéraire, au nom de l'or) que las marchandise, (1) diffère son *usage* immédiat, (2) diffère son *échange* immédiat, – et *désire* de rapporter son prix à la monnaie frappée, entrant dans le détour d'échange de la circulation instauré par la loi' (Goux, 1973: 84, his emphasis).
14. 'L'équivalent général est le lieu d'une loi, le lieu d'où l'on nomme. Si le père est le commun dénominateur des sujets particuliers, – et que la transmission du nom se fait par le père – si les signes du langage, par leur fonction même de dénomination, d'articulation des *noms*, sont par excellence les dénominateurs communs de tous les signes du monde, pareillement *"l'argent est le dénominateur commun de toutes les marchandises"*, de même que le phallus est *"le plus petit commun dénominateur de ce qui est objet"'* (Goux, 1973: 84–5).
15. 'D'une façon générale l'institution monétaire oblige les relations entre "marchandises" à passer par un détour législatif. "L'argent devient par convention, écrit Aristote, l'unique moyen d'échange en vue de satisfaire des besoins réciproques. Aussi porte-t-il le nom de NUMISMA parce qu'il procède non de la nature mais de la loi" (nomos). Le détour monétaire est donc l'assomption de la loi. Si l'on pense au rôle (isomorphe à tout ce procès) des signes linguistiques, si l'on pense à la dénomination, est mise alors à jour une chaîne *numismatique*. Une chaîne législative et juridique qui réunit le nom, le numéraire, la numération, la nomination et la dénomination' (Goux, 1973: 84).
16. See Aristotle (1926: Bk. V, Ch. v, 285).
17. 'Il y a donc on le voit une homologie étroite entre l'aliénation des travaux des individuels dans le procès d'échange, comme corrélât de la législation *a priori* de tout échange dans le champ de la circulation marchande, et l'aliénation totale des individus comme condition *a priori* de tout échange (entre les droits et les devoirs)' (Goux, 1973: 104).
18. 'Dans tous les cas (économie, politique, sexualité) c'est l'aliénation qui permet, oblige, d'accéder à la norme sociale et aux échanges qu'elle réglemente suivant une certaine évaluation commune. Il apparaît ainsi que l'équivalent général, comme mesure des valeurs et étalon des prix, vient occuper précisément et *occulter* ce lieu transcendent et préalable, – où il y fonctionne comme le délégué sensible. De même que le Nom-du-Père vient occuper le lieu de l'Autre et représente la loi que ce dernier institue, l'*or* vient occuper le lieu de la loi régulatrice des valeurs marchandes, et le *monarque*, pour faire régner la justice, vient occuper le lieu du "contrat d'origine" (qui ne serait autre, de

Platon à Hegel, comme extrême du mystère philosophique, que celui *des lois non-écrites de la cité*' (Goux, 1973: 105).
19. As Freud outlines in the essay 'Fetishism', the fetish 'is a substitute for woman's (the mother's) penis that the little boy once believed in'. Refusing to give up on this symbolic phallus, 'a very energetic action has been undertaken to maintain the disavowal'. In the fetish, the fetishist has 'retained the belief [in the woman's phallus], but he has also given it up'. In Freud's account – and this supports Goux's analogy with the commodity – the fetish is fundamentally rather successful: 'We can now see what the fetish achieves and what it is that maintains it. It remains a token of triumph over the threat of castration and a protection against it' (Freud, 1927: 152–4).
20. 'La civilisation occidentale se définit formellement comme celle qui a poussé jusqu'à ses extrêmes limites, et dans tous les registres, cette solution de l'organisation des élément sociaux par la subordination à un équivalent' (Goux, 1973: 91).
21. 'La sphère de la production met en jeu des *forces* (libido – force de travail ... forces sociales, individuelles et collectives) qui se trouvent occultées par la sphère de la circulation – basée sur le *détour d'échange*. Mais les forces mises en jeu se *rétablissent* dans le monde de l'échange sous la forme de *valeurs* dont elles sont la *substance* méconnue' (Goux, 1973: 110).
22. '... circuit antagonique entre des investissements diversifiés et producteurs et les contre-investissements qui les refoulent et les universalisent' (Goux, 1973: 110).
23. 'Le *renversement matérialiste* remet dialectiquement le sens et la valeur dans le prolongement matériel direct de l'activité vitale socialisée. C'est le sens profond, généralisé d'une triple critique: philosophique – de l'*idéalisme*; économique – du *fétichisme* ; politique – du *capitalisme*' (Goux, 1973: 112–13).
24. 'Marx est donc bien le lieu d'une coupure radicale, en ce que son geste inaugure et préfigure toux ceux qui après lui vont tracer leur motif. Qu'il s'agisse de Nietzsche ou de Freud, c'est la lutte contre *le résultat hypostasié d'une genèse effacée*. La lutte contre le résultat d'une histoire, qui en établissant dans leur rôle à présent abstrait, idéalisé, les valeurs, fut l'effacement même de sa base matérielle' (Goux, 1973: 111).

9
Producing and Consuming Agricultural Capital: the Aesthetics and Cultural Politics of Grain Elevators at the 1937 Paris International Exposition

Guillaume Evrard

This chapter aims to explore the representation of capital – specifically agricultural capital – via architecture during the 1937 Paris International Exposition, by focusing on the Canadian pavilion at the foot of the Eiffel Tower and one building of the French *Centre rural* (Rural Centre) at the western edge of Paris at Porte Maillot.[1] Capital has historically encompassed a wide range of items, especially in agriculture, extending from finance – both fixed capital and investment – to a more grounded and open-ended signification that has included production processes, climate and the actual assets on a farm: livestock, plantations, land, buildings, machinery and equipment. Although both structures drew on the common building type of a grain elevator, I argue that they did so in distinctly different ways and thereby represented different moments of capital speculation and displacement; namely the two different stages of capitalist flow, production and consumption, as Michel de Certeau analysed them in *The Practice of Everyday Life* (1988). The Canadian grain elevator was artistic and aesthetic in nature, whereas the French structure was an accurate replica of a contemporary type. Considered together, the Canadian pavilion and French grain elevator are two different representations of agricultural capital in the late 1930s; the latter, a modernist and functionalist image of a technocratic nature, the former, a nationally connoted shape of a deeply emotional value.

The International Expositions organised in America, Europe and, more recently, in Asia, have been important historical events, creating opportunities 'to form a meaningful message' (Giberti, 2002: 1) by juxtaposing the world's natural wealth and human creativity in displays originally inspired by a scientific rationale but later they also, as 'a matter of government policy', featured national pavilions alongside the thematic international sections. As Burton Benedict underlined in *The Anthropology of World's Fairs*, 'the fairs were not only selling goods, they were selling ideas: ideas about the relations between nations, the spread of education, the advancement of science, the form of cities, the nature of domestic life, the place of art in society' (1983: 2). These exhibitions were vast affairs with dozens of pavilions and they reached a peak in the 1937 Paris *Exposition Internationale des Arts et Techniques dans la Vie Moderne*. Derived from Latin, a 'pavilion' is a 'tent, especially a large peaked one' (Sykes, 1986: 752). In its battlefield version, the light and ephemeral pavilion is set up at the forefront of, and as the focal point for, the control of the political entity it, and its army, stands for. As it later evolved with a diverse range of shapes and materials, the pavilion was used to represent power; individual or collective, political or economic. At every world's fair, different types of power are on show for the masses. Contemporary commentators on successive exhibitions have noted the iconic and symbolic strength of their architecture, '[each of them being] by definition a microcosm, a picture of the world in miniature' (Giberti, 2002: 12). Behind these pavilions and their contents are intriguing representational issues.

International exhibitions are about representation, how buildings stand for and symbolise groups and capital (material and intellectual wealth). They also deal with ideas of speculation, both as contemplation of the world through the exhibition's mirror and as expectations for the future as well as dealing with displacement, taken in its psychoanalytical sense – substitution of a building for an idea, 'the substitute object [being] less threatening than the original one, and the displacement [having] therefore the effect of avoiding or reducing anxiety' (Colman, 2001).

Instead of examining the Canadian and French buildings individually, I shall proceed with common fields of comparison: first considering their relationship to their audience, and then their aesthetic and architectural aspects in relation to the idea of a global market. The French and Canadian grain elevators shared the same objectives: commercial promotion, education and entertainment, while creating different sorts of 'relations between consumers and the mechanisms of production' (de Certeau 1988: xvii). However, they did not deal with identical economical, political and ideological issues because they were driven by different agenda. Featuring the building type of the grain

Figure 1 Centre rural, Le silo à grain (The Grain Elevator), from Jean Favier, *L'architecture, Exposition internationale, Paris, 1937* (Paris: Éditions Alexis Sinjon, [1938], Portfolio 3, Plate 41 (detail)).

elevator, both the French silo in the *Centre rural* and the Canadian pavilion at the foot of the Eiffel Tower relied on a common architectural history that goes back to the second half of the nineteenth century. Yet they conveyed two different understandings of everyday life and global market through their architecture.

Promoting, educating, entertaining within different relations to the audience

Both French silo and Canadian pavilion displayed features of a grain elevator, 'a tall tower [...] on a farm' (Soanes and Stevenson, 2003b) that protects 'a machine consisting of an endless belt with scoops attached, used for raising grain' (Soanes and Stevenson, 2003a) and provides storage space ahead of future transport by boat or train. In the exhibition, both buildings, within which visitors could find 'the work floor, located at ground level; the storage bins, defining the bulk of the building;

the distributing floor, directly above the bins; and the head-house, the isolated structure on top of the building' (Mahar-Keplinger, 1992: 70), contributed to the representation of agricultural capital in North America and Europe on the exhibition grounds.

In the *Centre rural* French organisers did not aim to create a mock picturesque district in a remote part of the exhibition. The *Centre régional* already created this kind of atmosphere on the left bank of the Seine, on the very western edge of the main exhibition area, in a project which aimed to support the creation of a modern architecture acknowledging local histories and traditions, and which was warmer and friendlier than the Modernist – international – architecture to be found elsewhere (Hurtt, 2004). Georges Monnet, then socialist Minister of Agriculture, was clear about the aims of the *Centre rural*: 'We exclusively aimed at showing what can be achieved, in every town of France, thanks to the associated action of public services and populations aware of their own interest, under the initiative of their councils and their professional organisations' (République Française, 1938: 155). Jean Favier put in plain words the aims of the *Centre rural* with three main verbs: 'showing',

Figure 2 Canadian Pavilion, overall view and plan, from *Exposition 1937: sections étrangères*, introduction de Jacques Gréber; présentation de Henri Martin (Paris: Éditions art et architecture, [1937], Plate 38).

Figure 3 Canadian Pavilion, Transports stand, from Edmond Labbé, *Exposition Internationale des Arts et Techniques dans la Vie Moderne* (1937): rapport général, T. 2 Album annexe, Plate LXIX (Paris: Imprimerie Nationale, 1938–1940).

'bringing to awareness' and 'making appreciate'. Paul Dupays explained that the *Centre rural* would be a 'well-argued synthesis of the [then] current rural techniques' (1938: 299).

The Minister dismissed any picturesque look or atmosphere because these were thought of as old-fashioned. Moreover this specific area on the outskirts of Paris and its Exposition was described as 'a kind of early living version of what [would] be, one day, the land of France' (République Française, 1938: 155), in the same spirit as the Exposition as a whole. Rather than the display of local aesthetic traditions the main point of the exhibit was the presentation of the role of progress in improving everyday life in rural areas. As the reproduction of a 1,500–2,000-person town, the life-scale exhibition included a town hall, a school, public baths, a library, a post office and a restaurant. Several buildings were open to show different kinds of rural cooperatives: milk, fruits, wine and cereals (*Le Guide Officiel*, 1937: 146). The grain elevator represented the cereals cooperative.

In this context, the silo was one of 'the realisations [...] enlightening both the social and technical effort that must go on, all over [French] rural areas, for their inhabitants to enjoy the advantages of well-being, safety, spiritual culture and leisure, that [were] no less valuable than the ones the inhabitants of the most modern cities [could] enjoy' (République Française, 1938: 155). The promotion of French goods was obvious through, for example, tasting sessions. There as on the central grounds, organisers expressed their intention to entertain visitors and use displays as a teaching instrument. The *Official Guide* explained the purpose of the Exposition thus: 'You are not a visitor only looking for entertainment. You are also certainly a worker who loves [their] job, keen on improving [their] skills, and who, when back home in the evening, [their] task fulfilled, dreams for [themselves] and for others of a more beautiful, more stable, and happier life. The Exposition will allow you to fulfil this proud will and these distinguished desires' (*Le Guide Officiel*, 1937: 23).

Paul Dupays emphasised the exhaustive nature of this area of the Exposition: 'Nothing is missing, neither the culinary arts, nor folklore songs, not even the ordinary life on the market square' (1938: 300). Indeed, the market hall was used to show examples of agricultural engines and products. Alongside the market hall, a cinema fitted in the Farmers' Hall showed propaganda movies. Visitors' attention was drawn towards the different buildings, which '[gave] several opportunities to gain a better awareness of the efforts' of the different cooperatives (*Le Guide Officiel*, 1937: 146–7). Sometimes entertaining, sometimes patronising, the main message of the *Centre rural* was about improvement of everyday life, and it was to be conveyed to the widest audience possible. Indeed, more than a million people visited it (République Française, 1938: 155).

What about the Canadian pavilion? According to the French organisers the function of national pavilions was threefold: technically, pavilions could be used as exclusive premises for national commissioners; spatially, the construction of national pavilions provided opportunities to display more products, specifically in a national setting, in addition to the exhibits in the thematic international buildings; and aesthetically, pavilions could be a projection of the specific architecture of each and every country (Labbé, 1938–40: 1. 240–58). While the French grain elevator was 26.5 metres high, the Canadian pavilion was only 15 metres high, to comply with the guidelines the Chief Architect, Jacques Greber, had laid out, which stressed the 'varied, colourful and functional' character of the Exposition's architecture (Labbé 1938–1940: 2. Annex, 13). The overall design brief of the event referred to ideas of balance and harmony. Both Greber and

General Commissioner Edmond Labbé were interested in a modern creation capable of keeping the past, history and traditions in mind.

When Canadian civil servants received the French invitation for the Paris Exposition, they were uncertain as to the exact purpose of the event. It did not seem to be a purely commercial event. The Department of Trade and Commerce pictured an exhibition of large dioramas to promote Canadian potential for tourism and natural resources (Evrard, 2003: 83–4). The Federal Tourist Bureau, the National Art Gallery, and the Departments responsible for the Mines, National Parks, Natural Resources and Fisheries were invited to cooperate in the preparation of the displays. Eventually, in the Canadian pavilion, thirty booths offered information about Canadian flours, canned fruits, silk and minerals. Extensive literary and photographic documentation was available in a dedicated area of the main hall of the pavilion (*Le Guide Officiel*, 1937: 59). Flooring and wall panels demonstrated the quality of Canadian wood finishing materials: Quebec maple, mahogany, and British Columbian pine (Lefort, 1937).

As a consequence of joint displays from private companies and the Department of Mines and Resources about the production process of several minerals, General Commissioner Labbé noted in his final report that Canada was a leading world producer of various minerals – silver, gold, zinc and nickel. Additional details were provided about salmon fishing; visitors could taste some samples and take away a recipe brochure. Further on, the reconstitution of a typical Quebec farm interior displayed the province's traditional crafts in line with the artistic and crafts dimension of the Exposition. The Canadian railway companies' stands left visitors with vibrant memories, thanks to the use of the most advanced display techniques.

Overall, the Canadian representation seems to have been well received by its audience. Like every other visitor, the General Commissioner was astonished by the sheer size of the Dominion. Among other enthusiastic visitors, the reporter for the *Manchester Guardian Weekly* praised the quality of the Dominion's display and its diversity: 'The Canadian pavilion [...] makes Canada live in the visitor's mind. [... It] give[s] the visitor a "feel" of Canada, and almost a longing' ('The Paris Ehibition', 1937: 98), and a Parisian Sunday newspaper noted the 'proud evocation, along its two immensely long rail tracks, of the boundless wheat fields, the mines, fur hunting, and fisheries of this amazingly wealthy Dominion' ('Je voudrais bien savoir...', 1937: 10). The reporter for *La Presse*, the main North American French-speaking daily newspaper published in Montreal, commented on the success of the Canadian

Figure 4 Battage du blé dans l'ouest canadien (Threshing the wheat in Western Canada), *Pavillon du Canada: Exposition Internationale Paris 1937/Canadian Pavilion: International Exhibition Paris 1937* [1937], p. 20, French side.

displays, and especially on the fascination of the French visitors in front of the rail companies' stands, considering that French visitors were 'more and more eager to travel' (Lefort, 1937).

However, not everybody spoke so highly of the Canadian displays. Andrew Hamilton, reporting for *The Windsor Star*, expressed his disappointment with the copious exhibition about natural resources and the lack of information about what Canada was able to do with them. The correspondent for *The Financial Post* was scathing about the Canadian displays, informed by a specific awareness of what could have been done instead:

> Canada, a great nation with a brilliant story, has been notably weak in its exposition advertising. Our national exhibits lack the punch and glamour of modern showmanship. They harp too much on the past – on the crude, primitive days. They overplay the Indian, the trapper and the things of yesteryear. These things have their place but they are not the Canada of today, they tell nothing of the promise of tomorrow. ('Showmanship', 1937)

In order to make sense of the similarities and distinctions between French and Canadian grain elevators as representations of capital, de Certeau's *The Practice of Everyday Life* (1988) provides a useful analytical framework. Analysing and characterising 'the relations between consumers and the mechanisms of production' (1988: xvii), he identifies two types of relations: 'tactics and strategies' (1988: xix). Both Canadian and French displays aimed at the same sort of communication: commercial promotion, education and entertainment. Still they differed in the content of the message they communicated. On the one hand, the French grain elevator was part of an ensemble picturing the impact of technical and social progress on national agriculture, 'what could be achieved' in the future, and possible successes with a new social and economic structure in rural areas that might be the result of the development of cooperatives. The grain elevator may be interpreted as a beacon to transform interior agricultural production and consumption, the place for a French national *strategy*, 'the calculus of force-relationships which becomes possible when a subject of will and power (a proprietor, an enterprise, a city, a scientific institution) can be isolated from an "environment"' (de Certeau, 1988: xix).

De Certeau explains that 'a strategy assumes a place that can be circumscribed as proper (*propre*) and thus serve as the basis for generating relations with an exterior distinct from it (competitors, adversaries, "clienteles", "targets", or "objects" of research)' (1988: xix). The building 'generates relations', giving a strong sign to French citizens – its 'clientèles' – to change their production habits, and, by visiting exporting countries – 'competitors' and 'adversaries' – to change the object of their speculation and ambitions. On the other hand, the Canadian pavilion put on display what had been achieved in the Dominion, the potential of its great natural resources and the stunning natural environment, which could be the setting for great holidays. The Canadian presentation not only came across as amazing, and breathtaking – with its dioramas and railway maps – but also as familiar and friendly, with the old farm interior and traditional handicrafts. In de Certeau's terms, the Canadian message may be thought of as a *tactic*:

> a calculus which cannot count on a 'proper' (a spatial or institutional focalization), nor thus on a borderline distinguishing the other as a visible totality. The place of a tactic belongs to the other. A tactic insinuates itself into the other's place, fragmentarily, without taking it over in its entirety, without being able to keep it at a distance. It has at its disposal no base where it can capitalize on its advantages, prepare its expansions, and secure independence with respect to circumstances. (1988: xix)

Although the pavilion was produced on behalf of the Canadian national authority, the place it was set in (the bank of the Seine) belonged to France. Emphasising national achievements in the exploitation of natural resources and the beauty of (the) landscape in its displays, the Canadian representation 'pinned its hopes on a clever utilization of time, of the opportunities it presents' (de Certeau, 1988: 38–9). It may therefore be argued that the message delivered by this tactic is closer to the audience than the message conveyed by the French strategy.

If the messages conveyed were so different, although manifested via the same building type, it is mainly because they were part of distinct overarching national constructs.

Different overarching narratives

In the *Centre rural*, the grain elevator was part of a wider setting designed for people to understand innovative ideas and to demonstrate the validity of the French national policy to support national agricultural development.

From the end of the First World War, French agriculture had been expected to provide all the food the country required as French soldiers returned to the farms to cultivate their land without delay, and at affordable prices. Production had to increase significantly to satisfy interior needs. Within a global market France had to mitigate within its own borders the effects of international competition, for instance with the negotiations on tariffs. Since one of the main priorities was the provision of affordable food, agricultural exports were limited for almost a decade while imports were allowed, so that prices could drop (Augé-Laribé, 1950: 394–5). From the end of the 1920s and the beginning of the Great Depression, agricultural imports were critical to the national market. The situation of national agriculture worsened as the sector did not adapt quickly enough to bear competition with foreign producers. At the same time, trade unions and left-wing parties were satisfied with the increase in industrial wages and the drop in food prices.

When the *Front populaire* came to power in June 1936 its agriculture programme was light. Smallholders were not endangered; socialists and communists had already acknowledged the owning of land on a small scale for a decade (Lynch, 1998). The main decision was the introduction of a policy of state direction and control of economic flows and markets. By then world agricultural prices had increased, consequently inflating French prices. Yet the creation of national boards did not improve the situation, since individual purchasing power did not improve as the authorities would have hoped. As a consequence, these boards were used to control prices, and imports went up further, while neighbouring countries like Germany and Italy closed their borders.

During this interwar period, one of the major changes in rural life and the economy was the rapid development of farming cooperatives, for goods such as wine, milk, butter and, most importantly, cereals (Augé-Laribé, 1950: 434–5). The grain elevator in the *Centre rural* is therefore not a surprise. In the French village of the future, it stood for the agricultural cooperative that would support the perennial existence of small agricultural properties gathering together their production. The Socialist Party fought for these small or mid-size properties against both the biggest landowners and the development of larger farms because they believed that small agricultural holdings were essential to French country life.

The French grain elevator was less an expression of the growing impact of the welfare state on everyday life than a political and administrative answer to issues French agriculture had had to face for decades, at that time more than ever with the adverse effects of the Depression and increasingly globalised markets. A representation of agricultural capital, the grain elevator became a landmark of the political agenda of the *Front populaire*: the smallholders were acknowledged and supported with the creation of cooperative organisations to guarantee fair and stable wages while the biggest land properties would have eventually have been more or less nationalised and distributed among small property owners working together in cooperation. Crucially, at the nexus between tradition and modernity and amidst fears for the future of French culture and identity that it gave rise to (Peer, 1999: 51–2), the French grain elevator was the expression of a tamed modernism; not threatening but enhancing the national way of life by supporting its prosperity. The staging of folkloric events and the display of elements of this national way of life such as a 'Burgundian cellar' within the *Centre rural* (Whalen, 2007, 2009) created a familiar hence favourable backdrop for this process of adaptation of global modernity to a local national context and vice versa.

The context of the Canadian grain elevator is different. There was no need for it to stand as a political statement about internal issues since foreign visitors were its main audience. Yet it shows evidence of a conceptual shift in Canadian presentations abroad, from a focus on immigration toward an interest in tourism.

Historically, Canada's participation in world exhibitions aimed to promote its products in order to improve their international prospects and also advertise Canada as the last frontier to open. From 1867 onward the Confederation had been competing with the United States to populate the wide, wild spaces of the Prairie. Millions of cultivable hectares and the prosperity of the Dominion were at stake. Expositions were valuable showcases for Canada – as they were for other countries and companies – to display natural resources both exploited and potential and promote opportunities that would persuade people from the United States and Europe to immigrate (Evrard, 2003). For instance, in Paris, in 1878, Canadian products from agriculture, forests, fishing and mining industries were displayed on a big trophy (Short 1967: 355) surrounded by three white, black and grizzly bears respectively standing for Canadian Arctic, Atlantic and Pacific coasts. The Canadian commissioner unambiguously described this display as 'the introduction of the Dominion to the nations of Europe as a field for immigration, and of Canadian products and manufactures to the markets of the world' (Keefer, 1881: 22).

In addition to the displays in the national pavilion and thematic international buildings, Canadian organisers gave out, more or less officially, brochures promoting the advantages of emigration to Canada (Knowles, 1992: 62–4). Meanwhile, advertisements were published in US newspapers, posters and brochures, and distributed to American citizens and immigration agents, hired in the Midwest – Minnesota, Michigan, Illinois, Missouri, Nebraska, North Dakota, South Dakota and Wisconsin – to encourage both farmers' emigration to Canada and the displacement of a capable population towards what was officially presented as 'the granary of the world' (Bruce, 2001: 3). These proactive methods were in fact successful, since three million people settled in Canada between 1896 and 1914 (Knowles, 1992: 91).

However, in the 1930s, encouraging immigration from Europe and the United States was no longer the principal aim of the Canadian authorities and Canadian immigration bureaus in the United States and in Great Britain were closed (Bruce, 2001). Thenceforth, the Dominion's exhibits were still about displacement of capital and people across the Atlantic Ocean and through North America, yet they showed a shift of content, no longer promoting permanent immigration but only the export of Canadian commodities and the reception of foreign tourists. Canadian trains were not meant to be used by immigrants but to take tourists across the Dominion from east to west coasts. Canada and its economy did not need additional foreign immigration towards the West Coast or the Prairie, as the workforce available inside the Confederation's borders was adequate. Tourism was an alternative way for the country to sell national products and create activity with new services at home.

Throwing an architectural icon into global capitalism: a common architectural history

The first design the Canadian authorities proposed to Chief Architect Greber, showed simple and unornamented areas, balanced by the vegetation inside a central court, and a glass walled corner gallery, inspired by the principles of the Modern Movement which promoted buildings balancing planes and voids, opaque plastered and transparent vitreous surfaces. It had to fit into the Chief Architect's general requirements and into its surroundings, at the foot of the Eiffel Tower, where Belgium, Switzerland, Sweden, Great Britain and Czechoslovakia had already followed the Chief Architect's instructions. The pavilion was to adopt an overall horizontal silhouette that would create a soft transition between the Seine and the Exposition on the left bank. The first design displayed tall freestanding columns with high reliefs of beavers alternately head up and head down. It is as if there was a will to create a new architectural order – one that would match the Canadian identity, with unique beaver-shaped capitals. During the 1936–7 winter, this project was significantly modified with the addition of a corner tower in the shape of a group of grain bins. The Exposition's organisers turned down both designs.

The final design of the Canadian pavilion was proposed by a Montreal sculptor, Jean-Émile Brunet (1899–1977) who had gained much praise in 1927 for creating a sculpture of Canadian Prime Minister Sir Wilfrid Laurier which was placed on Parliament Hill, Ottawa (Macdonald, 1997, vol. 1: 400a–401a) and had been associated with the Paris project by the then Prime Minister William Lyon MacKenzie King. It was a compromise between the horizontality the Chief Architect demanded and the verticality the Canadian government proposed to make its building clearly visible on the Exposition's grounds. Sixteen vertical plaster tubes were stuck to the metallic structure paid for by the French organisers so that the Canadian pavilion was able to present, presumably, a piece of characteristic national architecture. It may come as a surprise that a grain elevator may be approached in terms of aesthetics or visual enjoyment. This dimension of the grain elevator as a representation of capital arose earlier on, with the grain elevator becoming, little by little, from the second half of the nineteenth century onwards, an aesthetic phenomenon.

In 1861, the British writer Anthony Trollope (1815–82) commented disapprovingly upon the grain elevator saying that the 'elevator is as ugly a monster as has been yet produced' when he visited Buffalo, New York,

Figure 5 Under the Eiffel Tower: on the left, the Belgian Pavilion. On the other side of the Jena Bridge, the pavilions of Great-Britain, Canada, the Press, and Advertising (Sous la Tour Eiffel: A gauche, le pavillon de la Belgique. De l'autre côté du pont d'Iéna, dans l'ordre et en perspective: les pavillons de la Grande-Bretagne, du Canada, de la Presse, de la Publicité...). Pierre-Louis Flouquet (1937) 'Paris 1937: L'Exposition internationale des arts et techniques dans la vie moderne'. *Bâtir* (June): 1227–8 (1227) (Studio Lumière, Bruxelles).

the largest grain port in the United States, on Lake Erie's shore (quoted by Brown, 1993: 305). Even spoken of negatively, the grain elevator was nonetheless put in aesthetic terms at a time when grain elevators were still wooden constructions, after the prototype the businessman Joseph Dart and engineer Robert Dunbar developed in 1842 (Brown, 1993: 304). The wooden grain elevator, as designed by Dart and Dunbar, was a significant step in agricultural capital management. Eliminating a slow and intensive workforce, the mechanism housed in the elevator facilitated both the physical displacement of and a financial speculation in agricultural capital. Grains could be gathered, negotiated, sold and shipped more easily and swiftly, thanks to the acceleration of the whole process the grain elevator allowed.

It was also in Buffalo, New York, in 1906, that the first reinforced-concrete elevator was built. Buffalo was at the time the biggest transshipment point of grain in the world, between the Midwest and the

East Coast. This kind of reinforced-concrete elevator in turn became a motif of inspiration for the Canadian pavilion and the grain elevator of the French *Centre rural*. The Modern Movement in architecture quickly considered the building type as an iconic illustration of its principles. In 1913, Walter Gropius (1883–1969) travelled to Buffalo and published an article about grain elevators, emphatically demonstrating the transparency of their structure and, therefore, their modernity: without any meaning or superfluous ornament, their function commanded their shape (Brown, 1993: 306–7). In 1914, the German architect Erich Mendelsohn (1887–1953) associated the grain elevator with modernism, following Gropius's pioneer ideas (Brown, 1993: 307; Vanlaethem, 1998). Later on, Le Corbusier (1887–1965) used a 1920 image of the grain elevator No. 5 in Montreal's harbour in *Towards a New Architecture*, published in French in 1923, where he questioned revolution and architectural reform as alternatives to each other. At the end of his speculation about the role of architecture in contemporary society, Le Corbusier famously concluded a revolution could be avoided. He explained that the reinforced-concrete grain elevator was beautiful and could contribute to improving life, thanks to its elementary forms shaped by its function.

Contemporary painters also used the form of the grain elevator, alongside factories, as an icon to create a truly American visual culture. Artists involved in precisionism like Charles Demuth (1883–1935) and Charles Sheeler (1883–1965) incorporated the once meaningless silhouette into a meaningful visual context to create an independent modern art in the United States (Doss, 2002: 79–82).

What did contemporary critics think about the grain elevator in the specific context of the International Exposition in 1937? The Exposition's *Official guide* explained to the visitor that 'the Canadian pavilion, by its shape and proportions, is the reproduction of one of those granaries, so numerous in this country', while the unknown author underlined the fact that both the design of the pavilion and the aluminium reliefs which hung along the facade were the creation of a unique artist, Brunet (*Le Guide Officiel*, 1937: 59).

Evelyn Tufts, reporting for *The Halifax Herald*, noted that 'the Canadian pavilion, which is white cement, has the usual grain elevator front which we never seem to get away from, and which is, perhaps, as appropriate as any for a great wheat-producing country'. This comment echoed the analysis of the Toronto architect Eric Arthur who thought in 1929 that 'there is something distinctly Canadian about a grain elevator' (Brooker, 1929: 111). A reporter for a French newspaper dealing

Figure 6 Partie du Port de Montréal, le 5e port du monde (Partial view of Montreal Harbour, fifth harbour of the world), *Pavillon du Canada: Exposition Internationale Paris 1937/Canadian Pavilion: International Exhibition Paris 1937* [1937], p. 5, French side.

with commercial exports explained that 'the shape [of the grain bins] has been used as an ornamental motif for very harmonious main and lateral facades which look like composed of half-columns stuck to one another, floodlit in the evening by floor lamps hidden at their foot' ('Canada', 1937). This kind of analysis which implicitly refers to classical architecture may have developed because of the sketchy and poeticised design of the silo bins displayed by the Canadian pavilion's facade. Andrew Hamilton (1937) partly situated the Canadian grain elevator in the wider history of architecture. Commenting upon the Dominion's participation, he observed that 'the exterior has been fashioned after the design of a terminal grain elevator, probably a wise choice since the grain elevator is said by experts to be Canada's only contribution to modern architecture'.

Of what relevance are the Modern Movement's historiographers' analyses to the understanding of the grain elevator as representation of agricultural capital? The Canadian pavilion can be analysed as a manifestation of 'functional analogy', which Peter Collins defined as 'analogies with living organisms, machines, and bodily functions, such as human taste and speech', distinct from analogy with past architectures (Collins, 1965: 146). The Canadian building is an industrial analogy. French and Canadian buildings both match the main properties of 'modern' buildings, as described by Christian Norberg-Schulz (1975). They are both 'derived from simple stereometric shapes'; their vertical cylinders, 'appear as unitary volumes' with the accumulation of these cylinders, and 'show a puritan lack of material texture and articulating detail' with a mostly technical and functional design (Norberg-Schulz, 1975: 358). Moreover, the Canadian pavilion offered an aesthetic and synthetic interpretation of the reinforced-concrete grain elevator. Brunet, a sculptor and architect, appropriated the original concrete grain elevator, usually designed to be reproduced massively according to rational standards, in order to create an adaptation which fits within the historical continuum of architectural creativity, from antiquity to modern times (de Certeau, 1988: 31–2).

The grain elevator is not the typical building type to show the 'further development of the concepts of transparency and spatial continuity' between inside and outside and between the interior volumes, a characteristic which connects 'modern' buildings with the nineteenth century, according to Christian Norberg-Schulz (1975: 358). However, the elements in which it is related to the late eighteenth century are twofold. First, the vertical cylinders 'return to the elementary shapes and geometric relationships introduced by the revolutionary architects' (Norberg-Schulz, 1975: 358). Second, the structure can be considered as a specimen of *architecture parlante* – speaking architecture – that does not reflect the actual function of the building but refers to Canadian architectural identity and landscape.

One symbol of capital to represent two moments of everyday life

After this review and explanation of the aims and context of the French grain elevator and the Canadian pavilion, I would like to elaborate upon the interpretation one could propose of these two occurrences of the same building type identified with the concept of agricultural capital in the Paris 1937 Exposition, in terms of *production* and *consumption*.

The grain elevator allows for one stage in the physical displacement of and within the speculative process involved in cereals trading. The grain elevator had a major function in the expansion of what de Certeau called 'the scriptural economy' in his analysis of the importance of writing in a capitalist economy (1988: 131–53). The grain elevator is 'a transitional place' that receives and stores in its bins raw agricultural products to deliver ultimately a repackaged commodified product, just as 'the island of the page is a transitional place in which an industrial inversion is made: what comes in is something "received", what comes out is a "product"' (1988: 135). Both Canadian and French grain elevators stood at the crossroads. On one side there was the harvest, the *production*, 'rationalized, expansionist, and at the same time centralized, clamorous, and spectacular' (1988: xii) On the other side, there was the dispatch of goods, their sales, and then, 'another production, called "*consumption*"' described as 'devious, dispersed' and 'insinuat[ing] itself everywhere, silently and almost invisibly' (1988: xii).

Even if the type of the grain elevator inspired both buildings, the Canadian pavilion showed its different parts less distinctly than the French one did. According to Jean Favier, the facade of the Canadian pavilion 'symbolised the grain elevators', because 'agriculture is one of the resources of the country' (1938: 299), but the facade was actually

Figure 7 A Field of Golden Grain in Western Canada, *Pavillon du Canada: Exposition Internationale Paris 1937/Canadian Pavilion: International Exhibition Paris 1937* [1937], p. 24, English side.

not the reproduction, an exact replica, of a grain elevator. This dissociation from the standard model gives an opportunity for speculation and displacement. The difference between the Canadian pavilion and the French grain elevator shown in their level of detail and verisimilitude illustrates two different moments of 'the practice of everyday life', namely *production* and *consumption* (de Certeau, 1988).

The French grain elevator was a clear and faithful reproduction of a real silo which one might have found at the time in modern rural areas of France. It was not primarily a fanciful shell aimed at attracting as many visitors as possible but rather sought to educate and to promote innovation in agricultural practice. Visitors were able to follow the different steps that the grain collected by modern cooperatives went through (République Française, 1938: 164–5). The French grain elevator was at the cutting edge: technical, if not scientific. A rural engineer had been consulted to create a comprehensive example of this building in the Exposition (République Française, 1938: 164). It was a place for the *strategy* of the government to impose knowledge through symbolism (de Certeau, 1988: 32) and eventually develop in French rural areas a strategy that 's[ought] to create places in conformity with abstract models' (de Certeau, 1988: 29).

The position of power of French organisers in the exhibition allowed for the presentation of a replica of a grain elevator. The French building was victorious in spatial terms, because it presented a faithful replica of an actual grain elevator, detailing the different elements it was composed of. It conveyed ideas of modernisation, technological improvement, rationalisation and efficiency, as part of a mechanism of cultural production, within a strategy able to produce, tabulate, and 'impose [its] spaces'.

In the meantime, the situation of relative weakness of Canada as a host to visitors, but in turn a guest at an exhibition organised by the French authorities, led to the 'use, manipulation, and diversion of the space' (de Certeau, 1988: 30) – a common building type and the shared exhibition grounds, allied to the urban environment of Paris. The Canadian pavilion did not present a verisimilar replica of a grain elevator but a silhouette recalling characteristic features of the Canadian landscape and economy. The Canadian pavilion illustrated the moment of consumption in the everyday life of the grain elevator as a commodified space. The Canadian pavilion made obvious another kind of relation between the actual grain elevator and the culture it represented, by 'establish[ing] a degree of *plurality* and creativity' (de Certeau, 1988: 30) where one would first have thought in terms of standardisation – of architecture and trade. The design of the Canadian pavilion by Brunet 'metaphorized the dominant order'. Brunet became a 'practitioner manipulating knowledge and symbolism as object whereas he had not produced them' (de Certeau, 1988: 32). He appropriated the form of the grain elevator as a symbol, therefore showing his own familiarity with it, and perhaps, by extension, the proximity of Canadian society to this building type and the capitalist economy it stood for.

In a note more than likely written during the first months of 1937, an unknown Canadian civil servant explained: 'It has been our desire to make that spot as Canadian as possible and our contribution to the Exposition distinctive and outstanding.' Further on, the same writer noted: 'In form it is a replica of a Canadian grain elevator, typifying the Dominion as the world's chief supplier of wheat, and embellished by plaques, the work of a Canadian sculptor and symbolic of Canadian life and industry' (quoted in Evrard, 2003: 87). The grain elevator was an appropriate form for the exterior walls of the pavilion, since it was very common in the Canadian Prairie, especially near the rail tracks which linked the Western and Eastern Provinces of the Confederation: following the Canadian Commissioner's impression, the cylindrical silhouette of the grain bins gave an impression of the tremendous wheat producer that Canada was (Lefort, 1937). At the same time, the choice of the grain elevator reflected its common character all over the Dominion; the character of a structure that the French visitor might see while travelling across the Dominion, after having visited the Canadian exhibition in Paris.

Whereas modern architects looked for a standard architecture that would make humankind happier, some fought against this trend. The late 1930s somewhat marked the end for this international goal for modern architecture. A desire for local character was developing to inform contemporary architecture, 'International Style was the goal of the modern movement, but only a transitory stage. [...] Like any great historical movement, [Functionalism] was first of all concerned with meanings, that is, with the problem of giving man an existential foothold' (Norberg-Schulz, 1975: 388).

Actually, in the context of the 1937 Paris Exposition, the grain elevator itself provided this foothold. Essentially belonging to the kind of the *architecture parlante*, it conveyed two different messages for the two nations: the Canadian pavilion looked towards the past, with the silo becoming a landmark for the Dominion, the building most able to characterise its identity. The grain elevator had become an important illustrative form of the Canadian identity. Following a tradition that had seen early twentieth-century English-speaking painters – for instance the Group of Seven – look for the aesthetic translation of the Canadian identity in natural landscapes, the Canadian pavilion at the 1937 Paris Exposition used, more or less consciously, a striking element of the contemporary Canadian landscape to set the national identity of the Dominion on the bank of the Seine. In contrast, the French grain elevator looked forward, displaying national wealth that was to increase, and progress yet to come.

The association of parallel and displaced meanings with the form of the grain elevator is ironic when one considers that the Modern Movement's pioneers had unveiled this structure, now seen as an architectural icon, for its absence of meaning and its purely formal and functional appearance. By contrast, both French and Canadian grain elevators represented in the International Exposition a specific procedure in the commodification of the agricultural capital in a global capitalist economy.

In featuring an international standard design celebrated by the Modern Movement, the French grain elevator embodied a national *strategy* and imposed a rational symbolic order on national agriculture, in order to strengthen the national economy in front of the global agricultural market. Meanwhile, the Canadian pavilion proposed a creative design that referred to the building type of the grain elevator, and made visible a sort of national familiarity with the grain elevator. The Canadian *tactic* was international, speaking to the widest audience thanks to engaging displays and a popularised technical building type. Between past, present and future, Canadian and French grain elevator buildings were a striking case of both speculation and displacement in the representation of agricultural capital, one reflecting a recent but nonetheless strong history, and the other picturing the potential transformations of the economic and social environment.

Note

1. The author thanks the anonymous reviewers for their helpful suggestions, and Robert J. Balfour for his support in this project. Special thanks to Philip Whalen, Coastal Carolina University, for sharing his knowledge and thoughts about agricultural promotional techniques in 1930s France.

10
Finance and Film: Wall Street Myth and Mythopoeia

Elton G. McGoun

Introduction

There is a scene in the film *Boiler Room* (2000) in which the central characters are watching a scene from the 1987 film *Wall Street*. The character of Gordon Gekko is introduced in this scene. They are shown reciting the dialogue along with the characters on the screen. This explicit intertextual reference means that there is something about the scene in *Wall Street* that is relevant to *Boiler Room*. The scene in *Wall Street* is also relevant to the culture of financial markets. Gordon Gekko is a representation of a recurrent American archetype that is attractive not only to the characters in *Boiler Room* but also to participants in real financial markets. This archetype not only drives the plots of films, but also affects the performance of real financial markets in which manipulation is a well-publicised occurrence.

One of the puzzles of financial markets is the recurrent pattern of manipulation that has been observed over the past century and a half or so in the United States. Why is it that regulation and enforcement, however rigorous, have never been able to been able to eliminate it? The usual answer is that there will always be a few bad apples whose greed will get the better of them, and the best anyone can hope to do is to catch the miscreants quickly and punish them severely enough to deter others. Indeed, one of the most famous scenes in *Wall Street* is Gordon Gekko's speech extolling the virtues of greed. Is it so surprising that such a powerful drive as greed cannot easily be confined within legal boundaries by either individuals or institutions, especially when it may be not only beneficial if properly channelled, but may be necessary for the efficient operation of financial markets?

This chapter asserts that the manipulation of financial markets is not the exceptional excess of a few individuals but an underlying condition inherent in American culture that is magnified in certain environments such as that of the contemporary financial scene. Although regulation and enforcement may appear to suppress manipulation, they actually play a role in its perpetuation. In the next section I discuss the reasons why the apparently evil Gordon Gekko has such an attraction for the *Wall Street* audience and the expression of this attraction in *Boiler Room*. Section three describes the American myths which have influenced the delineation of the character of Gordon Gekko. I shall conclude in the final section with an explanation of the ongoing process of mythopoeia by which Wall Street reproduces Gordon Gekko of *Wall Street*.

Gordon Gekko in *Wall Street*

The character of Gordon Gekko in the film *Wall Street* was intended to represent conventional evil. In an interview published in the journal *American Film* (Cockburn, 1987), the writer and director Oliver Stone described *Wall Street* as 'basically a *Pilgrim's Progress* of a boy who is seduced, corrupted by the allure of easy money' (Cockburn, 1987: 22). Indeed, this is a mythic theme that runs throughout Stone's films (Mackey-Kallis, 1996), and there are frequent references in the literature on *Wall Street* to Stone's use of the same 'good father/bad father/ redemption' theme he used in his preceding film *Platoon* (Kagan, 1995; Stone, 2000).

At least one reviewer of the film comments on the skill with which Stone conveys the seductiveness of evil, and other reviews suggest that seductive villains are a cinematic staple at whose portrayal Stone is especially adept. In a piece written years after the release of the film, Stone discusses the attraction of Gordon Gekko:

> Several critics of Wall Street complained about its black–white moralizing. Some identified it as 'Wall Street bashing'. But if anything, in view of the responses I've received through the years, it seems to me the opposite is true. Gordon Gekko (Michael Douglas) turns out to be, perversely, the most seductive character in the piece ... Gordon Gekko became a devil, a Mephistopheles for the 1980s. And yet he was a hero to so many young people of that and this hyped-up time. People still come up to me all over the world, exclaiming, 'Great movie! I loved Gordon Gekko!' If he was so blackly painted, how was it that people liked him so much and Michael Douglas won an

Academy Award as best actor in 1987? Is this black and white? His oft-quoted 'Greed is good' speech is interesting, as he at many points represents a commonsense point of view. Sometimes the things that are the most dangerous to us are also the most seductive, as in the case of Charlie Sheen. The movie is about excess – the excesses of capitalism. (Toplin, 2000: 231)

In this quotation, Stone observes that Gordon Gekko is more than a character who displays the trappings of power and wealth with flamboyance and *brio*. He also makes sense, and he does so in a perverse way that mocks the capitalist system in which he thrives.

In the end, though, what makes the character of Gordon Gekko so attractive? Is it what he has, what he says, or what he does? Is he a well-written and well-played character who just happens to be evil or an even better-written and better-played character who skilfully shows the seductiveness of evil? If he is indeed still 'a hero to so many young people', as Stone claims, why is this? Do they want to own what Gordon Gekko owned? Do they want to do what Gordon Gekko did, in his business as well as in his private life? Do they subscribe to his philosophy that greed is good, at least in financial market activities? Do they admire his candour? Are they simply the latest in a long line of impressionable young people who have fallen under the mesmerising spell of evil?

The familiar answer is essentially 'yes' to all of the above. We have Gordon Gekkos who break laws and manipulate markets because the power to do so, and the wealth from doing so, are such temptations that there will always be those willing to do likewise. We can reduce the number of Gordon Gekkos by being more diligent at rooting them out and raising the price they must pay for their transgressions, but we can never eliminate them entirely. The real answer may be more subtle.

As Oliver Stone himself stated, Gordon Gekko did indeed become *a*, if not *the*, 'Mephistopheles for the 1980s'. Current references to him on the Internet are not rare, especially in reviews of the more recent film *Boiler Room*. It is to be expected that the references to *Wall Street* should appear in reviews of the film *Boiler Room*, since there are few films in which finance plays a central role and no others have been as popular as these two. It is difficult to make the subject of finance exciting enough for a film, let alone comprehensible enough for a non-specialist audience to figure out what is going on.[1] But a more prominent link between the two films is the reference mentioned at the beginning of this chapter. In the opening scene of *Boiler Room*, already described earlier in this chapter, the central characters watch a scene from *Wall Street* in which the character of Gordon Gekko is introduced. They are shown reciting the dialogue along with the characters on the screen within a screen. Many reviewers comment on this and draw parallels with obsessed fans of other films, books and music.

There are three possible explanations for this significant connection to *Wall Street* within *Boiler Room*. The first is that it attaches *Boiler Room* to the very successful *Wall Street* to benefit from the reputation of, and audience familiarity with, *Wall Street*. In the terminology of the 'Nashville Scene' review of *Boiler Room* in WeeklyWire.com (2000), such an explicit reference by one film to another is called a 'kickstand'. A kickstand allows one film to benefit from another without being accused of plagiarism, because the earlier film on which the later film is modelled is clearly named.[2] The second explanation for the connection is that the behaviour of the characters in *Boiler Room* is clarified for the audience through the implied comparison and/or contrast with Gordon Gekko. The third, and most provocative, explanation of the connection is its suggestion that our own behaviour is derived from the media we view. In other words, *Boiler Room* is telling us that Wall Street becomes *Wall Street*.

There are also similarities between Gordon Gekko and the character of Eric Packer in DeLillo's novel *Cosmopolis* (2003): their wealth, their power, their retinue, and at least at the beginning of both the film and the novel, their isolation in their office (Gekko) or limousine (Packer) from any world other than that of wealth, power and retinue. There might, however, be a stronger parallel between Packer and another character in *Wall Street*, Bud Fox. While *Cosmopolis* traces Packer's journey from the prestigious East Side of Manhattan to the derelict West Side, Wall Street follows Fox from his tiny apartment on the West Side to a spacious penthouse on the East Side. Yet if we consider Fox to be retracing the path of a younger Gekko, as the film clearly suggests, then the younger Packer is in fact the future of the older Gekko.

Wall Street and *Boiler Room* illustrate that a character in a film who exerts an attraction on an audience, in this case Gordon Gekko, can be perpetuated in the culture:

> films and TV programs are hardly simple mechanisms for reflecting reality; instead, they are the reality on which many viewers draw for ideas about the world around them. In other words, many spectators construct their views of the world in terms of the

mass-produced, profit-minded imagery that bombards them daily. (Norden, 2000: 52)

All characters in films come out of the culture of the writers, director and actors. Gordon Gekko is believed to have been modelled on an unnamed friend of Oliver Stone (Biskind, 1987; Cockburn, 1987) as well as on Ivan Boesky, T. Boone Pickens and Carl Icahn (Fridson, 2000). What specifically is it, though, about the character of Gordon Gekko that leads to his appearance in *Wall Street* and then allows him to achieve a life beyond that film, as suggested by *Boiler Room*?

The Wall Street Myth

On the strength of the evidence presented in the previous section concerning the cinematic significance of the role of Gordon Gekko in *Wall Street* and the cultural significance of the role which was perceived after the film's release, this section begins with the assertion that 'Gordon Gekko is a mythic figure'. This is one of those statements that on the surface seems to make perfect sense but which upon deeper reflection becomes problematic. What does it mean to say that someone, real or imaginary, is a 'mythic figure', and is Gordon Gekko indeed one of these? According to Joseph Campbell, 'When a person becomes a model for other people's lives, he has moved into the sphere of being mythologized' (Campbell, 1986: 15).[3] Gordon Gekko surely qualifies in terms of this simple criterion, to which the referential scene in *Boiler Room* attests. But 'myth' is a common term that is confusingly used in a number of ways.

Von Hendy (2002) identifies three modern uses of the word 'myth' that arose out of the original romantic use: the folkloristic, the ideological and the constitutive.[4] Folkloristic myths are familiar stories passed on within an oral culture. Ideological myths are widespread falsehoods which transform the historical into the natural and the contingent into the eternal (Barthes, 1972). Constitutive myths are any beliefs central to a culture.

> The romantic mode assumes the capacity for transcendental mythopoeia to be a permanent possession of humanity. The ideological agrees about the permanent possession but adopts a negative stance of suspicion toward its products. The constitutive ... accepts this mythopoeia, true or false, as a constant of consciousness. Only the folkloristic mode can be understood to imply that myth is solely or nearly always a thing of remote times or exotic cultures. (Von Hendy, 2002: 303)

Romantic myth

Although some may facetiously refer to Wall Street as an 'exotic culture', financial markets are iconic images of modernity. *Wall Street* was not set in a remote time or place, and it is not a folkloristic myth. Yet it could be argued that the characters and events of Wall Street and *Wall Street* are modern manifestations of the archetypal structures of human minds, and as such, *Wall Street* is a romantic myth. Indeed, the simple opposition of good (Carl Fox) and evil (Gordon Gekko) in *Wall Street* is characteristic of myth.

Jung (1968) believed that humanity shared a collective unconscious of archetypes, and that every culture from the primitive to the modern employs archetypal images, conscious representations of these unconscious instincts, in narratives (or myths) appropriate to the particular time and place (Walker, 1995). Consider the following, which could have been written about Carl Fox and Gordon Gekko as well as about Stevenson's *Dr. Jekyll and Mr. Hyde* (1963):

> When interpreting the story from a Jungian standpoint, it is important to notice that, for Stevenson's Dr. Jekyll, the figure of Mr. Hyde contains not only evil tendencies but also a kind of repressed *vitality* ('the liberty, the light step, leaping impulses and secret pleasures that I had enjoyed in the disguise of Hyde'). This vitality is in some ways potentially life-enhancing and if properly integrated could have been a valuable addition to Jekyll's conscious personality. For the shadow is not all evil. For Jung, 'the shadow is merely somewhat inferior, primitive, unadapted and awkward; not wholly bad. It even contains childish or primitive qualities which would in a way vitalize and embellish human existence, but convention forbids.' (Walker, 1995: 40)

Is this the attraction of Gordon Gekko? That he represents an instinct deep within all of us that, allowed to manifest itself in modest proportion, would 'vitalize and embellish' our lives but that allowed to become dominant would destroy us as it did Bud Fox and the *Boiler Room* brokers? Does rigorous financial market regulation and enforcement repress inherent tendencies towards market manipulation that would in measured doses 'vitalize and embellish' the *social*, if not necessarily the purely *economic* performance of financial markets?

The French structuralists Detienne and Vernant (1978) have discovered in Greek mythology a primary element they call 'cunning intelligence' (*mètis*) (Champagne, 1992). They believe cunning intelligence to be a universal trait and have identified it in Sumerian myths and relate it to the Jungian archetype of the 'trickster' (Detienne and Vernant, 1978). As a trait which is shared by humans and animals and which stresses the contingent rather than the absolute, they remark that its earlier recognition was hindered by Platonism and Christianity, with their beliefs in the superiority of humanity and the existence of absolute truth (Champagne, 1992; Detienne and Vernant, 1978). The animal names 'Gekko' and 'Fox' in *Wall Street*, on which reviewers frequently comment, may reflect the origins in the animal world of Gordon Gekko's and, subsequently, Bud Fox's cunning intelligence.[5]

It will be useful to quote a more detailed description of cunning intelligence offered by Detienne and Vernant:

> In every confrontation or competitive situation – whether the adversary be a man, an animal or a natural force – success can be won by two means, either thanks to a superiority in 'power' in the particular sphere in which the contest is taking place, with the stronger gaining the victory; or by the use of methods of a different order whose effect is, precisely, to reverse the natural outcome of the encounter and to allow victory to fall to the party whose defeat had appeared inevitable. Thus success obtained through *mètis* can be seen in two different ways. Depending on the circumstances it can arouse opposite reactions. In some cases it will be considered the result of cheating, since the rules of the game have been disregarded. In others, the more surprise it provokes the greater the admiration it will arouse, the weaker party having, against every expectation, found within himself resources capable of putting the stronger at his mercy. Certain aspects of *mètis* tend to associate it with the disloyal trick, the perfidious lie, treachery – all of which are the despised weapons of women and cowards [*sic*]. But others make it seem more precious than strength. It is, in a sense, the absolute weapon, the only one that has the power to ensure victory and domination over others, whatever the circumstances, whatever the conditions of the conflict. In effect, whatever the strength of a man or a god, there always comes a time when he confronts one stronger than himself. (Detienne and Vernant, 1978: 13)

The first part of this quotation may make us hesitant to attribute Gordon Gekko's attraction to his cunning. Throughout the movie, his palpable financial and personal power is expressed in many ways. For the most part, he is not the underdog and has no need of *mètis*.

But there are two forces in the film that are stronger. The first is Sir Lawrence (Larry) Wildman, whose takeover of Anacott Steel is impeded by Gekko's (and Fox's) cunning intelligence. The second is the US Securities and Exchange Commission (SEC). Throughout the film, Gekko displays his use of cunning intelligence to avoid government detection of his illegal trading activities and teaches his tactics to Fox. Although the film is deliberately vague concerning Gekko's fate, one cannot help but suspect that through cunning intelligence, he will manage, unlike Fox, to avoid spending time in prison for his crimes.

Does anyone who watches *Wall Street* really want Gordon Gekko to be caught and to be severely punished? His use of his cunning intelligence against the SEC, and our response to it, expresses a telling ambiguity in our attitudes towards government regulation. Certainly we regard what he does as 'disloyal tricks, perfidious lies, and treachery', and 'the rules of the game have been disregarded', but who did he hurt, and was this done maliciously? Wasn't he just testing his cunning intelligence against his opponents in the government? Are the regulators beneficent powers who are there to protect us and whom we want to obey, or are they adversarial powers there to oppress us which we are almost duty-bound to oppose?

Whether one believes in Jung's collective unconscious or not, one has to acknowledge that the characters and plots in contemporary films and novels frequently resemble the characters and plots in what we call myths. How is it that those characters and plots retain their appeal to us, independent of the times and places in which we set them? Myths can only survive because the values they express are the values of the cultures within which the myths are handed down. And of course the myths will also play a role in perpetuating those values. Are we attracted to Gordon Gekko because he displays the cunning intelligence we already admire and exhibit, or do we admire Gordon Gekko's cunning intelligence and seek to emulate it? Either way, something of the ancient Greeks' value for *mètis* survives and thrives within financial markets.

Constitutive myth

Recall that a constitutive myth is any belief central to a culture. As Wright puts it, 'Myths always offer instructive, entertaining models of appropriate social actions, actions that are compatible with dominant institutions' (Wright, 2001: 2). We may therefore search a little closer to home in time and place for evidence that Gordon Gekko is a mythic figure in the constitutive sense. The Western is clearly a constitutive myth of American culture, and there is a massive body of literature on the myths of the Old West which makes it clear that these myths are not just of that particular time and place but embody deeper American values, especially the individualism that underpins financial markets.

The mythical cowboy was born in the wide-open spaces of the frontier. With the closing of the frontier, however, substitute frontiers had to be discovered where deserving individuals could have equal opportunity for success, unencumbered by the disadvantage of having been born into the wrong social class. The cowboy can be transplanted to an urban environment, but not without certain changes in character. Whether on the Western range or on the Eastern streets, there is a strong anti-authoritarian streak in the cowboy, reflecting the same streak running through American culture.

> American popular culture tends to focus on heroes who defy established authority. They defy established laws and rules – government, corporations, bureaucracy – to defend individual freedom. The cowboy is the individualist hero, the symbol of market freedom, and he often has to break the law to maintain a decent society, a society of freedom and equality ... On the open frontier the citizens can be civil, but in the industrial city virtually no one can be trusted. The individualist hero is denounced as a 'cowboy' because he breaks laws and rules. (Wright, 2001: 44)

The notion of a 'hero' being denounced as a 'cowboy' is a peculiar one. Cowboys are not heroes in American culture in spite of their defiance of authority, but because of it. Yet the 'government, corporations, bureaucracy' and the 'laws and rules' that the cowboy defies are also part of American culture, which is apparently desirous of subverting that which it has created. The same culture which is responsible for the Securities and Exchange Commission that Gordon Gekko deceives also finds him attractive and emulates him, even in his extreme acts.

Perhaps the solution to this conundrum is that disruption is as much a social necessity as stability. We need rule-makers to preserve order and rule-breakers to prevent stagnation. This means, however, that rules and laws have no real moral force, but are more or less temporary expedients. It is always the duty of someone to challenge them and test them so that we know when it is time to overturn them. We have myths to help us with this conflict.

In this sense the cowboy version of charisma is fundamentally an image of individualist disruption, that is, of constant innovation and criticism. Weber envisioned charisma as disruption leading to order, and the cowboy is an image of disruption as a source of order, the market order of laissez-faire. All societies need stability and rules, but the market also needs innovation and criticism. It needs new ideas, new technology, entrepreneurs, even visionaries. People who do these things are always disruptive, but they also keep the market efficient and productive. The cowboy is the opposite of the bureaucrat, and both are necessary in a rational industrial society. (Wright, 2001: 119)

In short, the Western's myth of the cowboy in its guise as the myth of Wall Street essentially justifies market manipulation. There is nothing wrong with evading governmental constraints on the individual's freedom to pursue wealth in financial markets, and while physical violence is out-of-bounds, assaults on economic interests are allowed. Gordon Gekko is vindicated.

The Western is the market myth of origin and its imagery pervades market culture, the imagery of the lonesome cowboy and the wild frontier. It endorses market freedom, equal opportunity, private property, limited government, and constant expansion. It also endorses violence as a necessity of freedom, legitimate resistance to government, the need for an endless frontier, the need for wilderness purity, and white male superiority. (Wright, 2001: 189)

Gekko is not, however, completely vindicated. A law has to be seen to be corrupt in order for breaking it to be seen as justified. All attempts at an objective definition of manipulation lead to circularity (Easterbrook, 1986; Fishel and Ross, 1991). Fishel and Ross conclude that there can only be subjective definitions of manipulation, which must include intent. A manipulation without fraud can only be distinguished by the intent of the trader to engage in manipulation, which the trader is unlikely to reveal and which is difficult to prove without documents, wiretaps or the testimony of co-conspirators (Gastineau and Jarrow, 1991). Although it might not be corrupt, it is not so difficult to see the law concerning manipulation as unfair.

Clearly, then, Gordon Gekko displays the cunning intelligence of Greek myth and plays the role of the cowboy which originated in the Wild West myth. He might indeed be a mythic figure, as was asserted at the beginning of this section, in either the romantic or the constitutive senses but not in the folkloric sense. That this fictional character is admired and emulated is evidence that myth does play a role in financial market behaviour. But what of the remaining sense of myth, the ideological?

Wall Street mythopoeia

Recall that ideological myths are widespread falsehoods which transform the historical into the natural and the contingent into the eternal. How is it that Wall Street and *Wall Street* both engage in mythopoeia, and do those myths reflect the 'truth' or mask it with a falsehood that appears to be the 'truth'?

The following was written to describe the myths of the Wild West, but as explained in the preceding section, important elements of these myths are shared by Wall Street:

> If individuals are rational, they can live in a civil society as opposed to a sacred society. In a civil society, all social relations – all institutions, laws, and government – are based on rational agreements, not on sacred authority. A civil social order can only be arranged by rational citizens to serve their private interests. It cannot be imposed by a dominant class in the name of divine truth. A civil society, then, must be committed to individual equality, in the sense of equal opportunity ... This vision of civil society legitimated market ideas, the ideas of freedom and equality, the idea of private property. Rational individuals will generate social relations based on market competition, and market competition in turn will generate a civil society. (Wright, 2001: 3)

Certainly, rational behaviour is the *sine qua non* when financial behaviour is modelled, but is Wall Street really rational? This is apt to be a controversial question. If it were not, would so much time be spent modelling financial behaviour on a rational basis? But if it were, would not financial models have had greater empirical success and would there be such a thing as behavioural finance? The important point is that rationality is indeed an essential component of the ideology of Wall Street (Frankfurter and McGoun, 1999), and the point of behavioural finance seems to be less a positive description of how people behave than a normative prescription of how they ought to (Frankfurter, McGoun and Allen 2004). In effect, rationality is an ideological myth of Wall Street.

This myth of rationality is not the only Wall Street myth which can be challenged. Is it really a place where deserving individuals have equal opportunity for success, unencumbered by the disadvantage of having been born into the wrong social class? It is certainly not a place where they have equal opportunity for success if they are disadvantaged by the wrong gender. Annie Oakley (Riley, 1997) notwithstanding, cowgirls have never achieved the mythic status of cowboys, and no woman has been the hero of a finance film. Anna Schuman came the closest in the obscure 1989 film *Dealers*, but she eventually deferred to her 'cowboy' employee Daniel Pascoe. Lee Winters was a powerful figure in *Rollover*, but she managed to single-handedly destroy the global economic system, albeit without losing the love of Hubble Smith. The only significant female character in *Wall Street*, Darien Taylor, was a bimbo – the other women in the film being prostitutes or wives more concerned with bikini waxes than finance. And with the exception of Seth, who had a minor romance with the secretary Abby, the brokers in *Boiler Room* were blatantly misogynistic.

The film *Wall Street* was criticised for being unrealistic, or at most depicting a small minority of bad apples in an otherwise honest and hard-working barrel (Fabrikant, 1987). But realism is not the point of myth.

> In the cowboy myth the characters and actions reflect the legitimating concerns of individualist theory, not the historical reality of the American West. So the general cultural message concerns the proper social behavior for a rational market society. The myth offers images of success and happiness, risk and failure, and through these images it tells us how to think and act in a market individualist context … All mythical stories provide entertaining support for their social institutions. In the process, they expose and humanize the organizing principles of those institutions. In market society the mythical stories complete and reinforce market theory, turning abstract discussions of rational individuals into dramatic images of human people … The myth shows how the theory should work in ordinary social relations, so it often reveals dimensions of the abstract theory that were hidden behind the abstractions. (Wright, 2001: 141)

Perhaps Stone's objective was to portray Gordon Gekko as an archcapitalist who is in fact an anti-capitalist and who exposes capitalism's excesses.

> By turning outlaws into functional approximations of detectives, these dime novels augment the moral authority of the outlaw as symbol of a critical stance toward the ideology and practice of industrial

and finance capitalism. If not the agent of an identifiable class or coherent political party, the outlaw – when legitimated in this way – at least voices a generalized discontent with the managerial order and its leadership. (Slotkin, 1992: 150–1)

In the end, it is not so surprising that Gordon Gekko is a hero to be emulated, not only by the brokers in *Boiler Room*, but by members of the film audience who work or who aspire to work on Wall Street.

> The problem for those who attempt to destroy this hero is that the popular hero is in many of his guises a rebel, and remains so in resistance to efforts to formalize and domesticate him. America's great national heroes – Washington is the pre-eminent example – are rebels. They are men who do not conform, who think and act independently. The West gave scope to men like this. Men who found the institutions of the East constricting tended to go West, just as men who found Europe too slow-moving, tied to archaic social and political structures, tended to make hopefully for America … [T]he American people show an inclination to adopt men like Jesse James and Clyde Barrow, or men who exemplified the road from rags to riches, for both kinds of hero were challenging the existing structure of society. (Calder, 1974: 190)

Of course we can never prove or disprove the effect that Gordon Gekko and the myths he represents have on financial markets:

> Are they agents of social change, or passive mirrors? To drag an old chestnut out of the fire, do artists and filmmakers simply reflect, or transform their age? And who will ever prove in which order? … We are left with what common sense tells us: any art form or medium both reflects and shapes the culture around it … Their audiences respond, assimilate a created image, and sometimes act according to its message. (O'Brien, 1990: 20)

We can, however, still speculate. American culture values cunning intelligence, and perhaps never more than when it is employed to challenge authority and break the bureaucratic rules and laws that keep the individual from realising *his* (not yet *her*) full potential.

In his history of financial speculation, Chancellor (1999) quotes David Hume's conventional explanation for the recurrence of speculation: '[a]varice, or desire of gain, is a universal passion which operates at all times, in all places, and upon all persons', wrote Hume in the eighteenth century (Chancellor, 1999: 57). He later quotes Josephson's explanation, more in line with the one we have presented in this chapter:

> Like the generals of the Civil War, the leading operators attracted public adulation. As Matthew Josephson wrote in *The Robber Barons*, 'If the doctrine of the nation favored an ideal of free and equal opportunity for all, so its current folklore glorified the freebooting citizen who by his own efforts, by whatever method feasible, had wrested for himself a power that flung its shadow upon the liberties and privileges of others. (Chancellor, 1999: 160–1)

We admire Gordon Gekko of *Wall Street* and the other Gekkos of Wall Street for their audacious attacks on the *status quo*, and we are entertained by their activities. The manipulations on Wall Street are as diverting as the manipulations in *Wall Street*. And as one reviewer in the *New York Post* wrote, 'the laws are sort of like the referee in pro wrestling, part of the show'. At the same time, however, we cannot ignore the more serious message: that 'cowboy' iconoclasts are not merely entertaining but are socially and economically necessary. In order to avoid stagnation, we need the rules not only to be challenged, but even to be broken. Gordon Gekko of *Wall Street* and the Gekkos of Wall Street are not only perversely, but also justifiably, admired. There is good reason for their having become an important part of the myths of American culture. Wall Street itself, assisted by the media, is engaged in an ongoing process of mythopoiea in which we seek to accommodate our conflicting feelings concerning the opposition between the law-makers and law-breakers, both of which our culture has created and both of which it needs.

Notes

1. The 1979 film *Rollover* is an important predecessor of *Wall Street* and *Boiler Room* in the history of the genre, but it was not popular, and most reviewers found the plot incomprehensible. Oliver Stone has said that *Rollover* showed him 'what *not* to do' (Silet, 2001: 7).
2. A number of reviewers also note the plot elements that *Boiler Room* borrows from *Wall Street*. Supposedly Seth is driven to become a stockbroker in an effort to earn the respect of his father the judge, and the two brokers Chris and Greg could be considered the good and evil influences on him.
3. Later Campbell comments: '[Movies] might be our counterpart to mythological re-enactments ... but what is unfortunate for us is that a lot of the people who write these stories do not have the sense of their responsibility. These

stories are making and breaking lives' (Campbell, 1986: 82). MacDonald (1987) and Wallmann (1999) also comment on the use of media, including film, to propagate myths: 'Certainly in the case of the United States in the 1950s and 1960s, the [Western] genre was intended as neither calculated indoctrination nor historical reconstruction. Yet just as surely as the mythology of ancient Greece and Rome explained and sanctified the social arrangements of those civilizations, televised tales of the Old West were meaningful secularized American myths that analogously served their particular public' (MacDonald, 1987: 78). 'I do not mean myth in the sense of quaintly parochial stories like fables and fairy tales, but rather in the more profound sense as the spiritual and intellectual explanations of a culture's values – of how the people of a culture view themselves and how their culture fits into the world. This form of mythology is integral to every culture, including America, and is expressed through storytelling in literature and now in such media as film and television' (Wallmann, 1999: 8–9).
4. For simplicity, this chapter uses these terms as adjectives to describe myths. It is more accurate, however, to say that something is a 'myth in the romantic sense' or a 'myth from the perspective of the romantic mode', for example, rather than to say that it is a 'romantic myth'.
5. Along with the octopus, the fox is an animal outstanding for its *mètis* (Detienne and Vernant, 1992).

11
Conclusion: Re-presenting Capital in Culture: the Necessary Persistence of Memory in a New Century

Robert J. Balfour

In the first decade of the early twenty-first century, and despite the promises of globalisation, ideas about the value of labour, education, race and gender can still be gauged in terms of long-established conflicts. Walking down King Dinizulu Street in Durban (South Africa), one cannot help but read the signs. Wildly popular evangelical and Pentecostal churches advertise openly the relationship between membership of these communities and success in life; between leading a worthy life in the eyes of such communities, and the measure of rewards to be bestowed on the faithful. Such rewards are material and are spelt out for the reader in the following terms: freedom from financial worry, and the accrual of wealth in this life; success in relationships and a commensurate abundance of offspring. The list is long. Not far from the street corner churches of modern urban Africa, are the markets of herbalists; again the list of ills may be remedied by a list of cures associated with specified costs (and thus value); the price to be paid for 'curing a bad boss; failure in bed; childlessness, or an illness', and so on. In short, there is nothing to which a price cannot be affixed, and no cure beyond an ascribed value. Durban is an erstwhile colonial city, and while not the current or even historic legislative centre (its sister city in the interior, Pietermaritzburg, has a longer history and legislative function) it is nevertheless the economic centre for the province of KwaZulu-Natal and as such derives much of its current wealth from old relationships between land, labour and capital. The changing relationship between these three elements has been the subject of this book, portrayed variously with reference to cultural artefacts over the past three hundred years. And, as if to demonstrate the increasingly remote relationship between value and its signifier (money), the book presents each 'turn' as an opportunity for illumination of the tension inherent between that which is produced, its established worth or value in terms of its context (geographical, political, cultural and economic), and the agents responsible for its commodification. As speculative capital gained ascendancy over a period of three centuries, so too did the fissures become greater between value and its increasingly disassociated commodity base. The book represents this development as a historical continuity, but does not take as its evidence a history of industrial or economic development, or a history of discovery, conquest or migration, but rather the relationships between specific cultural artefacts, and the periods chosen for special focus.

In general, this book has taken as its unit of analysis a variety of genres and artefacts, not all of which are linguistically signified, but all of which have been explored in scholarship and variously described at different times in the past three centuries. It is such descriptions (whether of tombstone epithets as the subject of poems, of pamphlets about grain storage providers, or reportage of canals and railways cut deep into Panama, or films about megalomaniac millionaires, or novels about counterfeit value and speculative relationships) that this book focuses upon in order to create, paradoxically, out of its very variegated facets, a more considered understanding of value and worth, and capital, in relation to human endeavour and relationships over time. This evidence, I suggest, cannot be established merely through an analysis of economic trends, or through the impact of great conflicts and equally great enforced migrations (such as the indentured Indian labourers of KwaZulu-Natal who were imported in the 1860s to compensate for the more intransigent local population) (Henning, 1993). Rather, what is attempted here is a cultural history of capital, or the enculturation of capital to demonstrate its impact on behaviour, values and value over time. Examples provided in the book also attest to value as divorced entirely from any articulated system of values, or what is often referred to as the 'discipline of the market' which is 'self-regulating'.

In particular, this chapter reviews the arguments made in previous chapters and draws from each the threads which serve to enable a coherence of themes and concerns to emerge. The concluding sections draw these observations from phenomena that, while they might be associated with particular epochs (for example, colonialism), remain pertinent in the first few decades of the new century. What emerges is that old forms of conflict, competition and cultural worth, remain powerful, even if in residual form, in what has commonly come to be described as the age of globalisation (see Castells, 2000). The focus in this chapter on the features of globalisation is deliberate since the range of evidence presented, and the arguments created for its consideration, suggest that while discourse of globalisation suggests closer proximity, mobility and access to opportunities, the practices of globalisation appear to be influenced by ideas of race, gender and power associated with Western metropolitan centres, going back to the Renaissance and Enlightenment.

Chapter 1 opened with a description of the uses of Irish labour, produce and land, developed by Sir William Petty on the eve of the eighteenth century in which the connections between value, labour and the regulation of a colonised market within which the value of labour is predetermined, is speculated upon. The retrieval of the Irish colonial experience in demonstrating how the discipline of economics and its discourses and assumptions developed, as evident in the *Modest Proposal* by Sir William Petty, is a powerful start to the book. Many of the themes articulated by Petty are articulated in a discourse that is disturbing if only because it echoes down into the twentieth century's ideologies concerning race and intelligence, and race and gender and may be found in the writings of social scientists, anthropologists, novelists, artists, poets, indeed the whole spectrum of 'cultural practitioners'. The book takes its cue from this beginning and its organisation on a chronological basis has served to illustrate aspects of this, and related arguments, in subsequent chapters. However, because we have been concerned here with the representation of capital, the book has not restricted itself only to analyses of race and gender binaries in relation to value, worth and capital.

If Petty's argument serves to signal, at a critical juncture in the history of English imperialism, the value of speculation in terms of the precise commodification of an entire population (in this case the Irish) for purposes of exploitation, the *Autobiography* of Benjamin Franklin is another moment, this time serving to create and make clear those links that have come be established in the literature and cultural artefacts (film, art, products) of the West, between value and behaviour and the value of right behaviour in relation to the profits and losses associated with a system in which profit comes to be distinguished from luxury. The discussion of Franklin's *Autobiography* in Chapter 2 stands for the synchronising of behaviour with capital; a notion to which cultural studies and economics commentators returned even in the late twentieth century, to better understand the complexities and challenges associated with the impulse to measure worldly success in terms of moral standing and financial gain.

Great writers of this time such as Defoe or Swift were aware of the tensions between value and a changing notion of moral worth and it was Defoe who famously noted that this was the time when 'people who sell' began to matter more than 'people who make'. Even at these early moments in which the industrial revolution was already beginning to change relationships between produce, the land and people trading in both, the moral well-being of the populace was still an important focus of social commentary. And, far from revealing the thinking of these times to be less mature, or more muddled than our understanding of modern economic complexities, Chapter 3 shows that Swift and other commentators were concerned about the implications of increasing national debt, of conspicuous consumption (then referred to as luxury), moral retardation, unemployment (or what we refer now to as surplus labour) and exploitation, whether of a colonial or domestic kind. The inability of a nation, or community, or class of person, to 'live within its sphere' suggested to Defoe and Swift and many others of the day that society could not sustain itself and would ultimately unravel, waste resources, and reduce the quality of its relationships. Contemporary economic scholarship has given this concept to many other fields and we refer to it now in a number of guises not least of which is the term 'sustainability', which might equally have denoted the ability to live within one's sphere. In Swift's terms luxury comes to stand for speculative capital; in other words, that wealth which is produced not by labour, but rather by the profit which results from the trading of differing ideas of labour's value. These ideas of value are shown in the first instance to be understood by scholars as occurring within the common discourse of the day.

Thus while Franklin could equate behaviour and action with a commercial value, barely a century later the religious ideologies of a previous age were increasingly ascribed and associated with value as may be seen in the commodification of value in the discourse of epitaphic poetry; or poetry memorialising death as discussed in Chapter 4. Theoretically rich in its reflections on how language creates value and the extent to which profit may be gained from ideas of value which are deferred into the future based on the investments made in the present, the epitaphic poetry of Gray and Wordsworth was written at the same time that Adam Smith provided Western thought with its first modern approach to economics as dissociated from the private realm of human transaction as evident in the religious discourse (epitaphs on tombstones) of the eighteenth century. In the introduction to this book I referred to the deferred value encountered in paper money which stands for a social contract to provide to the bearer of the paper note the worth of the currency in gold. In this contract the state stands for God as the assurer of value, yet it is the corruption of such value which is extrapolated in later chapters which deal with the growing association of such values (whether of stock market bonds, or of national currencies) with speculation; speculation not only in the value of the currency or the bond itself, but also in the ventures underpinning such values which came to be removed from the gold standard in the early part of the twentieth century. That development was prefigured in the last half of the previous century in which bubbles, fevers and rushes characterised the heyday of colonial and imperial exploitation.

It is in the nineteenth century that anxieties articulated in the eighteenth century enter the popular imagination through fiction, travel writing and journalism. While Joseph Conrad explored the depths of depravity and greed in novels like *Lord Jim* (1899) and *Heart of Darkness* (1902), journalists such as Winthrop were developing a new genre – the travelogue which coincided with the heyday of empire. In this book it is suggested that the language of such reportage drew heavily on the literary tropes available at the time. Thus the associations of fever with economic and material avarice, illness, and exploits and adventures in alien climes, find their articulation in narratives such as *Isthmiana* (1863) accompanying the economic initiatives and expansion of a major capitalist power: the United States of America. Surveying the broad range of journalism about a phenomenon such as the Panama Railway, and its associated California Gold Rush, the chapters in the book that deal with the nineteenth century delineate the impact of speculation as an activity which was central to imperial exploits (whether these be diamond prospecting by British companies, or the gold prospectors of American companies around the globe). Of interest to the reader in Chapter 5 is that these themes echo those of the previous century in which it becomes clear that the economic, as a sphere (and later as a discipline), has never been able to divorce itself from the emotional (the speculative) precisely because notions of value become speculative when capital is divorced from product – a theme which recurs in the chapters dealing with the eighteenth and nineteenth centuries respectively.

Postcolonial and gender scholars have pointed to contradictions of imperial ideologies and the economic narratives of this period offer rich trajectories in which such contradictions are articulated. The conditions of 'fever' applied not only to the national and colonial imaginations in which such fevers are represented as madness in the journalism of the period, as bridges too far into the unknowns of unfettered ambition, avarice and pride. A fascinating account which brings to the fore the connections between these elements and the 'values' (laissez-faire capitalism) for which they come to stand, can be found in the book by Adam Hochschild entitled *King Leopold's Ghost* (1998) in which discourse, and its ability to shape and influence value, becomes a means to be manipulated towards an end; a greater exploitation for unchecked profiteering. In short the 'fever' associated with rushes came also to stand for the conditions under which millions of people were either enserfed, indentured or just enslaved, to create the railways to lend easier access to the fields of gold. Not coincidentally, the discourses of racism and sexism reach their apogee in the nineteenth century and within the imperial imaginary such fever comes also to stand for contagion, the bodies of the very natives pressed into labour, rather than in the bodies of the conquistadores, the prospectors, the travellers and the pioneers. Twentieth-century chronicles of contamination and fever did not quite manage to spring free of this matrix of value, echoing a point made by GoGwilt (1995) that the very notion of the West is implicated in earlier ideas and narratives concerning race and gender, where race is (infamously) not associated with colour (as Petty's perspective on the Irish attests) but with notions of language and culture. GoGwilt sums up the connections in the following terms: '[t]his idea of "the West" is still very much linked to a diverse set of *colonial and imperial practices*. It functions, however, by denying the assumptions of colonial and imperial power, and dispersing the assumed links between such powerful ideas as race, nation, and culture' (1995: 68).

The nineteenth century is perhaps the defining moment in which displacement occurs since earlier periods still bear close relationship between the subject and the object. There is no doubt in a reading of Gray or Wordsworth as to who the 'I' is, and indeed in Petty and Swift there is an idea of the 'I' writing on behalf of a benevolent society which shares the same ethical and moral base, even if the understanding of the outcomes of action and consequences is different. In the nineteenth century fevers, and rushes of other speculative and colonial endeavours, came with disease, and in turn provided covert commentaries on the perceived moral degeneration of the age. Just as the consequences of fever are visited upon the foreigners as an outcome of the moral degeneration (barbarism and savagery) of the natives, so too there remains a continuity of concerns regarding the relationships between behaviour, capital and value.

While fevers characterised dangerous speculation and consequently destabilised notions of value, in many European countries popular movements had grown for greater participation in representative institutions. In a previous age participation in Parliament had been largely dependent on birth but towards the end of the eighteenth century there occurred the growth of a prosperous merchant class keen on expansionist policies abroad and greater representation at home. The basis for the movement was the great prosperity of the merchant class, and the idea that effective government was to be measured by the extent to which a nation state could profit by economic as well as military means. With economic prosperity there arose better education systems and a literate public demanded access to culture and participation in its institutions. Given the prominence of the novel as the art form most associated with the nineteenth century it is also unsurprising that many of the issues concerning capital, culture and access were portrayed in the form of the novel. In the early 1800s participation in representative institutions had long been limited to those who possessed property, but with the burgeoning of the middle class there arose pressure to reform the existing conditions of suffrage. Perhaps no one popularised debates concerning male suffrage more than Dickens in the late nineteenth century by drawing attention to the alignment of money with personal value or 'quality'. Chapter 6 discussed Dickens's *Our Mutual Friend* (1864–5) in which the debates concerning the privileges of inherited power and position were commented on in relation to the need for an educated citizenry as the basis for participation in democratic systems. Many politicians believed that gender, money and property could be conjoined to form an equitable basis for participation. It was at this time that Disraeli's Reform Bill (1859) proposed male participation in elections on the basis of money invested in banks or property as sufficient evidence of foresight and responsibility. Then, as now, the suggestion that money signified quality, and that justice was for the rich, enjoyed wide popularity, and Dickens challenged received notions (evident in the writings of Swift and others) that prosperity was a marker of divine favour; ideas that would find their ultimate corruption in the bubbles of the early twentieth century where speculation (in the form of credit loans and multiple shares floated to raise funds), and the belief in fortunes to follow, were the cause of ruin for thousands of people hoping for better lives.

While in the 1700s it could be argued that speculation was linked to the morally questionable indulgence of luxury, and that moral worth could be deduced from the nature of transaction and labour in the

1800s, it could also be asserted (and demonstrated) that 'speculation is the great Business engine of the age' (Chapter 4). The twentieth century would continue to testify to this maxim in other more recent cultural artefacts (for example, film and photography). In the meeting of peoples brought about by migration and conflict, there has always been a need to control the market and to fix value. Indeed, while mercantilism may have been replaced by colonial-imperialism, and that in turn replaced by free market capitalism, still the inability of regulators to fix the value of goods in relation to the value of labour, or ideas pertaining to the value of goods themselves, continues to pose a structural and ideological challenge. Speculation, passion and emotion refuse the rationality prescribed by Petty, or attempted by Franklin, or articulated by Greenspan. What emerges in place of such efforts is not only an awareness of theory sometimes appallingly adrift from an ethical and moral base, but also the recurrence of anxiety concerning the failure of regulation to protect vulnerable people from the excesses of their own, or other people's greed. Typically, the fevered sensibility that 'goes native' in a previous age, or attends to 'conspicuous consumption' in the current age, is still evident in the speculation concerning, for example, the deleterious effects of migrant populations on the culture of Europe, the impact of the media on youth, the impact of materialism on traditional values, the consequences of 'women's lib' for the identity of men, and miscegenation's effects on the superiority of the white race.

Chapters 7 and 8 traced the attempts by two twentieth-century authors to not only problematise the relationships between culture, capital and representation, but also in the very form of the novel's structural and narrative devices to invite reflection on the nature of capital and its effects on representation and culture. Thus the book traces the development of a specific cultural form in these chapters and suggests that it came to be deployed as a 'way of understanding' rather than simply a 'way of seeing', just as in other places in the book authors have explored the development of capitalism, and its primary means of creating value (capital) and inferred connections between that trajectory and its mirrors, cultural and social life. The novels in question – Dreiser's *The Financier* (1912) and Gide's *Les Faux-Monnayeurs* (1925) – in form and narrative provide commentary on the great shifts in human and economic history that occurred in the century with the development of free market economies and communism as ideological counterpoints.

Postone (1993), drawing from the perspective offered by Marx when he suggested that finance capital is devoid of content, argues that surplus value is temporal, since finance capital (or what Postone refers to as capital that is generated via its surplus value) is temporal. We see critics and cultural commentators such as Dreiser exploring that temporality in society and the economy. One key purpose of exploring the very discourse of capitalism (finance, credit, mortgage, bond, interest and other terms) provides a measure of the link between time and speculation on value. Dreiser's *The Financier* offers a critique of the relationship between finance and time. The critical juncture explored in Chapter 7 requires that capital be separated from commodity and that the activities associated with finance capital are abstracted into interest accrued or dividends, or capital gains. Critically such activities point to a future time in which accumulation or accrual will have occurred; in other words to when 'money would have been made from money'. Dreiser's novel appeared at the time in which the term 'finance capital' came into common usage to refer to large-scale credit used to purchase value in the present in order to secure profit in the future. Arrighi (1994) traces the development of capitalism, as a system of representation, back to the fourteenth century in which the connections between land and money were made. Harvey (1982) and other economics theorists have described how the ascendance of finance capital and its associated activities (market speculation, interest rates and credit) attempt to control and narrow the gap between space and time, as signifiers not of history or social life, but rather of value. In *The Financier* finance capital serves to orientate activities to be achieved in time in relation to the value of wheat; in other words, to maximise the production of time from which future profit may be extracted. This chapter shows that as early as 1912 Dreiser attempted to describe and understand the temporal process of financial accumulation and his novel draws the readers' attention to Postone's (1993: 265) point that money appears as a symbol of value and that credit is a further obfuscation of that value.

Because the processes of financial capital are located as they are in the future, it is not uncommon for novelists or journalists to locate them in persons of character (a strategy which remains popular well into the twenty-first century). But, as noted in Chapter 7, this strategy detracts from another perspective in which the novel, as form, operates as a system of representation itself. *The Financier* then, in form, offers the reader a system of representation in which meaning is accumulated over time and the plot serves to describe what occurs when the relationship between time, production and value is destabilised. Thus when the market cannot sustain value, and a panic is induced, a fall occurs and the future profits as well as the present value are diminished. In many ways the speculation and speculated value of wheat is revealed as counterfeit; it stands for a value which can never be realised even as it is traded in. Dreiser's text demonstrates that even if markets are regulated, such regulation remains fragile and determined subjectively by matters that cannot be anticipated (such as the fire which destroys the wheat) or by the nuances and speculative drives of the financier; a theme which is taken up in Chapter 10 with an analysis of the film, *Wall Street*. It is telling that the dissociation experienced by the main character in *The Financier* is represented in the narrative itself which repeats the very term that most encapsulates the deferral of meaning for finance capital: time.

Within the genres available for cultural production developmental trajectories can similarly be traced where the ideas concerning speculation, worth and capital are brought together within a long-established genre, only for that very genre itself to be destabilised. This process can be seen, for example, in the novel by Gide, *Les Faux-Monnayeurs* (1925). The very moment at which the gold standard is abandoned in France is represented in a novel that deals with counterfeit value, thus offering social and economic commentary in both form (by implication the gold standard now corrupted, now outdated; the novel now redundant, now outmoded) as well as content. Of course, the abandonment of the gold standard may stand as the culmination of the final 'dissociation' of value from meaning since prior to 1925 in France the value of money, as already stated, stood in relation to gold, to which paper money was meant to ultimately refer. Without that external (and material) referent there occurred the possibility and nightmare of the Great Depression. In particular countries such as Germany the value of paper money came to possess no external referent whatsoever. This book makes no argument regarding the historical development of particular genres in relation to history itself. Thus while the pamphlet might have been the most popular genre of the seventeenth and eighteenth centuries, and the novel the most prominent artistic form of the nineteenth century, it is evident that there exists no neat correlation between form and purpose; though this is not to deny the development of new technologies (such as film or photography, for example), or even artefacts from other fields such as architecture, for example, which have served to manifest the continuities in representation delineated as part of this book.

If Chapters 7 and 8 have dealt with an exploration of representation and capital in relation to some reflections on the particular form of the novel, then Chapters 9 and 10 deal with artefacts that speak equally powerfully to the representation of identity and value, but in very different forms; the first in the form of the building (in this case the design of grain elevators as represented at the famous Paris International Exposition of 1937, and the representation of identity, capitalism and value in the iconic film *Wall Street* (1987) fifty years later. In the chapter dealing with the Paris International Exposition, the French and Canadian architectural displays are compared; both aspired to convey the idea of agriculture and agricultural capital(ism) in each country. Earlier in the book explicit reference has been made to architectural phenomena, whether these be descriptions of the homes of the nouveau riche in Dickens's *Our Mutual Friend* or the construction of the Panama Railway and the attendant fever of the California Gold Rush in the 1850s.

Just as texts and writing produce discourse and take particular forms or genres (which I have referred to as forms of cultural artefact here), so too have buildings and structures long been associated with ideas concerning culture and identity. Given the focus of the book on capital in representation, the international exhibitions, popular especially in the late nineteenth and early twentieth centuries, provide rich and highly nuanced ground for an analysis of those forms, or architectural representations, which are associated explicitly with capital in the popular media. The 1937 Paris Exposition embodied certain paradoxes of aspiration in the pavilions constructed to represent 'the nations' to each other at this event. What is evident in the descriptions of the grain elevators of the Canadian and French displays is that France wished to perceive such structures in relation to its sense of self as a thoroughly modern republic, one in which the associations with an imperial past were replaced by an idea of the 'modern', even though the colonies were still very much part of the greater national French imaginary.

The grain elevator was thus a modern, and as Chapter 9 suggests, thoroughly technocratic invention, constructed to suggest the power of the French economy and with little reference to the mixed heritage of empire in its architectural references. For Canadians, on the other hand, still part of an empire and with a young and relatively unknown architectural history, the grain elevator embodied a more ideological purpose, testifying in the commentary of the time to an idea of nationhood and purpose in the world. Such buildings embody a sense of style, function, greater purpose, religious significance and identity that speak widely to the context and period in which they are located. Imperial cities were created on the basis of the desire for world prestige, nowhere more evident perhaps than in the Brussels of Leopold II, or the Forbidden City of imperial China. International exhibitions were meant to bring the world to a particular place (be it London, Paris, or more recently Dubai), and also, as argued by Benedict (1983) to signify to the world the importance of that host location or particular city. Thus an edifice is as much a cultural artefact as a novel, or political pamphlet, poem, or film, and indeed, as Giberti (2002) acknowledges, the pavilions of various international exhibitions were meant to convey a symbolic sense of national identity.

The decision to focus on artefacts of a less obvious kind (grain elevators convey first a sense of utility rather than symbolism) is deliberate in Chapter 9 since there already exists a multitude of writing and commentary on buildings with more obvious symbolic import (such as the palaces of dynasties, and palaces of justice), but in relation to this book, focused as it is on culture, capital and representation, there exists very little on the representation of agricultural capital – that form of capital which is linked to the land in ways alluded to at the beginning of this book where Petty and Swift comment on the value (moral as well as economic) of capital that is derived from agricultural labour and produce. For France, the 1937 Exposition was a means of representing the modernity of France in a changing view of its relationship to the agricultural heartlands, so often associated with a very deep conservatism. Thus the grain elevator was very much a projection of the future for the French on the 'role of progress' in relation to profit for the state. Indeed, as this chapter points out, the discourse of French officials and the Exposition documents charts an increasing tension between the state and small and private landholders; at this time international trade barriers and protectionism were common, and thus the pressures to achieve greater self-reliance were mounting. In Canada, the design of the grain elevator was expressed in strictly capitalist terms to maximise profit and efficiency. Large amounts of grain could be stored, shifted and traded at any time, with least reliance on labour.

A focus on improving the means of consumption, both in terms of the utility value of the elevator, and in terms of the consumption of iconic imagery by the public (the grain elevator was accompanied by presentations aimed at increasing immigration to Canada) recalls a point made in Chapter 9 in relation to the shift in focus from the means of production to the means of consumption and the latter's association with the development of finance and speculative capital. Since grain elevators served a communal function, they were cooperatively owned and managed and as such served the interests of larger or state-owned agricultural capital. The point of this chapter is in part to suggest that gigantism in modern architecture is necessarily focused on consumption, since whether in the form of downtown skyscrapers, or in the form of grain elevators, the sheer scale of construction articulates a discourse of consumption that is 'tactical' or 'strategic', to use de Certeau's terms (1988: 30). The French construction for the 1937 Exposition was a visible strategy to impose 'knowledge through symbolism'. The discourse generated in relation to the Canadian pavilion focused on the representation of the elevator as a signifier of the Dominion, and as a symbol of the past, but the same could not be said of the purpose of the representation. In de Certeau's (1988) terms, the Canadian pavilion represented a tactic, meant to convey a message about the past, the identity of the nation, and its immigration and tourist possibilities.

Reflections on consumption in the critical literature in economics and cultural studies are taken further in the analysis developed in Chapter 10 in which the effects of finance capital, as divorced from any context other than its own movement, are shown to have devastating consequences for people, both in terms of the dissociation produced in the individual, and the resulting displacement of emotion and value. In Chapter 10 the representation of (American) culture, and the form of capital which has come to be associated with its financial centre (speculative and financial capital in Wall Street), is reflected upon: How do cultural artefacts, whether in forms such as the novel, or in narrative and description, such as the journalism associated with the Panama Railway, reflect widespread beliefs and contradictions within these artefacts, interrogating the 'the discipline of the market' and raising questions sometimes neglected in scholarship whether in economics or media studies? How does one account for greed as a primary motivation for profiteering, other than through a moral lens? And, to what extent do profiteering practices, associated most frequently with brokerage, assume hubris and greed as primary motivations, despite regulatory frameworks designed to 'rein in' such practices and 'protect' investment? As with the novel (discussed in Chapter 7), the strategy of containing and also attempting to understand the opaque practices of finance capital, whose characters attempt to manipulate time and space to maximise value and profit, is not new. One of the significant strengths of this book is not only in posing such questions for further interrogation, but also its exploration of these themes across a range of genres. *Wall Street* (1987) is rich in intertextual references, and the later film *Boiler Room* (2000) contains several references to *Wall Street*, but aside from the obvious play on intertextuality between the films, and the obvious echoes between both films, and novels such as *Cosmopolis* (De Lillo, 2003) or even *The Financier* (Dreiser, 1912), the intra-referentiality, as well as the intertexuality of these cultural forms suggests another more challenging problematic: through their recreation of each other, and particularly through their powerful focus on character rather than action and process, it emerges that human agency remains profoundly resistant to systems-based regulation when it deals only with symptoms or aberrations (encapsulated by the representation of the individual person) rather than values. Furthermore, even if the range of cultural artefacts (buildings, newspapers, books, films) are approximations of reality, their superabundance in any age, and the evident return to issues that challenge our understanding of behaviour and motivation, remain beyond either the most profound forms of speculation (as hypotheses must be, for example) or the most mundane and banal of observations. If a marker of any civilisation is the variety and sophistication of the cultural artefacts it produces, and that such production interrogates both the nature and purpose of identity and agency in a plethora of activities at a given time, then it is equally obvious that such production becomes reality itself, rather than simply a reflection or contestation of an externalised system of representation and value. In other words, the creation of typologies of value, and of types (or characters) that participate in and embody aspects of such typologies, serves also to accentuate the complexity not only of the system of representation of value, but also the significance to be extracted from it for purposes of reflection and development.

What is evident in the texts of the twentieth century, as opposed to those of the nineteenth century (but similar to those of the eighteenth century), is a profound distrust of power not evidently accountable to people, but rather to 'markets'. If the discourses focused upon in the nineteenth century are different, they differ only to the extent to which ideology (imperialism or racism, for example) was able to coerce and dominate the production of meaning and thus value. The success of ideological systems to absorb all meaning and thus attempt to define value comprehensively (everything from right behaviour to right production and consumption), is always partial, but the examples that are still evident in popular imaginations are communism and fascism. The former has enjoyed a longer and more developed history but perhaps the most salient observation to be made in relation to the focus of this book is that systems of representation that serve to regulate and delimit meaning, and to prescribe value and meaning, have not enjoyed longevity.

This phenomenon is partly alluded to in Chapter 10, and also in Chapter 2, in which it was argued that even within the dominant ideology of capitalism, and the attempts to regulate its practices, there occurs a resistance to, and suspicion of corruption in the exercise of power through regulation. In other words, and within the context of the twentieth-century film *Wall Street*, there occurs a form of defiance which is expressed as speculation (and risk-behaviour) on the futures market in order to derive profit from speculation itself. This form of defiance is at once an act of exploitation as well as resistance, but it cannot ever (unlike a revolutionary act) serve as a sufficient threat to the very system from which it attempts to extract both value and meaning. If the practice of imperialism depended, as Swift suggested, on the expansion of an empire, and the sustainability of empire depended in turn on the captivity of newly acquired markets, then internal to this accumulation of power to a centre (and of luxury as its outward manifestation so abhorred by Swift and others), is also the ever-present will to its opposites: an ever more narrowly prescribed system of value and representation, or an ever widening sense of suspicion and subversion of those very impulses – a point to which I return in the concluding parts of this chapter. If capitalism is founded upon a myth (to borrow from, but also to extend the argument of Chapter 10), of ever expanding markets and ever available resources, then the threats, either internal or external, to that myth are likely to provoke a range of crises in representation. The vehicles for representation of such crises must be the popular artefacts of the time, allowing also for the continuity of representation across a wide variety of forms, or even in the development of new forms altogether.

In Chapter 10 it has been argued that perhaps one of the most distinguishing aspects of capitalism (as opposed to communism, or fascism, for example) is that defiance in the face of regulation remains a heroic value, whether in the tragic heroes of *Wall Street*, or *The Financier*, or in the voice of social commentators (such as Swift in Chapter 2), or in the person of the novelist (such as Dickens in Chapter 6). But the conditions for that voice to speak its truth to power (Said, 1978) are mediated, despite their not being controlled or regulated. For even if the actions of Gordon Gekko compromise his absent investors, and the totally absent markets in which they speculate, the system of representation allows for the containment of their meaning in a manner which renders their revolutionary potential insignificant. Furthermore, the manipulators of markets, whether as representations in popular fiction or film, or as employees in stock exchanges, are hardly likely ever to be female, and almost certainly not black or gay. In *Wall Street* what emerges as the subject of critique in relation to the 'characters', is the ability of the system to generate excess, or to allow for surplus wealth to be created and thus also potentially exploited (in earlier centuries this would have been referred to as luxury, and its associations with gambling, or speculation, are many and have been described variously in this book as most likely to occur frequently in 'big business', big government' and 'big power'). Variously vilified (Bernard Madoff), or adulated (George Soros), successful market speculators stand for a deepening sense that commerce exists for many as the highly profitable regulation of avarice. And, even if the speculative movement of surplus wealth serves to disenfranchise and render vulnerable surplus populations (a feature of imperialism which has survived to become also a feature of late twentieth-century capitalism), then as a society, as a civilisation there lies at the heart of our practices a form of violence that is condoned and indeed sanctioned as necessary for the development and advancement of humankind.

Nowhere have the global implications of such behaviours become more evident as empires have given way to nation states, and nation states have themselves slowly given way to the 'global village'; a trajectory which is historically documented even if it forms the wider and unspoken context for this book. It is to the global manifestations of these highly localised and selective accounts provided in the book that I turn now. According to Amin, in the aftermath of decolonisation and at the onset of globalisation in the latter half of the twentieth century:

> all ... institutions [associated with the state] have lost part or all of their legitimacy. In their place a variety of 'movements' have taken centre stage, focusing on the demands of environmentalists or women or the struggle for democracy or social justice, or asserting community identities (ethnic or religious) ... Extreme instability is therefore a characteristic of this new political life. (1999: 25)

In this book culture, capital and representation have been the focus of an interrogation of capital and twentieth-century capital is most closely associated with free market trade, deregulation of markets, and the movement of speculative capital around the globe. Globalisation then is the necessary aftermath of decolonisation, and decolonisation is the aftermath of empire (an idea disputed by Rosenberg, 2000 but supported by Hobsbawm, 2000), and as previous chapters demonstrate, the notion of continued expansion is linked to that of deferred value. For the first time, and freed from the obfuscation of nationalist or imperialist ideologies, it is possible to see that the movement and creation of surplus wealth is not in fact disembodied from context, and has consequences for the value of labour, and thus commodities in any region across the globe.

Amin argues that three features characterise globalisation: 'Massive and permanent unemployment has reappeared within the Triad (US, Europe, and Japan), the welfare state has been eroded, and a new phenomenon of exclusion/marginalisation has become a permanent feature of the landscape' (1999: 17).

Marginalisation and the continued exploitation of what Adams, Gupta and Mengisteab (1999) refer to as the 'domestic working class' in the post-colonies, and nowadays within former imperial centres, is not an accidental consequence of the collapse of empires, but rather, a prerequisite for their reformulation and survival. It is not that a 'new phenomenon' in the form of globalisation has been produced, as suggested by Amin (1999). What has happened is that it is no longer incumbent on the individual to experience the guilt of empire, since the agency associated with the continued exploitation of the 'domestic working class', is no longer visibly associated with former metropolitan centres, but is abstracted into the market. Recognition (both moral and economic) of past guilt remains, however – even though the obvious links to these centres (cultural, ideological and even economic) have been broken – as seen in the strategic movement of De Beers and Anglo American stock from the South African Stock Exchange to the Wall Street and London exchanges.

In the late twentieth century the ideology associated with the new 'social order and free market economics' was paralleled by a discourse replete with suggestion that the dismantling of protectionist policies and the welfare state made possible the accessibility of technology, promotion of democracy, free market systems, and the narrowing of the gap between the rich and poor, settled and displaced. Weeks describes the process:

> The 'story' [or spin] derives from the premise that the countries of the world are now integrated through trade and capital flows to an extent that national economic policy is ineffective in so far as it does not follow a common set of highly restricted policies. Those who deviate from that set of policies can anticipate swift and terrible punishment by the impersonal discipline of *markets*, and most notably the *financial markets*. (1999: 50)

Hobsbawm makes this point: 'The interesting thing about the current phase of the global economy is that it has taken place under conditions of immigration control imposed by all the large capitalist countries' (2000: 64). Liberalisation of state economies encourages what theorists refer to as a drive towards the bottom as countries compete to offer cheaper labour, fewer taxes and relaxed restrictions on the movement of capital. These tend to support a class that already enjoys access to the benefits of a global economy, whilst undermining any protection the state might offer to those who do not. This process is massive, and is rendered personal in the new century through the tracing of such links through artefacts from the previous three centuries described in this book. According to Halliday:

> the lived experience of globalisation draws on conceptions of power and inequality derived from earlier periods – the cold war and, before that, colonialism. Indeed the whole discourse of conflict within globalisation reflects the continued impact of these times, since that very discourse is in large measure phrased in a vocabulary and conceptual system derived from earlier conflicts. (2001: 21)

To return to Petty, Franklin, Dickens, Winthrop and others referred to in this book, we make two claims. First, that the ideology of capitalism, and its various manifestations (or stages) through the last three centuries, remains heavily complicit in the ideologies of racism and cultural superiority that, whilst perhaps not evident in the 'impersonal discipline of the markets', remain powerful predicators of value and worth which find their realisation in these markets. New writings and cultural artefacts (as argued by Balfour, 2007) associated with the age of globalisation are equally revealing of the fictions of globalisation, because despite the relative absence of such arguments in economic accounts, it is evident that markets and capital cannot easily be detached from the historical processes (industrialisation, speculation, colonisation) out of which they arise, and the question of individual identity is not easily disentangled from these social, economic and political forces. And, second, that it is imperative that a greater focus on interdisciplinary scholarship of the kind articulated in this book become normative in higher education so as to achieve an integration of insights in the general understanding of the relationship between culture and capital and the historical phenomena shaping both.

Bibliography

Adams, F., Gupta, S. D. and Mengisteab, K. (eds) (1999) *Globalization and the Dilemmas of the State in the South*. Basingstoke: Palgrave Macmillan.
Adorno, Theodor ([1941] 1981) 'Veblen's Attack on Culture', in *Prisms: Studies in Contemporary German Social Thought*, trans. Samuel Weber and Shierry Weber Nicholsen. Cambridge, MA: MIT Press, pp. 73–9.
Aglietta, Michel (1979) *A Theory of Capitalist Regulation: the US Experience*. New York: Verso.
Amin, S. (1999) 'For a Progressive and Democratic New World Order', in F. Adams, S. D. Gupta and K. Mengisteab (eds), *Globalization and the Dilemmas of the State in the South*. Basingstoke: Palgrave Macmillan, pp. 17–32.
Anon. (1859a) 'A Great Meeting of Creditors', *All the Year Round* 1(7): 153–6.
Anon. (1859b) 'Our Eye Witness at Gloucester', *All the Year Round* 1(29): 51–3.
Appleby, Joyce (1992) *Liberalism and Republicanism in the Historical Imagination*. Cambridge, MA: Harvard University Press.
Ariès, Philippe (1981) *The Hour of Our Death*, trans. H. Weaver. Oxford: Oxford University Press.
Aristotle (1926) *The Nichomachean Ethics*, Loeb edition, trans. H. Rackham. London: William Heinemann.
Arrighi, Giovanni (1994) *The Long Twentieth Century*. London: Verso.
Ashcroft, B., Griffiths, G. and Tiffin, H. (1989) *The Empire Writes Back: Theory and Practice in Post-Colonial Literatures*. London and New York: Routledge.
'Aspinwall and the Panama Railroad' (1866) *Harper's Weekly*, Volume 1866 (Issue 01/27), 0062bc–0062bc.
Aspromourgos, Tony (1996) *On the Origins of Classical Economics: Distribution and Value from William Petty to Adam Smith*. London: Routledge.
Aspromourgos, Tony (2000) 'New Light on the Economics of William Petty (1623–1687): Some Findings from Previously Undisclosed Manuscripts', *Contributions to Political Economy* 19: 53–70.
Augé-Laribé, Michel (1950) *La politique agricole de la France de 1880 à 1940*. Paris: PUF.
Bagehot, Walter (1867) *The English Constitution*. London: Chapman and Hall.
Baker, Jennifer Jordan (2000) 'Benjamin Franklin's *Autobiography* and the Credibility of Personality', *Early American Literature* 35: 274–93.
Balfour, R. J. (2007) 'V. S. Naipaul's "Half a Life", "The Magic Seeds" and Globalisation', *Literator* 28(1): 1–22.
Baran, Paul and Sweezy, Paul (1963) *Monopoly Capital*. New York: Monthly Review Press.
Barthes, Roland (1972) *Mythologies*. New York: Hill and Wang.
Benedict, Burton (ed.) (1983) *The Anthropology of World's Fairs: San Francisco's Panama Pacific International Exposition of 1915*. London and Berkeley: The Lowie Museum of Anthropology in association with Scholar Press.
Benjamin, Walter (1969) 'On Some Motifs in Baudelaire', in H. Arendt (ed.), *Illuminations: Essays and Reflections*. New York: Schocken Books, pp. 155–94.

Benjamin, Walter (1977) 'Über einige Motive bei Baudelaire', in S. Unseld (ed.), *Illuminationen*. Frankfurt am Main: Suhrkamp, pp. 185–229.
Bhabha, Homi K. (1994) *The Location of Culture*. New York: Routledge.
Bindon, D. (1712) *A Letter from a Merchant Who has Left Off Trade to a Member of Parliament, in which the Case of the British and Irish Manufacture of Linen, Threads, and Tapes, is Fairly Stated; and All the Objections Against the Encouragement Proposed to be Given that Manufacture, Fully Answered*. London, pp. 279–83.
Biskind, P. (1987) 'Stone Raids Wall Street', *Premier* (December): 33–8.
Black, J. (2002) *The Reality Effect: Film, Culture, and the Graphic Imperative*. New York: Routledge.
Bolingbroke, Viscount (1740) 'On Bribery and Corruption', in *A Collection of Political Tracts*. London, pp. 279–83.
Bomstad, Linda (2004) 'Money, Meaning and Method in John Locke', paper presented at the conference on Money, Power, and Prose: Interdisciplinary Studies on the Financial Revolution in the British Isles, 1688–1756. Regina, SK, University of Regina (25 June).
Bowlby, Rachel (1985) *Just Looking: Consumer Desire in Dreiser, Gissing and Zola*. London: Methuen.
Braddick, Michael J. (2000) *State Formation in Early Modern England, c.1550–1700*. Cambridge: Cambridge University Press.
Bradshaw, Brendan (1989) 'Nationalism and Historical Scholarship in Modern Ireland', *Irish Historical Studies* 26: 329–51. Reprinted in Ciaran Brady (ed.), *Interpreting Irish History: the Debate on Historical Revisionism, 1938–1994*. Dublin: Irish Academic Press, 1994, pp. 191–216.
Brands, H. W. (2000) *The First American: the Life and Times of Benjamin Franklin*. New York: Doubleday.
Brantlinger, Patrick (1996) *Fictions of State: Culture and Credit, 1694–1994*. Ithaca: Cornell University Press.
Brewer, J. (1990) *The Sinews of Power: War, Money and the English State, 1688–1783*. Cambridge, MA: Harvard University Press.
Brewer, J. (1997) *The Pleasures of the Imagination: English Culture in the Eighteenth Century*. London: HarperCollins.
Briggs, Peter M. (2005) 'John Graunt, Sir William Petty, and Swift's *Modest Proposal*', *Eighteenth-Century Life* 29: 3–24.
Brooker, Bertram (ed.) (1929) *Yearbook of the Arts in Canada, 1928–1929*. Toronto: McMillan Company of Canada.
Brooks, Peter (1976, repr. 1995) *The Melodramatic Imagination: Balzac, Henry James, and the Mode of Excess*. New Haven: Yale University Press.
Brown, William J. (1993) 'Walter Gropius and Grain Elevators: Misreading Photographs', *History of Photography* 17 (Autumn): 304–8.
Bruce, Jean (dir.) (2001) *The Last Best West: Advertising for Immigrants to Western Canada, 1870–1930*. © Canadian Museum of Civilization Corporation. Created: 7 February 2000. Last update: 9 August 2001. http://www.civilization.ca/hist/advertis/ads1-01e.html#menu
Burke, Edmund (1987) *A Philosophical Enquiry into the Origin of our Ideas of the Sublime and Beautiful*, ed. James T. Boulton. Oxford: Blackwell.
Calder, J. (1974) *There Must Be a Lone Ranger: the Myth and Reality of the American Wild West*. London: Hamish Hamilton.

Campbell, Joseph (1986) *The Power of Myth*. New York: Doubleday.
'Canada' (1937) *L'Exportateur français* (1 August).
Carlin, Norah (1993) 'Extreme or Mainstream? The English Independents and the Cromwellian Reconquest of Ireland, 1649–1651', in Brendan Bradshaw, Andrew Hadfield and Willie Maley (eds), *Representing Ireland: Literature and the Origins of Conflict, 1534–1660*. Cambridge: Cambridge University Press, pp. 209–26.
Carlyle, Thomas (1867) *Shooting Niagara: And After?* London: Chapman and Hall.
Cash, Thomas M. (1872) 'A Plain Statement of Facts for the Perusal of Those Interested'. New York: n.p.
Castells, M. (2000) *The Power of Identity*. Oxford: Blackwell.
'Central America' (1857) *Harper's Weekly*, Volume 1857 (Issue 02/21), 0113ad–0113ad.
Champagne, R. (1992) *The Structuralists on Myth*. New York: Garland Publishing.
Chancellor, E. (1999) *Devil Take the Hindmost: a History of Financial Speculation*. New York: Plume Books.
Chandler, R. (1742–4) *The History and Proceedings of the House of Commons*, 14 vols. London, vol. 7.
'Character' (1989) *Oxford English Dictionary*, 2nd edn. Online at http://www.ed.com, accessed March 2005.
Childs, P. and Williams, P. (1997) *An Introduction to Post-colonial Theory*. London: Longmans.
Cockburn, A. (1987) 'Oliver Stone Takes Stock', *American Film* 13: 20–6.
Cole, T. (1761) 'Six Discourses on Luxury, Infidelity, and Enthusiasm'. Quoted in John Brewer, *The Pleasures of the Imagination: English Culture in the Eighteenth Century*. New York: Farrar, Straus & Giroux (1997).
Collins, Peter (1965) *Changing Ideals in Modern Architecture, 1750–1950*. Montreal: McGill University Press.
Colman, Andrew M. (2001) 'Displacement, noun', in *A Dictionary of Psychology*. Oxford: Oxford University Press. Oxford Reference Online. 20 August 2005, http://www.oxfordreference.com/views/ENTRY.html?subview=Main&entry=t87.e2383
Conrad, J. (1983–) *The Collected Works of Joseph Conrad*, ed. Frederick R. Karl and Laurence Davies, 4 vols to date. Cambridge: Cambridge University Press.
Corry, Montague (ed.) (1867) *Parliamentary Reform. A Series of Speeches on that subject delivered in the House of Commons by The Right Hon. B. Disraeli (1848–1866)* [repr. from *Hansard*]. London: Longmans, Green.
Coughlan, Patricia (1990) '"Cheap and common animals": the English Anatomy of Ireland in the Seventeenth Century', in Thomas Healy and Jonathan Sawday (eds), *Literature and the English Civil War*. Cambridge: Cambridge University Press, pp. 205–23.
Covey, Stephen R. (1990) *The 7 Habits of Highly Successful People: Powerful Lessons in Personal Change*. New York: Fireside/Simon & Schuster.
Davenport, T. H. and J. C. Beck (2001) *The Attention Economy: Understanding the New Currency of Business*. Boston: Harvard Business School Press.
de Angelis, Massimo (2000) *Keynesianism, Social Conflict, Political Economy*. New York: St. Martin's Press.

de Certeau, Michel (1988) *The Practice of Everyday Life*, trans. Steven Rendall. Berkeley: University of California Press.
de Man, Paul (1984) 'Autobiography as De-Facement', in *The Rhetoric of Romanticism*. New York: Columbia University Press, pp. 67–81.
DeGategno, Paul J. and Stubblefield, R. Jay (2006) *Critical Companion to Jonathan Swift: a Literary Reference to his Life and Works*. New York: Facts On File.
DeLillo, D. (2003) *Cosmopolis*. New York: Scribner.
Derrida, Jacques (1993) *Given Time: I. Counterfeit Money*, trans. Peggy Kamuf. Chicago: University of Chicago Press.
Derrida, Jacques (1994) *Specters of Marx: the State of the Debt, the Work of Mourning, and the New International*, trans. Peggy Kamuf. London and New York: Routledge.
Detienne, M. and Vernant, J.-P. (1978) *Cunning Intelligence in Greek Culture and Society*. Sussex: Harvester Press.
Dickens, Charles ([1864–5], repr. 1997) *Our Mutual Friend*. Harmondsworth: Penguin.
Dickens, Charles (1965–2002) *The Pilgrim Edition of the Letters of Charles Dickens*, ed. Madeline House, Graham Storey and Kathleen Tillotson, 12 vols. Oxford: Clarendon Press.
DiPiero, T. (1988) 'Buying into Fiction', *Diacritics* 18(2): 3–15.
'Domestic Intelligence: the New Granadian Dispute' (1857) *Harper's Weekly*, Volume 1857 (Issue 08/08), 0502ad–0503a.
Doss, Erika (2002) *Twentieth-Century American Art*. Oxford and New York: Oxford University Press.
Downie, J. Alan (2005) 'Public and Private: the Myth of the Bourgeois Public Sphere', in Cynthia Wall (ed.), *A Concise Companion to the Restoration and Eighteenth Century*. Oxford: Blackwell, pp. 58–79.
Downie, J. Alan (2008) '*Gulliver's Travels*, the Contemporary Debate on the Financial Revolution, and the Bourgeois Public Sphere', in C. Ivar McGrath and Chris Fauske (eds), *Money, Power, and Print: Interdisciplinary Studies of the Financial Revolution in the British Isles*. Newark: University of Delaware Press, pp. 115–34.
Dreiser, Theodore ([1912] 1995) *The Financier*. New York: Meridian Press.
Dupays, Paul (1938) *L'Exposition internationale de 1937: ses créations et ses merveilles*. Paris: Henri Didier.
Earle, P. (1976) *The World of Defoe*. New York: Atheneum.
Easterbrook, F. (1986) 'Monopoly, Manipulation, and the Regulation of Futures Markets', *Journal of Business* 59(2) (Supp.): 103–7.
Eddy, George Simpson (1929) *Account Books Kept by Benjamin Franklin: Ledger "D," 1739–1747*. New York: Columbia University Press.
Ekelund, Robert B. Jr. and Tollison, Robert D. (1981). *Mercantilism as a Rent-seeking Society: Economic Regulation in Historical Perspective*. College Station, TX: A & M University Press.
Eliot, T. S. (1917) 'The Love Song of J. Alfred Prufrock', in *Prufrock and other Observations*. London: The Egoist Press, pp. 4–10.
Enright. D. J. (1986) 'Swift, Fielding, and Bad Taste', in *The Alluring Problem: an Essay on Irony*. Oxford: Oxford University Press, pp. 75–8.
Evrard, Guillaume (2003) 'Les pavillons du Canada lors des Expositions internationales et universelles de 1867 à 1939: création d'une architecture,

construction d'une image', unpublished Art History MA dissertation, Université Marc-Bloch, Strasbourg.

Exposition 1937: sections étrangères, introduction de Jacques Gréber; présentation de Henri Martin. Paris: Éditions art et architecture [1937].

Fabens, Joseph W. (1852) *A Story of Life on the Isthmus*. New York: George P. Putnam and Co.

Fabrikant, G. (1987) 'Wall Street Reviews *Wall Street*', *New York Times*, 10 December, pp. D1, D5.

Fauske, C. (2002) *Jonathan Swift and the Church of Ireland, 1710–1724*. Dublin: Irish Academic Press.

Favier, Jean (1938) *L'architecture, Exposition internationale, Paris, 1937*. Paris: Éditions Alexis Sinjon.

Ferguson, Frances (1977) *Wordsworth: Language as Counter-Spirit*. New Haven and London: Yale University Press.

'Financial and Commercial to Stock Information' (1857) *Harper's Weekly*, Volume 1857 (Issue 05/09), 0303a–0303a.

Finn, Margot (1993) *After Chartism: Class and Nation in English Radical Politics, 1848–1874*. Cambridge: Cambridge University Press.

Finn, Margot (2003) *The Character of Credit: Personal Debt and English Culture, 1740–1914*. Cambridge: Cambridge University Press.

Fischel, D. and Ross, D. (1991) 'Should the Law Prohibit "Manipulation" in Financial Markets?' *Harvard Law Review* 105: 503–53.

Flouquet, Pierre-Louis (1937) 'Paris 1937: L'Exposition internationale des arts et techniques dans la vie moderne', *Bâtir* (June): 1227–8.

Fox, Christopher (ed.) (2003) *The Cambridge Companion to Jonathan Swift*. Cambridge: Cambridge University Press.

Frankfurter, G. and McGoun, E. (1999) 'Ideology and the Theory of Financial Economics', *Journal of Economic Behavior and Organization* 39: 159–77.

Frankfurter, G., McGoun, E. and Allen, A. (2004) 'The Prescriptive Turn in Behavioral Finance', *Journal of Socio-Economics* 33(4): 449–68.

Franklin, Benjamin (1987) *Benjamin Franklin Writings*, ed. J. A. Leo Lemay. New York: Library of America.

Franklin, Benjamin (2003) *The Autobiography of Benjamin Franklin*, 2nd edn, ed. Louis P. Masur. Boston and New York: Bedford/St. Martin's Press.

Frenkel, Stephen (1996) 'Jungle Stories: North American Representations of Tropical Panama', *Geographical Review* 86(3): 317–33.

Freud, Sigmund (1927) 'Fetishism', in J. Strachey (ed.), *Standard Edition of the Complete Psychological Works of Sigmund Freud* (1961 edn). London: Hogarth, Volume 21, pp. 152–7.

Fridson, M. (2000) 'Wall Street', in R. Toplin (ed.), *Oliver Stone's USA*. Lawrence: University Press of Kansas, pp. 120–34.

Gallagher, Catherine (2006) 'The Bio-Economics of *Our Mutual Friend*', in *The Body Economic: Life, Death, and Sensation in Political Economy and the Victorian Novel*. Princeton, Princeton University Press, pp. 86–117.

Gastineau, G. and Jarrow, A. (1991) 'Large-Trader Impact and Market Regulation', *Financial Analysts Journal* 47: 40–51.

Giberti, B. (2002) *Designing the Centennial: a History of the 1876 International Exhibition in Philadelphia*. Lexington: University Press of Kentucky.

Gide, André ([1925] 1966) *The Counterfeiters*, trans. Dorothy Bussy. London: Penguin.
Goblet, Yann-Morvran (1930) *La transformation de la géographie politique de l'Irelande au XVIIe siècle, dans les cartes et essais anthropogéographiques de Sir William Petty*, 2 vols. Paris: Berger-Levrault.
Godden, Richard (1997) *Fictions of Capital: the American Novel from James to Mailer*. Cambridge: Cambridge University Press.
GoGwilt, C. (1995) *The Invention of the West: Joseph Conrad and the Double Mapping of Europe and Empire*. Stanford, CA: Stanford University Press.
Goldhaber, M. H. (1997) 'The Attention Economy and the Net', *First Monday* 2(4), http://www.firstmonday.org/issues/issue2_4/goldhaber/, accessed 15 July 2005.
Goodacre, Hugh J. (2005) 'William Petty and Early Colonial Roots of Development Economics', in Kwame Sundaram Jomo (ed.), *Pioneers of Economic Development*. New Delhi: Tulika Books; London: Zed Press, pp. 249–68.
Goodacre, Hugh J. (2009) 'Economics, Geography and Colonialism in the Writings of William Petty', in Richard Arena, Sheila Dow and Matthias Klaes (eds), *Open Economics: Economics in Relation to Other Disciplines*. London: Routledge, pp. 228–42.
Goodlad, Lauren (2003) *Victorian Literature and the Victorian State: Character and Governance in a Liberal Society*. Baltimore: Johns Hopkins University Press.
Goux, Jean-Joseph (1973) *Économie et Symbolique: Freud, Marx*. Paris: Éditions du Seuil.
Goux, Jean-Joseph (1984) *Les Monnayeurs du Langage*. Paris: Galilée.
Goux, Jean-Joseph (1990) *Symbolic Economies: After Marx and Freud*. Ithaca: Cornell University Press.
Goux, Jean-Joseph ([1973] 1994) *The Coiners of Language*, trans. Jennifer Curtiss Gage. Norman: University of Oklahoma Press.
Goux, Jean-Joseph (1999) 'Cash, Check, or Charge?' in Martha Woodmansee and Mark Osteen (eds), *The New Economic Criticism: Studies at the Intersection of Literature and Economics*. London and New York: Routledge, pp. 114–28.
Gray, Thomas and Collins, William (1977) *Poetical Works*, ed. R. Lonsdale. Oxford: Oxford University Press.
Greenfield, A. (2005) *A Perfect Red Empire: Espionage, and the Quest for the Color of Desire*. New York: HarperCollins.
Greider, William (1988) *Secrets of the Temple: How the Federal Reserve Runs the Country*. New York: Simon & Schuster.
Guttman, Robert (1996) *How Credit Money Shapes the Economy*. Armonk, NY: M. E. Sharpe.
Habermas, Jürgen (1989) *The Structural Transformation of the Public Sphere: an Inquiry into a Category of Bourgeois Society*, trans. Thomas Burger. Cambridge: Polity Press.
Hadfield, Andrew and Maley, Willie (1993) 'Irish Representations and English Alternatives', in Brendan Bradshaw, Andrew Hadfield and Willie Maley (eds), *Representing Ireland: Literature and the Origins of Conflict, 1534–1660*. Cambridge: Cambridge University Press, pp. 1–23.
Halliday, F. (2001) *The World at 2000*. Basingstoke: Palgrave Macmillan.

Hamilton, Andrew W. (1937) 'Empire in Background at Exposition', *The Windsor Star* (23 August).
Hardt, Michael and Negri, Antonio (2001) *Empire*. Cambridge, MA: Harvard University Press.
Hartley, J. (2008) 'The Chameleon Daniel Defoe: Public Writing in the Age before Economic Theory', in C. Ivar McGrath and Chris Fauske (eds), *Money, Power, and Print: Interdisciplinary Studies of the Financial Revolution in the British Isles*. Newark: University of Delaware Press, pp. 26–50.
Hartman, Geoffrey H. (1970) 'Romantic Poetry and the Genius Loci', in *Beyond Formalism: Literary Essays, 1958–1970*. New Haven and London: Yale University Press, pp. 311–36.
Hartman, Geoffrey H. (1987) 'Inscriptions and Romantic Nature Poetry', in *The Unremarkable Wordsworth*. Minneapolis: University of Minnesota Press, pp. 31–46.
Hartz, P. (1991) 'On Symbolic Economies', *American Journal of Semiotics* 8(1–2): 137–47.
Harvey, David ([1982] 1998) *The Limits to Capital*. London: Verso.
Harvey, David (1989) *The Condition of Postmodernity*. Oxford: Blackwell.
Headley, J. T. (1855) 'Darien Exploring Expedition under Command of Lieut. Isaac C. Strain', *Harper's Monthly Magazine*, 10 (58), October 1855: 577–590. Reprinted in Michael LaRosa and Germán R. Mejía (eds), *The United States Discovers Panama: the Writings of Soldiers, Scholars, Scientists, and Scoundrels, 1850–1905*. Lanham, MD: Rowman and Littlefield (2004), pp. 45–82.
Hellman, J. (1986) *American Myth and the Legacy of Vietnam*. New York: Columbia University Press.
Henning, C. G. (1993) *The Indentured Indian in Natal: 1860–91*. New Delhi: Promila and Co.
Henwood, Doug (1996) *Wall Street: How it Works and for Whom*. London: Verso.
Hertz, Neil (1985) *The End of the Line: Essays on Psychoanalysis and the Sublime*. New York: Columbia University Press.
Hilferding, Rudolf (1981) *Finance Capital*. London: Routledge.
Hobsbawm, Eric (2000) *The New Century: In Conversation with Antonio Polito*. London: Abacus.
Hochschild, Adam (1998) *King Leopold's Ghost: a Story of Greed, Terror and Heroism in Colonial Africa*. London: Pan Macmillan.
Horwitz, H. (1982) 'To find the value of X: *The Pit* as a Renunciation of Romance', in E. Sundquist (ed.), *American Realism: New Essays*. Baltimore: Johns Hopkins University Press, pp. 215–37.
House, Humphrey (1961) *The Dickens World*. Oxford: Oxford University Press.
Howard, June (1985) *Form and History in American Naturalism*. Chapel Hill, NC: University of North Carolina Press.
Hull, Charles H. (ed.) (1899) *The Economic Writings of Sir William Petty*, 2 vols. Cambridge: Cambridge University Press.
Hurtt, Deborah D. (2004) 'Simulating France, Seducing the World: the Regional Center at the 1937 Paris Exposition', in Medina Lasansky and Brian McLaren (eds), *Architecture and Tourism: Perception, Performance and Place*. Oxford and New York: Berg, pp. 147–64.
Isaacson, Walter (2003) *Benjamin Franklin: an American Life*. New York: Simon & Schuster.

Jaffe, Audrey (2002) 'Trollope in the Stock Market: Irrational Exuberance and *The Prime Minister*', *Victorian Studies* 45(1): 43–64.
James, Simon J. (2003) *Unsettled Accounts: Money and Narrative in the Novels of George Gissing*. London: Anthem.
Jameson, Fredric (1971) *Marxism and Form*. Princeton: Princeton University Press.
Jameson, Fredric (1981) *The Political Unconscious: Narrative as a Socially Symbolic Act*. Ithaca, NY: Cornell University Press.
Jameson, Fredric (1991) *Postmodernism, or the Cultural Logic of Late Capitalism*. Chapel Hill, NC: Duke University Press.
Jameson, Fredric (1998) *The Cultural Turn*. London: Verso.
'Je voudrais bien savoir ... ce qu'on peut voir de neuf à l'Exposition?' *Le Dimanche Illustré* 10 (11 July 1937).
John, Juliet (2001) *Dickens's Villains: Melodrama, Character, Popular Culture*. Oxford: Oxford University Press.
Johnson, M. (1952) 'A Literary Chestnut: Dryden's "Cousin Swift"', *PMLA* 67: 1024–34.
Johnson, S. (1755) *A Dictionary of the English Language*. London.
Jones, Kristine L. (1986) 'Nineteenth Century British Travel Accounts of Argentina', *Ethnohistory* 33(2): 195–211.
Jones, T. (2004) 'Pope's "Epistle to Bathurst and the Meaning of Finance"', *Studies in English Literature 1500–1900* 44(3) (Summer): 487–504.
Joyce, Patrick (1991) *Visions of the People: Industrial England and the Question of Class*. Cambridge: Cambridge University Press.
Joyce, Patrick (1996) 'The Constitution and the Narrative Structure of Victorian Politics', in James Vernon (ed.), *Re-reading the Constitution: New Narratives in the Politics History of England's Long Nineteenth Century*. Cambridge: Cambridge University Press, pp. 179–203.
Jung, Carl (1968) *The Archetypes and the Collective Unconscious*. Princeton: Princeton University Press.
Kagan, N. (1995) *The Cinema of Oliver Stone*. New York: Continuum.
Keefer, Thomas C. (1881) *Report for the Canadian Commission*. Ottawa: MacLean, Roger and Co.
Kelly, Patrick Hyde (1998) '"Conclusions by no means calculated for the circumstances and condition of Ireland": Swift, Berkeley and the Solution to Ireland's Economic Problems', in Aileen Douglas, Patrick Hyde Kelly and Ian Campbell Ross (eds), *Locating Swift: Essays from Dublin on the 250th Anniversary of the Death of Jonathan Swift, 1667–1745*. Dublin: Four Courts, pp. 47–59.
Kelly, Patrick Hyde (ed.) (1991) *Locke on Money*, 2 vols. Oxford: Clarendon Press.
Kenderdine, Thaddeus S. (1888) 'A California tramp and later footprints; or, Life on the plains and in the Golden state thirty years ago, with miscellaneous sketches in prose and verse ... Illustrated with thirty-nine wood and photo-engravings'. Philadelphia: Press of Globe Printing House. Available at: http://hdl.loc.gov.loc.gdc/calbk.005
King, Nicholas B. (2002) 'Security, Disease, Commerce: Ideologies of Postcolonial Global Health', *Social Studies of Science* 32(5–6) (October–December): 763–89.
King, T. Butler (1850) 'Report of Hon. T. Butler King: 22 March 1850', Appendix (Taylor, Bayard (1850)), *Eldorado, or Adventures in the Path of Empire*. New York: George Putnam and Co.

Knowles, Valerie (1992) *Strangers at our Gates: Canadian Immigration and Immigration Policy, 1540–1990.* Toronto and Oxford: Dundurn Press.
Kramnick, I. (1968) *Bolingbroke and His Circle: the Politics of Nostalgia.* Cambridge, MA: Harvard University Press.
Krippner, Greta (2005) 'The Financialization of the American Economy', *Socio-Economic Review* 3(2): 173–208.
Labbé, Edmond (1938–40) *Exposition internationale des arts et techniques dans la vie moderne, Paris 1937: rapport général.* Paris: Imprimerie nationale.
Lacan, Jacques (1966) *Écrits.* Paris: Seuil.
Lacan, Jacques (1977) *Écrits: a Selection,* trans. Alan Sheridan. London: Tavistock.
Landa, Louis A. (1942) 'A Modest Proposal and Populousness', *Modern Philology* 40: 161–70. Republished in L. A. Landa (ed.), *Essays in Eighteenth-Century Literature.* Princeton: Princeton University Press, 1980, pp. 39–48.
Lanham, Richard A. (1994) 'The Economics of Attention', *Proceedings of the 124th ARL Membership Meeting (The Research Library the Day After Tomorrow,* Austin, Texas, 18–20 May 1994), Association of Research Libraries, http://www.arl.org/resources/pubs/mmproceedings/124mmlanham, accessed 21 June 2009.
Lanham, Richard A. (1997) 'The Economics of Attention', *Michigan Quarterly Review* 36(2): 270–84.
Lanham, Richard A. (2006) *The Economics of Attention: Style and Substance in the Age of Information.* Chicago: University of Chicago Press.
LaRosa, Michael and Mejía, Germán (eds) (2004) *The United States Discovers Panama: the Writings of Soldiers, Scholars, Scientists, and Scoundrels, 1850–1905.* Lanham, MD: Rowman and Littlefield.
Latour, Bruno (1988) 'The Politics of Explanation: an Aternative', in S. Woolgar (ed.), *Knowledge and Reflexivity: New Frontiers in the Sociology of Knowledge.* London: Sage, pp. 155–76.
Lebergott, Stanley (1980) 'The Return to US Imperialism, 1890–1929', *Journal of Economic History* 40(2): 229–52.
Ledger, Sally (2007) *Dickens and the Popular Radical Imagination.* Cambridge: Cambridge University Press.
Lefort, Pierre (1937) 'Le Pavillon du Canada aura un succès marquant', *La Presse* (28 June).
Le Guide Officiel, Exposition international, Paris 1937, Arts et Techniques dans la vie moderne (1937). Paris: Éditions de la Société pour le Développment du Tourisme.
Lenin, Vladimir (1939) *Imperialism: the Highest Stage of Capitalism.* New York: International Publishers.
Letwin, William L. (1963) *The Origins of Scientific Economics: English Economic Thought, 1660–1776.* London: Methuen.
LiPuma, Edward and Lee, Benjamin (2003) *Derivatives and the Globalization of Risk.* Chapel Hill, NC: Duke University Press.
Locke, John (1690) *Second Treatise on Civil Government.* London.
Looby, Christopher (1986) '"The Affairs of the Revolution Occasion'd the Interruption": Writing, Revolution, Deferral, and Conciliation in Franklin's *Autobiography*', *American Quarterly* 38(1): 72–96.
Lucey, Michael (1995) *Gide's Bent: Sexuality, Politics, Writing.* Oxford: Oxford University Press.

Lukács, Georg (1971a) *History and Class Consciousness*. Cambridge, MA: MIT Press.
Lukács, Georg (1971b) *Writer and Critic*. New York: Grosset & Dunlap.
Lynch, Édouard (1998) 'Le Parti socialiste et la paysannerie dans l'Entre-deux-guerres: pour une histoire des doctrines agraires et de l'action politique au village', *Ruralia* 3. Accessed 1 June 2005 at http://ruralia.revues.org/document54.html
Macdonald, Colin S. (1997) 'Brunet, Emile', *A Dictionary of Canadian Artists*, 5th edn. Ottawa: Canadian Paperbacks.
MacDonald, J. (1987) *Who Shot the Sheriff?* New York: Praeger.
Mackey-Kallis, S. (1996) *Oliver Stone's America*. Boulder, CO: Westview Press.
Mahar-Keplinger, Lisa (1992) *Grain Elevators*. New York: Princeton Architectural Press.
Mandel, Ernest (1975) *Late Capitalism*. London: New Left Books.
Manthorne, Katherine (1989) *Tropical Renaissance: North American Artists Exploring Latin America, 1839–1879*. Washington: Smithsonian Institution Press.
Marangoly-George, R. (1996) *The Politics of Home: Postcolonial Relocations and Twentieth-Century Fiction*. Cambridge: Cambridge University Press.
Marx, Karl (1976) *Capital, Volume 1*, trans. Ben Fowkes. London: Penguin.
Marx, Karl (1978) *Capital, Volume 2*, trans. Ben Fowkes. London: Penguin.
Marx, Karl (1981) *Capital, Volume 3*, trans. David Fernbach. London: Pelican Books.
Masur, Louis P. (2003) 'Introduction: the Life of Benjamin Franklin', in Louis P. Masur (ed.), *The Autobiography of Benjamin Franklin*, 2nd edn. Boston and New York: Bedford/St. Martin's Press, pp. 1–26.
Maurice, Frederick Denison (1866) *The Workman and the Franchise*. London: Alexander Strachan.
McClelland, Keith (2000) 'England's Greatness, the Working Man', in *Defining the Victorian Nation: Class, Race, Gender and the British Reform Act of 1867*. Cambridge: Cambridge, University Press, pp. 71–118.
McCormick, Ted (2006) 'Alchemy in the Political Arithmetic of Sir William Petty (1623–1687)', *Studies in History and Philosophy of Science* 37(2): 290–307.
McCullough, David (1977) *The Path Between the Seas: the Creation of the Panama Canal, 1870–1914*. New York: Simon & Schuster.
McGrath, C. I. and Fauske, C. (eds) (2008) *Money, Power and Print: Interdisciplinary Studies on the Financial Revolution in the British Isles*. Newark: University of Delaware Press.
McMickle, Peter L. (1984) 'Young Man's Companion of 1717: America's First Book on Accounting', *Abacus* 20(1): 34–52.
Michaels, Walter Benn (1987) *The Gold Standard and the Logic of American Naturalism*. Berkeley, CA: University of California Press.
Miller, David (1989) *Dark Eden: the Swamp in 19th Century American Culture*. Cambridge: Cambridge University Press.
Miller, Peter (1994) 'Accounting as Social and Institutional Practice: an Introduction', in Anthony G. Hopwood and Peter Miller (eds), *Accounting as a Social and Institutional Practice*. Cambridge: Cambridge University Press, pp. 1–39.
Montag, W. (1994) *The Unthinkable Swift*. London: Verso.

Moore, Earl E. (2000) 'The Panama Rail Road Company', *Manuscripts* 52(3) (Summer 2000): 209–18.
Moore, John Robert (1971) *A Checklist of the Writings of Daniel Defoe*, 2nd edn. Hamden: Archon.
Morgan, Hiram (1985) 'The Colonial Venture of Sir Thomas Smith in Ulster, 1571–1575', *Historical Journal* 28(2): 261–78.
Morgan, Hiram (1999) 'Beyond Spenser? A Historiographical Introduction to the Study of Political Ideas in Early Modern Ireland', in Hiram Morgan (ed.), *Political Ideology in Ireland, 1541–1641*. Dublin: Four Courts Press, pp. 9–21.
Muller, J. Z. (2002) *The Mind and the Market: Capitalism in Modern European Thought*. New York: Random House.
Nackenoff, C. (1994) *The Fictional Republic: Horatio Alger and American Political Discourse*. New York: Oxford University Press.
'Nashville Scene' (2000) *WeeklyWire.com*, 28 February.
Norberg-Schulz, Christian (1975) *Meaning in Western Architecture*. London: Studio Vista.
Norden, M. (2000) 'Introduction: the Changing Face of Evil in Film and Television', *Journal of Popular Film and Television* 28(2): 50–2.
Norris, Frank (1958) *The Octopus*. Cambridge: Riverside Press.
'Notice of new books' (1860) *The New York Times*, 26 October, p. 2.
Novak, M. (2001) *Daniel Defoe: Master of Fictions*. Oxford: Oxford University Press.
O'Brien, T. (1990) *The Screening of America: Movies and Values from Rocky to Rainman*. New York: Continuum.
O'Regan, P. (2000) 'William King to William Wake, 31 March 1721'. TCD Ms 750/6/213, in Philip O'Regan, *Archbishop William King of Dublin (1650–1729) and the Constitution in Church and State*. Dublin: Four Courts Press, p. 291.
Oran (1859) 'Panama Railroad: Tropical Journeyings', *Harper's New Monthly Magazine*. September, Volume 19 (Issue 112), pp. 145–69.
'Panama Railroad' (1859) *Harper's Weekly*, Volume 18 (Issue 104).
Pascal, Blaise (1910) *Blaise Pascal, Thoughts [Pensées]*, trans. W. F. Trotter. Harvard Classics. New York: Collier.
Pavillon du Canada: Exposition Internationale Paris 1937/Canadian Pavilion: International Exhibition Paris 1937, introduction de Philippe Roy, n.1, [1937].
Peer, Shanny (1999) 'Les provinces à Paris: le Centre régional à l'Exposition internationale de 1937', *Le Mouvement social* 186 (January–March): 45–68.
Petty, Sir William (1899) *The Economic Writings of Sir William Petty*, ed. Charles H. Hull, 2 vols. Cambridge: Cambridge University Press.
Petty, Sir William (1927) *The Petty Papers: Some Unpublished Writings of Sir William Petty*, edited from the Bowood Papers by the Marquis of Lansdowne, 2 vols. London: Constable.
Petty, Sir William (1928) *The Petty-Southwell Correspondence, 1676–1687*, edited from the Bowood Papers by the Marquis of Lansdowne. London: Constable.
Pfeiffer, Ida (1856) *Lady's Second Journey round the World*. New York: Harper and Brothers.
'Philo-dicæus' (1647) *The standard of equality in subsidiary taxes and payments, or a just and strong preserver of publique liberty conducing towards the most happy government of kingdomes and states*. London: printed by D. H.
Pim, Bedford (1869) *Dottings on the Roadside in Panama, Nicaragua, and Mosquito*. London: Chapman and Hall.

Pizer, Donald (1976) *The Novels of Theodore Dreiser: a Critical Study*. Minneapolis: University of Minnesota Press.
Poovey, Mary (1995) 'Speculation and Virtue in *Our Mutual Friend*', in *Making a Social Body: British Cultural Formation, 1830–1864*. Chicago: University of Chicago Press, pp. 155–82.
Poovey, Mary (2002) 'Writing About Finance in Victorian England', *Victorian Studies* 45(1): 17–41.
Postone, Moishe (1993) *Time, Labor and Social Domination: a Reinterpretation of Marx's Critical Theory*. Cambridge: Cambridge University Press.
Rawson, Claude Julien (1978) 'A Reading of *A Modest Proposal*', in J. C. Hilson, M. M. B. Jones and J. R. Watson (eds), *Augustan Worlds*. Leicester: Leicester University Press, pp. 29–50.
Rawson, Claude Julien (1985) 'A Reading of *A Modest Proposal*', in *Order from Confusion Sprung: Studies in Eighteenth-Century Literature from Swift to Cowper*. London: Allen & Unwin, pp. 242–52.
Rawson, Claude Julien (2001) *God, Gulliver, and Genocide: Barbarism and the European Imagination, 1492–1945*. Oxford: Oxford University Press.
République Française, Ministère du Commerce et de l'Industrie (1938) *Livre d'or officiel de l'Exposition internationale des arts et techniques dans la vie moderne, Paris, 1937*. Paris: Éditions Spec.
Reynaud-Pactat, P. (1988) 'Jean-Joseph Goux and the Metaphor of the Promissory Note in Gustave Flaubert's *Madame Bovary*', *Diacritics* 18(2): 69–80.
Rice, Grantland S. (1997) *The Transformation of Authorship in America*. Chicago: University of Chicago Press.
Riley, Glenda and Etulain, Richard W. (eds) (1997) *By Grit and Grace: Eleven Women Who Shaped the American West*. Golden, CO: Fulcrum Publishing.
Roff, S. (1995) Review: *The Coiners of Language*, *MLN* 110(4): 1007–10.
Rogers, P. (ed.) (1983) *Jonathan Swift: Complete Poems*. The English Poets. New Haven: Yale University Press.
Rosenberg, J. (2000) *The Follies of Globalisation Theory*. London and New York: Verso.
Russell, F. (1998) *Northrop Frye on Myth*. New York: Garland Publishing.
Said, Edward (1978) *Orientalism*. London: Penguin.
Sanders, Andrew (1999) *Dickens and the Spirit of the Age*. Oxford: Clarendon Press.
Schmitt, Cannon, Henry, Nancy and Arondekar, Anjali (2002) 'Introduction: Victorian Investments', *Victorian Studies* 45(1): 7–16.
Schneider, Claire (1999) *Gerrit Engel: Buffalo Grain Elevators*. Buffalo, NY: Albright-Knox Art Gallery. Albright-Knox Art Gallery's website, accessed 10 June 2005, http://www.albrightknox.org/pastexh/Engel/essay.html
Schor, Esther (1993) *Bearing the Dead: the British Culture of Mourning from the Enlightenment to Victoria*. Princeton: Princeton University Press.
Schott, Joseph L. (1967) *Rails Across Panama: the Story of the Building of the Panama Railroad, 1849–1855*. New York: Bobbs-Merrill Co.
Schuster, L. (2003) *The Use and Abuse of Political Asylum in Britain and Germany*. Berlin: Frank Cass.
Scodel, Joshua (1991) *The English Poetic Epitaph: Commemoration and Conflict from Johnson to Wordsworth*. Ithaca and London: Cornell University Press.
Sedgwick, Eve Kosofsky ([1985] 1993) *Between Men: English Literature and Homosocial Desire*. New York: Columbia University Press.

Shell, Marc (1982) *Money, Language, and Thought*. Berkeley: University of California Press.

Shonkwiler, A. (2005) 'An Early View of Capitalism: Why We Still Read Dreiser', paper presented to 'The Representation of Capital 1700–2000: Speculation and Displacement' Colloquium. Institute for English Studies, Institute for Commonwealth Studies, London, 14–15 September.

Short, Audrey (1967) 'Canada Exhibited 1851–1867', *The Canadian Historical Review* 48(4) (December): 353–64.

'Short Cuts Across the Globe' (1850) *Harper's New Monthly Magazine*, Volume 1 (Issue 1), pp. 79–81.

'Showmanship' (1937) *The Financial Post* (20 November).

Silet, C. (ed.) (2001) *Oliver Stone Interviews*. Jackson: University Press of Mississippi.

Slotkin, R. (1992) *Gunfighter Nation: the Myth of the Frontier in Twentieth-Century America*. New York: Atheneum.

Smith, Adam ([1776] 1976) *An Inquiry into the Nature and Causes of the Wealth of Nations*, ed. E. Cannan. Chicago: University of Chicago Press.

Smith, Adam ([1759] 1984) *The Theory of Moral Sentiments*, ed. D. D. Raphael and A. L. Macfie. Indianapolis: Liberty Fund.

Soanes, Catherine and Stevenson, Angus (eds) (2003a) 'Elevator, noun', *The Oxford Dictionary of English*. Oxford: Oxford University Press. Oxford Reference Online. Oxford University Press, accessed 3 July 2005 at http://www.oxfordreference.com/views/ENTRY.html?subview=Main&entry=t140.e24243

Soanes, Catherine and Stevenson, Angus (eds) (2003b) 'Silo, noun', *The Oxford Dictionary of English*. Oxford: Oxford University Press. Oxford Reference Online. Oxford University Press, accessed 3 July 2005 at http://www.oxfordreference.com/views/ENTRY.html?subview=Main&entry=t140.e71563

Sohn-Rethel, Alfred (1978) *Intellectual and Manual Labour: a Critique of Epistemology*. London: Macmillan.

Sontag, Susan ([1978; 1988] 1990) *Illness as Metaphor and AIDS and its Metaphors*. New York: Anchor Books/Doubleday.

'Speculation' (1853) *The New York Daily Times*, 7 May, p. 4.

Stevenson, R. (1963) *Dr. Jekyll and Mr. Hyde and Other Stories of the Supernatural*. New York: Scholastic.

'Stocks and Speculation' (1860) *The New York Times*, 31 August, p. 4.

Stone, J. (2000) 'Evil in the Early Cinema of Oliver Stone: *Platoon* and *Wall Street* as Modern Morality Plays', *Journal of Popular Film and Television* 28(2): 80–7.

Stone, O. (1987) *Wall Street* [film].

Stone, O. (2000) *Boiler Room* [film].

Sundquist, Eric (1982) *American Realism: New Essays*. Baltimore: Johns Hopkins University Press.

Swift, Jonathan (1696–1707) 'A Digression Concerning Madness', section ix of *A Tale of a Tub*, in *The Prose Works of Jonathan Swift*, Vol. 1, *A Tale of a Tub With Other Early Works 1696–1707*, ed. Herbert Davis. Oxford: Blackwell (1948), pp. 1–135.

Swift, Jonathan (1708) 'Letter from a Member of the House of Commons in Ireland to a Member of the House of Commons in England, Concerning the Sacramental Test', in *The Prose Works of Jonathan Swift*, Vol. 2, *Bickerstaff Papers and Pamphlets on the Church*, ed. Herbert Davis. Oxford: Blackwell (1957), pp. 109–26.

Swift, Jonathan (1720) 'Proposal for the Universal Use of Irish Manufacture in Cloaths and Furniture of Houses, &c., Utterly Rejecting and Renouncing Every Thing Wearable that comes from England', in *The Prose Works of Jonathan Swift*, Vol. 9, *Tracts Relating to Ireland, 1720–1723*, ed. Herbert Davis. Oxford: Blackwell (1957), pp. 13–22.

Swift, Jonathan (1726) *Travels into Several Remote Nations of the World by Lemuel Gulliver*. London.

Swift, Jonathan (1728) 'A Short View of the State of Ireland', in *The Prose Works of Jonathan Swift*, Vol. 12, *Irish Tracts, 1728–1733*, ed. Herbert Davis. Oxford: Blackwell, 1971, pp. 1–12.

Sykes, J. B. (1986) 'Pavilion', *The Concise Oxford Dictionary of Current English*, 7th edn. London: Guild Publishing.

Tambling, Jeremy (1995) *Dickens, Violence and the Modern State*. Basingstoke: Macmillan.

Taylor, Bayard (1850) *Eldorado, or Adventures in the Path of Empire*. New York: George Putnam and Co.

Taylor, Miles (1995) *The Decline of British Radicalism, 1847–1860*. Oxford: Clarendon Press.

'The Last Instance of British Filibusterism' (1857) *Harper's Weekly*, Volume 1857 (Issue 05/30), 0338ab–0338ab.

'The Paris Exhibition. Criticisms of the British Pavilion. From our Paris Correspondent' (1937) *The Manchester Guardian Weekly* (30 July), p. 98.

'The Season of Speculation' (1860) *The New York Times* (11 August), p. 4.

Tomes, Robert (1855a) *Panama in 1855: An Account of the Panama Rail-road; of the Cities of Panama and Aspinwall; with Sketches of life and Character on the Isthmus.* New York: Harper and Brothers.

Tomes, Robert (1855b) 'A Trip on the Panama Railroad', reprinted in Michael LaRosa and R. Mejía (eds), *The United States Discovers Panama: the Writings of Soldiers, Scholars, Scientists, and Scoundrels, 1850–1905*. Lanham, MD: Rowman and Littlefield (2004), pp. 5–14.

Tompkins, J. (1992) *West of Everything: the Inner Life of Westerns*. New York: Oxford University Press.

Toplin, R. B. (2000) *Oliver Stone's USA: Film, History, Controversy*. Kansas: University of Kansas Press.

Trotter, David (1988) *Circulation, Defoe, Dickens and the Economics of the Novel*. London: Macmillan Press.

Tufts, Evelyn S. (1937) 'Exhibits from Dominion are Disappointing', *The Halifax Herald* (July).

Turner, F. (1920) *The Frontier in American History*. New York: Henry Holt and Company.

Vanlaethem, France (1998) 'Le silo à grain en béton, un modèle idéal pour l'architecture moderne', *Le silo n°5 du port de Montréal et son secteur: le passé, l'avenir*, Montreal (September).

Vaughn, Karen I. (1992) 'The Economic Background to Locke's *Two Treatises of Government*', in *John Locke's* Two Treatises of Government: *New Interpretations*, ed. Edward J. Harpham. Lawrence: University Press of Kansas, pp. 118–47.

Von Hendy, A. (2002) *The Modern Construction of Myth*. Bloomington: Indiana University Press.

Walker, Joanna (1996) 'Concepts of Retirement in Historical Perspective', in J. Walker (ed.), *Changing Concepts of Retirement: Educational Implications*. Aldershot: Arena, pp. 3–21.
Walker, S. (1995) *Jung and the Jungians on Myth*. New York: Garland Publishing.
Wallmann, J. (1999) *The Western: Parables of the American Dream*. Lubbock: Texas Tech University Press.
Walter, Carrie Stevens (1897) 'A Panama Riot', *In California's Garden*. San Francisco.
Warner, Michael (1986) 'Franklin and the Letters of the Republic', *Representations* 16: 110–30.
Wasserman, Renata R. M. (2001) 'Financial Fictions: Émile Zola's *L'argent*, Frank Norris's *The Pit*, and Alfredo de Taunay's *O encilhamento*', *Comparative Literature Studies* 38(3): 193–214.
Waters, Catherine (1997) *Dickens and the Politics of the Family*. Cambridge: Cambridge University Press.
Weber, Max ([1930] 2004) *The Protestant Ethic and the Spirit of Capitalism*, trans. Talcott Parsons. London and New York: Routledge.
Weber, Max (1968) *Economy and Society: an Outline of Interpretive Sociology*. New York: Bedminster.
Webster, Albert A. (1876) 'The Isthmus and Panama', 19 February, available at http://www.trainweb.org/panama/i&p.html
Webster, Charles (1979) 'Utopian Planning and the Puritan Revolution: Gabriel Platte, Samuel Hartlib, and Macaria'. Oxford: Wellcome Unit for the History of Medicine: Research Publications, 2. With a facsimile reprint of *A description of the famous kingdome of Macaria*.
Weeks, J. (1999) 'The Essence and Appearance of Globalization: the Rise of Finance Capital', in F. Adams, S. D. Gupta and K. Mengisteab (eds), *Globalization and the Dilemmas of the State in the South*. Basingstoke: Macmillan, pp. 107–15.
Whalen, Philip (2007) 'Burgundian Regionalism and French Republican Commercial Culture at the 1937 Paris International Exposition', *Cultural Analysis* 6: 31–69.
Whalen, Philip (2009) '"Insofar as the Ruby Wine Seduces Them": Cultural Strategies for Selling Wine in Inter-war Burgundy', *Contemporary European History* 18(1): 67–98.
Williams, Aubrey (1969) 'Alexander Pope, "Epistle to Bathurst"', in Aubrey Williams (ed.), *Poetry and Prose of Alexander Pope*. Boston: Houghton Mifflin, pp. 176–88.
Williams, Raymond (1971) *The English Novel: From Dickens to Lawrence*. London: Chatto & Windus.
Winthrop, Theodore (1863) *Isthmiana, The Canoe and the Soldier and Isthmiana*. Boston: Ticknor and Fields.
Wittkowsky, George (1943) 'Swift's Modest Proposal: the Biography of an Early Georgian Pamphlet', *Journal of the History of Ideas* 4: 75–104.
Wood, Gordon S. (2004) *The Americanization of Benjamin Franklin*. New York: Penguin Books.
Wood, P. R. (1991) 'Going off Gold', *Stanford French Review* 15: 395–7.
Woolley, J. (ed.) (1999–2008) *The Correspondence of Jonathan Swift, D.D.* 5 vols. Frankfurt: Peter Lang.
Wordsworth, William (1969) *Poetical Works*, ed. T. Hutcheon and E. de Selincourt. Oxford: Oxford University Press.

Wordsworth, William (1974) *The Prose Works of William Wordsworth*, 3 vols, ed. W. J. B. Owen and J. W. Smyser. Oxford: Clarendon Press.
Wordsworth, William (1979) *The Prelude: 1799, 1805, 1850*, ed. Jonathan Wordsworth et al. New York and London: Norton.
Wortley, Lady Emmeline Stuart (1851) *Travels in the United States, etc.* New York: Harper and Brothers.
Wright, W. (1975) *Six Guns and Society: a Structural Study of the Western.* Berkeley: University of California Press.
Wright, W. (2001) *The Wild West: the Mythical Cowboy and Social Theory.* London: Sage Publications.
Yamey, Basil S. (1974) 'Pious Inscription; Confused Accounts; Classification of Accounts: Three Historical Notes', in Harold C. Edey, Basil S. Yamey and William T. Baxter (eds), *Debits, Credits, Finance and Profits.* London: Sweet & Maxwell, pp. 143–60.
Zayani, Mohamed (1999) *Reading the Symptom: Frank Norris, Theodore Dreiser, and the Dynamics of Capitalism.* New York: Peter Lang.

Index

accounting
  ledgers *see* ledgers
  methods   38
  proverbs   39
  writing   40
accumulation, finance   11
Adams, E. et al., *Globalization and the Dilemmas of the State in the South*   14
Adorno, Theodor   6, 43, 47
Aguiar, Marian   xii, 10, 100–15
Anne (Queen)   52
architecture, capitalism   12
Arrighi, Giovanni   119, 120
Arthur, Eric   162
Ashcroft, B. et al., *The Empire Writes Back*   14
Aspinwall, Lloyd   102
Aspinwall, William H.   102
Aspromourgos, Tony   20
attention economy, epitaphs   8–9, 67–82

Bagehot, Walter   87–8, 90–1
Baker, Jennifer Jordan   36
Balfour, Robert J.   xii, 1–15, 184–200
Beck, John C.   67
Benedict, Burton   149, 195
Bindon, David   58–9
Bolingbroke (Viscount)   55–6
Bomstad, Linda   51
Brantlinger, Patrick   129
Brewer, John   56, 57, 59
Bright, John   87
Brunet, Jean-Émile   160, 162

Campbell, Joseph   182
Canada
  grain elevators   12, 148–68, 194–5
  International Exposition (Paris, 1937)   12, 148–68
capital
  cultural studies   1–2

culture   184–200
  epigrams   6, 37–44
  finance capital   116–31, 191–2
  money *see* money
  producing time   118–22
  self-evident truths   37–44
  speculative capital   14
  unregulated capital   2
  see also wealth
capitalism
  accounting capital   38
  architecture   12
  flow of attention   9, 67–82
  Franklin (Benjamin)   6–7, 35–48, 187
  gender   7
  habits of mind   6–7, 35–48
  industrial revolution   7
  objects of production/value   11
Carlyle, Thomas   86
cash flow, epitaphic   67–82
Cash, Thomas M.   108–9, 113
Chancellor, E.   181–2
Charles V (King of Spain)   101
Chauncey, Henry   102
Christianity
  money   1
  Puritans   40
  Quakers   45–6
  Wars of Religion (1562–98)   8
Cole, Thomas   59
colonialism
  colonised peoples   5–6, 19, 25–7
  cultural representation   25–7
  diaspora   10–11
  economic development   26
  utopia   28–30
commodification
  commodity exchange   136–7, 138, 140
  discourse   8
Comstock, Samuel   102
Conrad, Joseph   188
  'other'   14

corruption 89, 91, 97, 98
Covey, Stephen R. 37
credit
  credit relations 86
  financial 85, 93
  political 88
  representation 85–9
  social 85
credit/debit
  colour 44–7
  ledgers 40–1
Cromwellian period, Ireland 6, 16–34
cultural assumptions, fiction 4–5
cultural representation, Ireland 25–7
cultural studies, capital 1–2
culture
  capital 184–200
  international investment 103–6
custom 88, 90, 91, 93, 98

de Certeau, Michel, *The Practice of Everyday Life* 12, 156–7, 164–7, 196
Defoe, Daniel
  Moll Flanders 7
  morality 8, 187
  prolific writing 53–4
Demuth, Charles 162
Derrida, Jacques 12, 68, 135, 136, 143, 144, 145
Detienne, M. 174, 175
Dickens, Charles
  money 83–91, 93, 95–8
  Our Mutual Friend 9–10, 83–99, 190
discourse, commodification 8
displacement 2, 4, 5, 6, 8, 9, 10, 11, 12, 14, 15, 17, 31–2, 40, 57, 68, 69, 72, 73, 74, 81, 148, 149, 159, 161, 165, 166, 168, 189, 196
  see also migration; movement
Disraeli, Benjamin 9, 88, 89, 90, 93, 95, 190
Downie, Alan 53
Dreiser, Theodore, *The Financier* 11, 118, 122, 123, 125–8, 191–3, 198
Dunbar, Robert 161
Dupays, Paul 152, 153

Earle, Peter 53
economic polity, emergence 49–66
economics
  colonial economic development 26
  Cromwellian Ireland 23, 25–7, 28–9
  epitaphic tradition 8–9, 67–82
  global economy 14
  history of economic thought 31–3
  political *see* political economy
  Symbolic Economies 11
  well-informed state 31
England, Constitution 87–91, 95
Enright, D. J. 54
epigrams, capital 6, 37–44
epitaphs
  attention economy 8–9, 67–82
  commonplace 68–80
  epitaphic cash flow 67–82
  Gray (Thomas) 9, 68–73
  Wordsworth (William) 9, 73–9
Evrard, Guillaume xii, 12

Fauske, Christopher J. xii, 7–8, 10, 49–66, 105
Favier, Jean 166
fetishism 136, 137, 138, 142, 143
fiction, cultural assumptions 4–5
films
  Boiler Room 169, 170, 171, 172, 173, 174, 180, 181, 196
  constitutive myth 176–9
  finance and film 169–83
  romantic myth 174–6
  Wall Street 12–13, 169–83, 193–4, 196, 198
  Wall Street Myth 173–9
  Wall Street mythopoeia 179–82
finance
  accumulation 11
  finance capital 116–31, 191–2
  financial credit 85, 93
  financial temporality 118–22
  reading finance capital 122–9
Finn, Margot 85
Fisher, George 39
Fogarasi, György xii, 8–9, 10, 67–82
franchise *see* suffrage

Franklin, Benjamin
  Autobiography (1793) 6–7, 35–48, 186
  capitalism 6–7, 35–58, 187
Franklin, William Temple 39
Frenkel, Stephen 100, 102, 104, 115

Gassendi, Pierre 55
gender, capitalism 7
George I (King) 57
Gide, André, *The Counterfeiters* 11, 132–5, 143, 144, 191, 193
globalisation 4, 5, 158, 184, 185–6, 199, 200–1
Goblet, Yann-Morvran 29, 32
GoGwilt, C. *The Invention of the West* 3, 14, 189
gold standard, money 11–12, 132–47
Goldhaber, Michael H. 67–82
Goodacre, Hugh xii–xiii, 5, 16–34, 105
Gordon Gekko 13, 169–83
Goux, Jean-Joseph
  The Coiners of Language 11–12, 132, 136, 143
  money and language 132–47
  settlement by writing 40
grain elevators
  audience relations 150–3
  International Exposition (Paris, 1937) 12, 148–68, 194–5
Gray, Thomas
  Elegy written in a Country Church-Yard 9, 68–73
  epitaphs 9, 68–73
  value 8
Greber, Jacques 153, 160
Greenspan, Alan 111
Gropius, Walter 162
Grotius, Hugo 10

Habermas, Jürgen 4, 5
Hamilton, Andrew 163
Harris, Joseph 50
Hartley, James 53–4
Hartman, Geoffrey 73–4
Harvey, David 117–19, 121, 125
Headley, J. T. 104
Hochschild, Adam 189

Horwitz, Howard 123, 124
Hume, David 181
hypotheses 3–4

immigration 158, 159, 195, 196, 200
individual agency 37, 40, 43, 45
industrial revolution, capitalism 7
International Exposition (Paris, 1937)
  Canadian pavilion 153–7
  different overarching narratives 157–60
  grain elevators 12, 148–68, 194–5
Ireland
  Connaught 6, 17, 18
  Cromwellian period 6, 16–34
  cultural representation 25–7
  economic activity 23, 25–7, 28–9
  labouring people 22–5
  land appropriation 17
  population movement 17, 18, 24
  transplantation 17, 18, 24
  utopia 28–30

Jaffe, Audrey 105, 111–12
James II (King) 51
Jameson, Fredric 117, 124, 125
Jefferson, Thomas 42, 101
John, Juliet 10, 94
Johnson, Viscount 55
Johnson, William B. 113
journalism, railway development 10
Joyce, Patrick 96
Jung, Carl 174, 175, 176
Junto 44
justice, rights-based 10

Kelly, Patrick Hyde 49–50, 52–3
King, Nicholas 109, 110
King, William 58
King, William Lyon MacKenzie 160

La Berge, Leigh Claire xiii, 11, 116–31
Labbé, Edmond 153, 154
Lacan, Jacques 137, 138, 139
Lanham, Richard A. 67
LaRosa, Michael 103, 105, 108, 109
Latour, Bruno 48

Laurier, Wilfred 160
Law, George 102
ledgers
  credit/debit 40–1
  gain/loss 35
  social order 41
literature, money compared 4
Livesey, Ruth xiii, 9, 83–99
Locke, John 50–1
Looby, Christopher 48
Lucey, Michael 143–4
luxury
  morality 7
  ostentatious extravagance 59–65, 187

Macready, William Charles 87
Madoff, Bernard 199
manhood
  melodramatic narrative 93–8
  suffrage 9–10, 84, 87, 88, 95
Maragoly-George, R, *The Politics of Home* 15
markets
  manipulation 13
  natural liberty 33
Marx, Karl
  Capital 24, 116, 139
  commodity exchange 136–7, 138, 140
  fetish 139
  finance capital 116–17, 119–20, 191–2
  graveyard rhetoric 68
  political economy 19, 24, 143
  science of money 139
Marxism
  class consciousness 124
  political economy 11, 19, 24, 143
Massie, Joseph 50
Masur, Louis 41–2
Maurice, Frederick Denison 9, 84, 89, 95
McGoun, Elton G. xiii, 13
Mejía, Germán R. 103, 105, 108, 109
memory, persistence 184–200
Mendelsohn, Erich 162
mercantilism 49–50, 52–3, 60–2, 65
methodology, choices 2–3

Michaels, Walter Benn 117, 123, 124, 126
migration 15, 27, 31, 185, 191
  see also displacement; movement
Miller, David 108
Modern Movement 148–68
money
  Christianity 1
  counterfeit 11–12
  Dickens (Charles) 83–91, 93, 95–8
  fetishism 136, 137, 138, 142, 143
  gold standard 11–12, 132–47
  language 132–47
  literature compared 4
  money suffrage 9, 88, 95, 190
  money/personal estates 19, 20
  usury 1
Monnet, Georges 151
Montag, Warren 55
morality
  Defoe (Daniel) 8, 187
  luxury 7
  Smith (Adam) 70–1
  Swift (Jonathan) 8, 187
More, Thomas, *Utopia* 28
movement
  capital 13, 121–2, 196, 199, 201
  peoples 14, 110
  see also displacement; migration
Morris (Governor) 45, 46, 47
Muller, J. Z. *The Mind and the Market* 1, 7, 10, 12, 14

Norberg-Schulz, Christian 164, 167
'Norman yoke' 96, 97
Norris, Frank 123

Panama
  borderless states 106–11
  door of the seas 101–3
  fever 100–1, 107–10, 112–15
  feverish speculation 111–15
  international investment culture 103–6
  railway development 10, 100–15
  speculation 100–15
  travel narratives 100, 103, 104, 106, 107, 108, 110, 112

Paris Exposition *see* International
   Exposition (Paris, 1937)
Pascal, Blaise 59
Petty, William 5, 6, 16–34, 186
Pfeiffer, Ida 104, 108
Plato, *Republic* 29
poetry
   epitaphic tradition *see* epitaphs
   graveyard poetry 68
political arithmetic 16, 17
political economy
   Marxism 11, 19, 24, 143
   Smith (Adam) 25, 187
politics
   economic polity 49–66
   political arithmetic 16, 17
   political credit 88
   Western identity politics 14
Poovey, Mary 117
Pope, Alexander 64
post-colonialism, race and identity 14
postmodernism, fact/fiction 4–5
Postone, Moishe 116, 119, 121–2, 124, 191–2
producing time 118–22
property
   suffrage 86, 88, 190
   trust 91–3
Pulteney, William 57

railway development, Panama 10
representation
   credit 85–9
   labouring people 22–5
   material wealth 19–21
   propaganda and colonised peoples 25–7
Rice, Grantland C. 36
Roberts, Ben xiii, 11–12, 132–47
Roosevelt, Theodore 103
Rosha, Rekha xiii–xiv, 6, 35–48

Schor, Esther 68, 71–2
Seacole, Mary 104
Shakespeare, William 1, 7
Sheeler, Charles 162
Shonkwiler, Alison 118, 125
slavery
   abolitionists 36–7, 43

indebtedness 7, 37
passive endorsement 43
state-supported 8
Smith, Adam
   graveyard poetry 68
   moral circulation 71
   natural liberty 33
   political arithmetic 16
   political economy 25, 187
   sympathy 70–1
   Theory of Moral Sentiments 70–1
Sohn-Rethel, Alfred 117
Soros, Georges 199
speculation 2, 3, 9, 10, 13, 80, 85, 92, 126, 129, 148, 149, 161, 181–2, 186, 190–1, 192–3, 197, 198, 199, 201
   and displacement 8, 9, 10, 13, 15, 57, 68, 166, 168
   feverish speculation 10, 111–15
   global economy 14
   Panama railway 100–15
Spenser, Edmund 27
Spinoza, Baruch 55
states
   borderless states 106–11
   increasingly intrusive state 56–9
   well-informed state 31
Stephens, John Lloyd 102
Steuart, James 50
suffrage
   Disraeli (Benjamin) 9, 88, 89, 90, 93, 95, 190
   manhood 9–10, 84, 87, 88, 95, 190
   mass 86
   money suffrage 9, 88, 95
   professional 89, 93, 95, 190
   property 86, 88, 190
Swift, Jonathan
   A Tale of a Tub 54–5, 63
   cannibalism satire 16
   increasingly intrusive state 56–9
   madness 55
   modern economic polity 49–66
   morality 8, 187
   ostentatious extravagance/luxury 59–65, 187
   poetry 7
   radical discontinuity 49–56

satire 16–18, 32–3
trade 8
Symbolic Economies 11

taxation
  excise duties 57
  national income 19–21
  war 57
Taylor, Bayard 104, 108, 113
Temple, William 60
Thomas Aquinas 12
Tomes, Robert 104, 105, 108, 110
travel 13, 102, 155
  expectations 10, 103
  narratives 10, 100, 103–6, 107, 108,
    109, 110, 112–13, 114–15, 188
Trollope, Anthony 161
trust, property 91–3
Tufts, Evelyn 162
Twain, Mark 104

utopia, colonialism 28–30

values 1, 8, 12, 43, 93, 97, 98, 126,
  138, 142–3, 176, 183, 185, 188,
  189, 191, 197
  American 13, 177, 181
Vaughn, Karen Iversen 51
Vernant, J.-P. 174, 175
von Hendy, A. 173
von Humboldt, Alexander 101

wages
  excessive levels 22
  representation of labouring
    people 22–5
Wall Street *see* films
Walter, Carrie Stevens 104, 113
Warner, Michael 36, 48
Wars of Religion (1562–98) 8
Waters, Catherine 85
wealth
  money/personal estates 19, 20
  representation of material
    wealth 19–21
Weber, Max 37–8, 40, 43
Webster, Albert 114
Western identity politics, ideology 14
William III (King) 51, 52, 57
Winthrop, Theodore 100, 110
Wordsworth, William
  capitalist flow of attention 9, 73–9
  epitaphs 9, 73–9
  Essays upon Epitaphs 9, 75–6
  The Prelude Book VII 9, 76–9
  Tintern Abbey 9, 73–5
  value 8
Wortley, Emmeline Stuart 112–14
Wright, W. 176, 177, 178, 179, 180
writing
  accounting 40
  epitaphic *see* epitaphs
  unregulated capital 2